Schutzbrief(e)	protective letter(s)
Schutzhaus (-häuser)	protective house(s)
Schutzpass	protective passport
Sonderkommando	special unit SS
Untermenschen	subhuman beings
Wehrmacht	German army

DANGEROUS DIPLOMACY

DANGEROUS DIPLOMACY

The Story of Carl Lutz,
Rescuer of 62,000 Hungarian Jews

Theo Tschuy

Foreword by
Simon Wiesenthal

William B. Eerdmans Publishing Company
Grand Rapids, Michigan / Cambridge, U.K.

© 2000 Wm. B. Eerdmans Publishing Co.

Wm. B. Eerdmans Publishing Co.
255 Jefferson Ave. S.E., Grand Rapids, Michigan 49503 /
P.O. Box 163, Cambridge CB3 9PU U.K.

Printed in the United States of America

05 04 03 02 01 00   7 6 5 4 3 2 1

Library of Congress Cataloging-in-Publication Data

Tschuy, Theo.
[Carl Lutz und die Juden von Budapest. English]
Dangerous diplomacy: the story of the Swiss consul Carl Lutz:
Budapest 1944-45/ Theo Tschuy; foreword by Simon Wiesenthal.
p.   cm.
ISBN 0-8028-3905-3 (alk. paper)
1. Jews — Persecutions — Hungary. 2. Holocaust, Jewish (1939-1945) —
Hungary. 3. World War, 1939-1945 — Jews — Rescue —Hungary.
4. Lutz, Carl. 5. Diplomats — Switzerland — Biography.
6. Righteous Gentiles in the Holocaust — Hungary — Biography.
7. Hungary — Ethnic relations. I. Title.

DS135.H9 T7713 2000
362.87'81'092 — dc21
[B]   00-063626

www.eerdmans.com

In memory of our cousin Taudo, 17,
who in 1944 was murdered by the Gestapo

CONTENTS

FOREWORD

When we founded the Federation of Jewish Persecuted by the Nazi Regime (Bund Jüdischer Verfolgter des Naziregimes) in 1963, some of our members of Hungarian origin suggested that we invite Swiss Consul General Carl Lutz to give a talk in Vienna as part of our cultural program. He accepted this invitation. The consul general came to Vienna with his wife and we listened to a highly interesting presentation about the situation in Hungary after the German occupation of 1944. Consul General Lutz also spoke about the partly successful attempts to save Hungarian Jews from deportation to Auschwitz. He had been in Budapest since 1942, where he remained until 1945. Having been in Swiss diplomatic service in Palestine, he was acquainted with the problem of Jewish immigration. As long as the Hungarian government was still in control, Hungarian Jews were able to obtain emigration certificates, and it was Consul General Lutz — at that time still vice consul — who cooperated with the authorities of that country on this issue. His efforts were so successful that week after week 50 to 100 persons, mostly children and young people, obtained exit permits from the Kallay government to leave for Palestine. The young emigrants travelled by rail via Romania or on Danube boats to the Black Sea, where they boarded steamers for the Holy Land. According to the records of the Swiss Federal Archives, Consul Lutz helped approximately 10,000 emigrants to leave Hungary up to March 19, 1944, the day of the German occupation. Thanks to his interventions with the Hungarian bureaucracy, these transports functioned quite well for no less than two years. While the emigration candidates awaited their departure, Vice Consul Lutz gave them *Schutzbriefe*, letters of protection, which kept them from being drafted into labor service or from becoming arrested.

The situation changed dramatically with the German occupation of March 19, 1944. The new masters installed the government of Prime Minister Sztojay, and Hitler's envoy to Budapest, Veesenmayer, dictated his orders. All emigration was immediately suspended.

This interdiction led to a protest of the Swiss legation (embassy), which represented twelve other foreign governments at war with Hungary, especially the United States and Great Britain, against the one-sided cancellation of an international agreement that had been co-signed by Hungary. Veesenmayer enquired how many emigrants were still registered with the Swiss, and Lutz said 8,000. The Germans consented that these 8,000 emigrate, provided the Swiss consul did not insist on saving more. He refused, for the proposed deal was treacherous: It would have meant that the Swiss consul agreed to the murder of the rest of the Jews. Without making it known, Lutz began to issue additional tens of thousands of Schutzbriefe far beyond the 8,000 figure. In order to hide this undercover action, he kept formally "negotiating" with Veesenmayer, Eichmann, and the subservient Hungarian authorities on the 8,000. As a result, thousands of those now under his protection stayed alive and were not deported. In order to facilitate these procedures, he established a special Emigration Department of the Swiss legation. Carl Lutz knew that in challenging Nazi power so directly, he was taking enormous personal risks. Veesenmayer and Eichmann became his enemies.

But Consul Lutz and the other neutral diplomats in Budapest were largely powerless against the deportation of 350,000 Hungarian Jews to Auschwitz between May 15 and July 8, 1944. This was stopped under international pressure, when Horthy, Hungary's regent, suspended the deportations temporarily. His order was largely the result of an unprecedented press campaign in neutral and western countries, which — with the indirect help of Consul Lutz — George Mandel-Mantello, a Hungarian Jewish refugee in Switzerland, had unleashed in neutral and western countries. Tragically, however, the Hungarian province had in the meantime become *judenrein*, cleansed of Jews, to use a horrible Nazi expression. Only a quarter of a million Jews of Budapest survived for the time being.

Consul Lutz wisely used the short, quiet interval in mid-1944 in order to increase his protection of Jews. He placed no less than 30,000 *Schutzbrief* holders in seventy-six *Schutzhäuser*, protective houses, for which he obtained diplomatic immunity. This was another, unprecedented feat of his, to be expanded by other diplomats later.

But the tragedy of Hungary's Jewry soon entered its final stage. While the Red Army crossed the eastern frontier Veesenmayer instigated a second putsch on October 15, 1944. He replaced the Horthy regime with the Arrow Cross, the Hungarian Nazis, and their leader, Szalasi, became the new Nazi puppet in Hungary. The Arrow Cross now set out to destroy the Jews of Budapest. They went on killing sprees throughout the city and refused all previous agreements with the Swiss consul concerning Schutzbriefe and protective houses.

Undaunted, Consul Lutz renegotiated everything with the uncouth and illiterate Arrow Cross. He was repeatedly called out to free kidnapped Schutzbrief holders or to defend protective houses which had been invaded by the Arrow Cross. He was in danger of death more than once. During this dangerous final period Carl Lutz was no longer alone, because he now was able to count on the effective cooperation of Angelo Rotta (apostolic nuncio), Friedrich Born (International Committee of the Red Cross), Raoul Wallenberg (Sweden), and Peter Zürcher (his temporary representative in Pest) among others. This was a remarkable and mutually supportive team, which attracted Hungarians who were ashamed of what their country was doing to the Jews. Thus, together they saved several thousand Jews who had been deported on foot along the Vienna Road in November 1944. They also saved the inmates of the large ghetto of Pest in January 1945. This dedicated group, of which Consul Lutz was the leading figure, saved no less than 100,000 Hungarian Jews. Altogether 124,000 Budapest Jews survived the war.

After his return to Switzerland General Consul Lutz — instead of being acclaimed a hero — was accused of having exceeded his authority in Budapest. Narrow-minded, jealous government bureaucrats called his independent humanitarian spirit high-handed disobedience. Carl Lutz was not punished by his superiors. He was, in fact, given new diplomatic assignments until his retirement in 1961. But the memory of his action was suppressed, and for almost fifty years it remained buried in the archives. The consul became a non-person. However, if anyone must be reproached for misbehavior it would be those who, in the name of the Swiss people, arrogantly delivered countless Jews to Germany, who had crossed the borders "illegally." Symbols of dishonor remain Dr. Rothmund, director of the Swiss Foreign Police Department, and his superior, Federal Councillor von Steiger, who coined the fateful phrase, "the boat is full." It had been their idea to suggest to Nazi Germany in 1938 that passports of German and Austrian Jews be stamped with the letter "J." Their holders became thus fair game, and most perished in Nazi death camps.

The attitude of the Swiss authorities deeply hurt Consul General Lutz. Various foreign states, including Israel, honored him, however, and his home town, Walzenhausen, made their famous native son an honorary citizen. He was even nominated for the Nobel Peace Prize. The Swiss Parliament finally recognized his great deed in 1957, and in 1995 the Swiss Federal Government officially apologized for its long neglect, declaring the consul general to be one of the outstanding citizens in the nation's history. For Carl Lutz this apology came twenty years too late. He had died in 1975.

I hope that through this new English version the story of Carl Lutz, whose unique deed has become part of world history, will inspire those who struggle for racial justice and for world peace in our generation.

Simon Wiesenthal

ACKNOWLEDGMENTS

The idea of writing a book on Carl Lutz germinated during two long conversations I had with the consul during the period of the Eichmann trial. Professional commitments and the inaccessibility of original documents impeded the realization of the project for many years. In the meantime, in 1975, Mr. Lutz passed away, as have most of the eyewitnesses of the Holocaust. However, in recent years documentary evidence has become more fully available. About ten years ago Dr. Simon Wiesenthal encouraged me to engage in such a biographical project. I published a larger, more scientific study in 1995 at the Buchverlag der Neuen Zürcher Zeitung in Zurich, Switzerland, under the title *Carl Lutz und die Juden von Budapest* (ISBN 3 85823 551 2). The present new English version is not a translation but a shorter and more personalized account of the dramatic events in Budapest. It includes new elements which have come to my attention more recently. It limits the dramatic events described to the period from March 1944 to February 1945. I am grateful to the publisher in Zurich for letting me use parts of the original version as a base for the new work.

I would like to acknowledge the help of the following archives for providing the basic materials: The Swiss Federal Archives in Berne (official papers of Carl Lutz), the Archives for Contemporary History of the Federal Technical University in Zurich (private papers and photographic work), the Swiss Eastern Europe Library in Berne (background history), and the Hungarian Academy of Sciences, Department of History, in Budapest (official Hungarian documents). I would also like to thank the members of the Lutz family for additional documents and personal recollections: Gertrud Lutz (died in 1995) and Agnes Hirschi, the consul's stepdaughter. Special thanks go to Alexander (Sandor) Grossman, Harald Feller, Enrico Mandel-Mantello, the son of George, Christina Koerner-Feine, the daughter of Gerhart Feine, Hanspeter Zürcher and Hansjörg Vonrufs from the Zürcher and Vonrufs families, and to several others, who took part in or were close to the dramatic events of 1944/45. The writing of the two books has been a profoundly rich and rewarding, yet disturbing personal experience.

A special word of thanks goes to Ruth and to our children for their stimulating comments and patient support.

Then King Nebuchadnezzar said to his counselors, "Did we not cast three bound men into the fire?" They answered the king, "True, O king." He answered, "But I see four men loose, walking in the fire, and they are not hurt; and the appearance of the fourth is like a son of the gods."

(DANIEL 3:24-25)

Reliable Jewish Hungarian sources credit Swiss consul Carl Lutz (1895–1975) with having saved 62,000 Jews from death. His action was the largest of the kind ever undertaken in Nazi-dominated Europe.

1. THE FORGED PASSPORT

On Sunday, March 19, 1944, Rafi (Raphael) Friedl, a young eighteen-year-old Slovak Jew, alias Janos Sampias, a Catholic Christian, had every reason to fear for his life. Early on that cold, clear spring morning he had been awakened by a distant humming, which grew louder by the second, until all of a sudden a squadron of German Messerschmidts burst forth from behind the silhouette of Buda. In tight formation the planes thundered low across the hill on which stood the historic city. They raced across the Danube and made a wide curve over the vast, flat expanse of Pest, returning in a westerly direction. The Messerschmidts flew so low that Rafi could see the black crosses on the wings with the naked eye. Another squadron followed, and then another. By the time the first unit had described its circle it dovetailed in with the last one of the three, which now flew in front, so that hundreds of planes seemed to be streaking in the sky above Budapest, instead of just a few dozen.

The Germans had to fake strength at this late stage in the war. Their fuel stock was nearly exhausted, but they were anxious that the people of Budapest did not know that. It was the effect which counted. In the course of a few minutes the German airforce had beaten the one and a half million inhabitants of the Hungarian capital into mental submission, the result of an ingrained old habit, dictated by a cruel history, that it was better to submit and to survive than to resist and to die. The German Führer, the leader, knew the psychology of the peoples with whom he dealt.

3

Some years earlier, Rafi Friedl remembered, Hitler had made his planes circle low over Vienna and Prague in a similar way. They were in the air for hours, replete with bombs and rounds of ammunition. If the threatened governments had not capitulated at the last moment, their ancient capitals would have been devastated. No one in Budapest knew why the Messerschmidts had been sent. All kinds of rumors were flying about the town of some disagreement between Hitler and Count Nicholas Horthy, the aged regent of Hungary. They were supposed to be friends. But while official propaganda was abundant, there was no concrete news. Certainly, the promises of easy victory and new greatness had dissolved long ago. From the looks of things, peace seemed as far removed as ever. Everyone craved for an end to the cursed war, because there was not a single family which had not lost a son, a father, or a husband. They had gone to their death in the vast expanse of the Soviet Union. The airplanes would surely be followed by marching boots.

Rafi Friedl was afraid. He had come to Hungary two months earlier, in January, hoping to be safe. His family, his father, his mother, and his brothers and sisters — their memories be blessed — and most of his friends had been pushed into cattle wagons in 1942 and were deported. He himself had escaped only by sheer wits and by his looks. That is, he was tall, blond, and blue-eyed. He did not look how a Jew was supposed to look, short, black eyes, black hair, and so forth. He had heard of death camps, of course, but did not really know what they were, except that they must be something unspeakable. It was better not to think of them, because they reminded him of his family. The *Chalutzim,* the Jewish pioneers, became his new family. Before the war, this organization had fostered emigration to Palestine. When the great disaster took place, the order went out to forget about emigration and to save Jewish lives at all costs, especially children and young people. Jewish substance, the remnant of Israel, must be preserved as a sacred trust. Back and forth Rafi went with other Chalutzim and brought hundreds of Polish and Slovak children across the border to Hungary. This was a dangerous assignment. More than one pioneer was caught and executed, together with the children whom he or she (girls were equal partners) had accompanied. Thus, as a teenager Rafi had passed through more dangers and seen more horrors than most adults in a lifetime. In January 1944 he felt, however, that pressure was mounting and that he himself could be caught. The border police and the secret services were aided by a treasonable anti-semite populace on both sides of the frontier. This is why he fled to Hungary with a fresh document. It was a forged Slovak passport made out in the name of a Christian called Janos Sampias, from whom he had bought it. The only authentic part of the passport was his own photograph, which he had carefully glued in.

All day on that fateful Sunday Rafi remained locked up in his room. Sure enough, by the time the pealing church bells called Christians together for worship, their sounds became interspersed with those of the grinding chains of armored cars and the noise of soldiers' steps and staccato-like orders of officers. There were no explosions. There was no shooting. Hungary really seemed to submit without protest. From behind the curtains of his room, Rafi observed the timid worshippers as they found their way to the churches, a habit which even the momentous event of an occupation could not break. But then these people did not have to worry as much as a Jew.

There was an air raid alarm during the day. The sirens went off, and several bombs exploded. This seemed to be the way the Americans protested against the German occupation, Rafi believed. He remained locked up in his small rented room in the crammed apartment house in Josephtown on the Pest side of the Danube, waiting for "the" knock, which could mean the end. But there was silence. Perhaps because his landlady really believed Mr. Sampias to be a Slovak, as he had told her. She had shown his passport to the police, as any landlady was required, and she noticed his blond hair and blue eyes. Apparently neither the landlady nor the police had suspected anything to be wrong. They did not even notice that the original photograph had been replaced. Rafi had moreover told the woman that he was really an American citizen, because his father had emigrated to the United States years earlier. Had not the war come in between, he would have followed him across the ocean. She seemed impressed and said that she also had relatives in the United States. How could he tell her that his father had been deported, because he was a Jew? Rafi was of course aware that any trained security man would see that his papers were not in order. When "they" had doubts, they could always pull down his pants and look whether he was circumcised or not. Sampias said, after Rafi had given him the money, he would simply tell the Slovak authorities that his passport had been lost or stolen. He would, at any rate, run little risk, even if the authorities did not believe him. Yet Rafi never knew what his landlady really thought. Once or twice he had cracked antisemitic jokes, in order to test her. But like most people in such a position, she had a closed face. He could assume that she, like all landladies, landlords, and doorkeepers worked hand in glove with the police.

Sunday passed, and a night.

Rafi shook visibly as he left the apartment house early on Monday morning, the 20th. Before he closed the door behind him, he hesitated and looked up and down the street. Then he walked away jauntily, sure that the landlady's eyes were following him. Few people scurried about. They, too, seemed to be afraid. Rafi walked in measured steps. Running or even hasty steps would attract attention. He whistled and tried to look cheerful, just like the few gendarmes, who were out in the streets, together with the Nyilas, those frightful teenagers in their green uniforms of the Arrow Cross party, the Hungarian Nazis. The previous government had kept them under tight control. Now they were coming out in the open. Luckily, no one paid any attention to Rafi. The gendarmes and the Nyilas stood in small groups, apparently debating what the occupation could mean for them, admiring the armored vehicles of the Germans and looking at the occasional passing officers with the ominous rune-like SS insignia. Henceforth, Rafi thought, no one would restrain the gendarmes from showing their power. Assisted by the uncouth Nyilas, they would annoy the passersby, demanding identification papers, bringing them to police posts, and pushing people around in general. Looking over to the Danube, Rafi noticed that German troops had positioned themselves at both ends of the bridges which connected Pest with Buda. The public buildings were also surrounded by Germans. He looked up at the royal castle and Gellert Hill across the river. If he squinted, he could see that these historic points, too, were in the hands of the Nazi invaders.

Rafi Friedl headed towards Szabadsag-tér, Freedom Square, a tree-studded open space in downtown Pest, not far from the Danube. One side of the square was bordered by the stock market, now closed, and the other by a large six-floor office building constructed during the 1920s. This imposing structure was the former American legation. Ever since late December 1941, when Hungary and the United States found themselves in a state of war, the building had been administered by neutral Switzerland. The small Alpine republic was the "protective power" of American interests in Hungary as long as the war lasted. The building retained its extra-territorial status. The person in charge of the operation was Consul Carl Lutz, who had replaced the American minister. He had come to Budapest at the beginning of 1942 and directed his activities from the former office of the American minister on the second floor. The consul's tasks were manifold. He took care of American, British, and other foreign citizens or dual nationals, who had been stranded in Hungary after the outbreak of the war. He saw to it that their papers were in order. He made arrangements concerning claims and inheritances. He looked after prisoners of war, mostly downed airmen. Above all, he cooperated with the Budapest office of the Jewish Agency of Palestine in providing protective letters and emigration papers to Jewish children and young people, who had sought safety in Hungary, but whom the Chalutzim wanted to get out. All in all, at this moment the consul was responsible for no fewer than 3,000 persons. On occasion he passed on diplomatic notes to the Hungarian government from the United States, Great Britain, Romania, Egypt, Belgium, Chile, and several other Latin American states. If a note was of a certain importance, Lutz would request his immediate superior, the Swiss representative in Hungary, Minister Maximilian Jaeger, to accompany him on visits to the Hungarian foreign minister or to the regent, Horthy, the chief of state. The Swiss foreign ministry in Berne received such notes and sent them to Budapest via the diplomatic pouch. In return, Hungarian notes were transmitted to the concerned powers in the same way. It was Switzerland's task to ensure that communication channels remained open despite the war, while trying to avoid direct contacts between the belligerents.

This was the man, no less, whom Rafi Friedl wanted to see on this morning.

Rafi had never met Carl Lutz, but he knew that if there was anyone in the city of Budapest who could deliver him from danger, it was the Swiss consul. Rafi had often been told by his contacts at the Budapest office of the Jewish Agency for Palestine about the involvement of this Swiss diplomat, with whose help hundreds if not thousands of children and young people had reached safety in Palestine. Among Budapest Jews, Rafi knew, Carl Lutz was a household name. He had heard that both the consul and his equally remarkable wife, Gertrud, had always taken the time to see the children off from the Danube pier, when, about once a week, a train or boat was about to leave.

The young Slovak had reached the vast expanse of Freedom Square, when he noted an unusual scene near the former American legation. Despite the early hour, several dozen men, women, and children were anxiously pushing towards the main entry. They were loudly arguing with two consular employees, who blocked their way. These people were obviously Jews, because Rafi heard them say that they were afraid and wanted the consul to get them out of Hungary. The quicker the better. If not, the Germans would arrest them all before the day was over. Rafi had seen this same fear before in Slovakia, when the Jews were deported. The Hungarian Jews, he remembered, had never taken seriously the tales of the persecution of Jews in other countries. Such horror stories had been spread about the Germans during the previous war, they said. Had the shamefaced Allies not been forced to admit after the war that these tales had been nothing but propaganda? Even if they were true now, neither deportations nor death camps could possibly happen in this country where Christians and Jews had lived together in happy symbiosis for a thousand years. Now, on this morning, the faces of the frightened Jews showed that the myth had exploded. They could not even flee. The radio had announced that the borders were closed to all Jews. The presence of gendarmes and Nyilas on the square increased their sense of fear and helplessness.

As Rafi approached the entry to the legation he rehearsed for the tenth time what he would say to the consul. That his name was Janos Sampias. That he had an American father. That the representative of American interests in Hungary should give him papers, which would prove that he was an American citizen. The Swiss consul should place

8

him under his formal protection. This would place him beyond the reach of any Hungarian gendarme. He could no longer be arrested simply because he was a Jew. No one would draft him into forced labor. Above all, no one could deport him. Rafi told himself that he really was in a privileged position; he did not have to fear for his life like these poor people, who were like beggars for life. He edged forward, through the crowd. He looked up at the Swiss coat of arms, the white cross in the red field, which was attached to the wall above the entry. There was an inscription next to the door, written in Hungarian and in German, which said that this building was administered by the Swiss legation and enjoyed extraterritorial status. Inside that door, he would be as good as inside Switzerland, where a reasonable people had built up a reasonable society with fair laws for all and with no war and no dictators. Rafi had often dreamt of a country which had realized the vision of Plato's *Republic*. He had read it in school, ages ago, when his mother and his father were still alive, wondering why most governors were so utterly incapable of following the ancient philosopher's advice. Switzerland must be like that.

Rafi ignored the angry recriminations of those who had waited for hours to enter the legation. He said to the two employees that he was an American citizen and wanted to see "his" consul. It seemed easy to lie, but then Rafi had lied all the time with the Chalutzim as he had crossed the border with the children again and again. He had become hardened beyond his age. The employees asked for his papers. Rafi showed them his Slovak passport. They told him to wait like everyone else. But Rafi insisted that they had to take him at his word. He would protest to the consul in person if he was kept waiting much longer. After a further battle of words, the irritated guards finally let him enter. One of them took him up to the consul's secretary on the second floor. She was at that moment involved in conversation with Gertrud Lutz, the consul's wife, a medium-sized chestnut-haired young woman in her early thirties. The secretary told Rafi curtly to wait, because Mr. Lutz was engaged in an important conference. The two women returned to their conversation. They talked in Swiss-German, which Rafi could not understand, but he gathered from an occasional word that they spoke about the events of the last two days and of the Jews waiting below. Once in a while they looked out of the window and studied the people.

The meeting in the consul's office took time and Rafi became impatient. He wanted to open the door to his office and to speak to him. The secretary held Rafi back and told him to take a chair and to wait. There was an angry exchange between the two, because Rafi said that his business was serious. The secretary answered that all business these days was serious. Gertrud Lutz came to Rafi's side and patted his arm. She said in a quiet though straightforward way that everyone, including herself, was impatient nowadays and that they were all on edge. Her husband, the consul, would surely answer all questions to his satisfaction as soon as he could. Rafi was taken aback. The consul's wife possessed an inborn authority, he thought, to which he readily submitted. For the first time since he had seen the Messerschmidts on the day before he felt less nervous.

Finally the door of the consul's office opened. Carl Lutz stepped into the reception office. He was tall, thin, and dark-haired. His glasses gave him a reserved, professorial, even a shy look, perhaps more severe than he intended. He was in his late forties, older by some years than Gertrud, Rafi noted. The consul was still engaged in a low-voiced conversation with three distinguished-looking gentlemen, who were right behind him. One of them Rafi knew, Moshe Krausz, the secretary of the Budapest office of the Jewish Agency for Palestine. He was the one to whom he had turned over the Polish and Slovak Jewish children after crossing over into Hungary. Krausz was about forty. Rafi knew him to be an annoyingly meticulous and fussy administrator, given to gossip. But in his slow bureaucratic way Krausz did get things done. Rafi exchanged a brief glance with him and nodded. The other two men he did not know, but from their conversation he soon could guess who they were. The first was a man in his fifties of impressive bearing. He had a straightforward look and was clearly in charge of the three. This was Otto Komoly, the president of the Palestine Office. He was a well-known engineer. As an officer he had fought with great distinction in the Austro-Hungarian army during the previous war. Today he demonstratively wore his silver Militärverdienstkreuz, first class, medal, which Habsburg emperor Charles had pinned on him for bravery in the field, even though he had been a Jew. Surely no fanatic would lay his hand on him, he, who had risked his life for Hun-

10

gary. The third person was a young, bespectacled lawyer in his thirties, clearly an intellectual. He had a German-sounding name, Rezsö (Rudolf) Kasztner. Rafi had vaguely heard of him. This lawyer had arrived in Budapest only recently, coming from Transylvania, which used to belong to Romania. But already he was making a name for himself within the Jewish community. Kasztner was the vice president of the Palestine Office. Only later would Rafi learn that Krausz led behind-the-scenes intrigues against Kasztner, who was so much more brilliant than he, and — more seriously — that Komoly and Kasztner were also at odds. Komoly wanted to organize Jewish resistance, while Kasztner preferred to work out a "deal" with the enemy, in order to save Jewish lives. However, on this second day of the German occupation all three were united in trying to avert the grave danger for Hungarian Jewry.

The consul and his three visitors kept talking, standing together in the middle of the reception room. They conversed in German, although the visitors sometimes fell into Hungarian, when they wanted to explain a special point to each other. Rafi gathered that the Palestine Office had been ransacked by gendarmes and German SS that morning. Some important lists of potential émigrés had been taken away. This was a bad omen. Lutz repeated what he apparently had said before, that he was prepared to take the Palestine Office into the legation, until they all could see their way more clearly. The three men eagerly nodded their approval. Lutz continued, saying that this was an unusual offer for a diplomatic representative to make, but that he would somehow try to straighten out the matter with the Hungarian foreign ministry, assuming the government still functioned. He was also sure that his superior, Minister Jaeger, would approve. Then he gave instructions to his secretary that an office or two be turned over to Mr. Krausz and his staff.

But then Lutz mentioned a figure of 8,000, and his face became grave. Rafi almost jumped from his seat when he realized that the consul was talking about the children and young people who were registered for emigration to Palestine at this moment. Had he, Rafi, not spirited some of them to Hungary at the risk of his own life? He heard the consul say that between 1942 and March 19, 1944, the Palestine Office had, with his help, transported no less than 10,000 Jewish children and young people out of

Hungary and dispatched them in the direction of Palestine. The 8,000 more were the next batch to follow. Rafi's mind became fully alert as he listened to Lutz express his concern about the radio news, that all emigration abroad for Jews was stopped. He had not yet received official confirmation, Lutz said, but he had no doubt this new decision had been made at the instigation of the German occupants and that it was a most serious matter. What was to be done? Clearly, there was no one else in the country to defend these young lives but he. The new people in power wanted to move not only against the Palestine Office but against the Swiss representative of foreign interests. It was part of an ugly game of international politics.

Gertrud Lutz did not hesitate to join the conversation. She wanted an answer to an even more immediate problem, she said. What was to be done with the people waiting outside, especially the women and children? Some had been there since the day before. They could catch pneumonia. She had been told that many Jews were expelled from their apartments. More would doubtless arrive. They would be getting hungrier as the day wore on, and their meager supplies were eaten up. Neither the consul nor his three visitors had an answer. It was obvious that the Jews would try to seek the safety of foreign diplomatic buildings. But could they be let in without causing serious diplomatic repercussions? The consul answered his wife that a solution had to be found, but he did not know yet what kind. The problem was that the authorities could suspend the extra-territorial status of the former American legation and declare him persona non grata. This would mean not only the end of the Department of Foreign Interests of the Swiss legation, but the end of all protection for Jews, including the 8,000. Lutz was obviously disturbed over the multiplicity of the problems, for which he saw no solution. His hesitations seemed to nettle Gertrud. She said she would go downstairs in order to see what she could do. Vaguely, Rafi heard the consul remark to his parting visitors that he was about to rush off in order see his superior, Swiss minister Jaeger. He needed his advice before the situation got out of hand. The secretary whispered into the consul's ear. He turned and looked at the young visitor.

Before Rafi knew it, he was ushered into the vast office of Carl Lutz. Although it was clear to the young man that the consul was under stress, he made Rafi sink into a leather sofa and gave him his full attention. Rafi, in the light of what he had just learned, felt embarrassed. He said that his problem was small and personal, compared with what he had heard before. Lutz smiled and ignored the remark. Rafi repeated his rehearsed story, while the consul leafed through the forged Slovak passport and listened. That his name was Janos Sampias. That his father had emigrated to the United States and had become an American citizen, which made him an American citizen, too. Could the consul certify his United States citizenship? Lutz put the passport down and his eyes quietly focussed on Rafi, as the young man kept talking. It seemed to him as if the consul could penetrate his thoughts and didn't believe a word. Lutz asked a few questions about Rafi's origins in Slovakia and his arrival in Budapest. He also said he noticed that he seemed to know Mr. Krausz, which Rafi affirmed. But the vice consul did not pursue this point, and Rafi wondered why he had asked.

Then the consul rose and walked to a cupboard. He pulled out a drawer and took out several forms. At the top it said United States Department of Justice. Then he asked Mr. Sampias whether he knew English. Rafi had said yes, although he had mastered little more than a smattering, which he had hastily acquired from a friend as soon as he had decided to visit the Swiss consul. He nearly lost his countenance when he glanced at the title of the forms and saw the abundance of questions, page after page. He heard the vice consul say, as from afar, that Mr. Sampias should take his time in filling out the questionnaire. Upon completion he would send it by diplomatic courier to the Swiss foreign ministry in Berne. From there it would go for verification to the American authorities in Washington. As soon as these gave their approval, which would doubtless take several months, he, Lutz, would issue a *Schutzpass,* a protective passport. This Swiss document would say that Mr. Sampias was a recognized American citizen living in Hungary, and that he enjoyed the full protection of Switzerland.

The consul gently pushed Rafi into the reception room. The secretary was alone. Lutz asked her to find a small office for Mr. Sampias so that he could fill out some American forms, undisturbed. He himself was rushing off to the Swiss legation on Stefania Street. Would she please call

Minister Jaeger, telling him that he was on his way. Lutz added that he would see Mr. Sampias again after his return.

*   *   *

Alexander (Sandor) Grossman, a merchant from Miskolc and a tested *Hechalutz,* a pioneer, who was to become a key aide to Consul Lutz, gave a vivid description of the mental condition of his fellow Jews at that fateful moment in Hungarian history:

> For the Jews the real tragedy of the German occupation on March 19 was at first not external and visible. Their first defeat was a loss of self-confidence. Only a small layer, that is, the young people belonging to the Chalutzim and their friends, judged the situation realistically. These young people began at once to organize actions of rescue and resistance. They cooperated with the leadership of the socialist, communist, and Small Landholder parties. However, the large majority of the Jews — including their official leaders — were helpless. Despite alarm signals, despite the close official friendship between Hungary and Germany and despite growing pressures, the Jews were never able to analyze their own situation properly. To a large extent this was due to the undignified Hungarian chauvinism, which Jewish officials had taught their fellow believers to accept "This is not possible here," the Hungarian Jews told themselves, as they listened to the horror stories filtering in from Germany, Austria, Czechoslovakia, Poland, etc. When, after the coming of the Germans, the danger became obvious, many Jews committed suicide. Most retreated into silent pain and utter passiveness. Jewry became fatalistic. When distress reached its peak, it was, finally, the pioneers and their circle, who, despite dangers to their lives, attempted to save their persecuted brothers and sisters.

Reszö Kasztner judged his fellow Jews even more severely. The Jews of Hungary, he said, though they were aware of the catastrophe of Jewry in neighboring countries, continued to lead a life of "prudent indifference."

The Budapest Jews, in particular, were individualists and had little sense of community. They were incapable of conceiving the kind of uprising like the one of the Jews of Warsaw in 1943. Not long before the Germans occupied Hungary, for instance, Otto Komoly gave a talk before the Society of Former Jewish Officers and the Society of Jewish War Veterans (of World War I) about the tragedy in Poland. He warned his listeners of a coming disaster in Hungary. They would not even listen and booed him out. Of course, the Hungarian Jews fully knew that any plan of resistance was difficult to prepare because of the antisemitic spirit of "Christian" Hungarians. These would hardly support a Jewish uprising. Moreover, "there were informers and agents provocateurs at every corner. The kindly neighbor and the good-natured door keeper were all anxious to see the Jews 'punished'." There was no spirit of solidarity as in Denmark, where an entire nation decided to save its Jews. This despair was doubtless dominant in Reszö Kasztner's mind when, at a given moment, he engaged in his ill-fated negotiations with the SS.

*   *   *

Two policemen who were on guard duty opened the gate of the Swiss legation when Consul Lutz pulled up in the black Packard, which he had inherited from the former American minister. Lutz got out of the car before Szluha, his driver, could open the door for him. He was only a consul, and not a high-ranking diplomat, he always told Szluha. No fuss must be made over his person.

The minister had been waiting. Maximilian Jaeger was in his late fifties. He was the jovial kind of diplomat, married into wealth and therefore not dependent on a salary. During the previous war, for instance, when he was first secretary at the Swiss legation in Paris, he pointedly liked to assert his independence by sauntering out of the legation whenever he was in no mood for work, and to pass hours in the nearby Jardins du Luxembourg, looking at young ladies. His superior, the Swiss minister to France, would complain to Foreign Minister Giuseppe Motta in Berne about this lack of discipline. But he added with resignation that no admonishment ever impressed Jaeger, because he knew that he had his own means. Motta, who was authoritarian but generous, let the matter pass. He knew Jaeger to be a potentially capable diplomat, who needed responsibilities of his own. After the war, in 1924, Motta sent Jaeger to Vienna, as Swiss minister to the two newly created Republics of Austria and Hungary. Here, his "independent means" came into their own because, above and beyond the meager expense allowances from Berne for representative purposes, Jaeger was able to give splendid receptions and dinners, which soon belonged to the most sought after social events of Vienna. Thus, during the troublesome years between the two wars, until the annexation of Austria by Hitler in 1938, Jaeger became the best informed diplomat in the former Habsburg capital. His reports to Motta bristled with sharp analyses of events and power holders. When, in 1938, the legation in Vienna was closed down, Jaeger moved to Budapest and concentrated on Hungary alone. Jaeger detested rightist politicians, but in his earlier years he sometimes expressed antisemite feelings in his reports to Motta, which was fashionable among the European elite of the time. To Jaeger's credit, it must be said that the National Socialist excesses which he had seen during the annexation of Austria caused him to change his outlook.

He was anxious just as Lutz was to talk about the momentous events that were shaking Hungary. Berne had already cabled for a full report. The minister seemed profoundly disturbed when the consul told him about the crowd of Jews waiting outside the former American legation and about the 8,000 children and young people who were registered for departure to Palestine and could not leave. So often in history, Jaeger said, reasons of state, or rather diplomatic custom, clashed with human considerations. That is, if the mad rantings of someone like Hitler had anything to do with reasons of state. His voice dropped to a whisper as he opened the door to his office. Lutz knew that whenever Jaeger spoke in a whisper, he always came up with behind-the-scenes tales about the high and mighty. The minister said that a member of Horthy's entourage had overheard some German at Schloss Klessheim say that the Führer was definitely suffering from terminal syphilis. As a young man he had years ago become infected by a Jewish prostitute in Vienna. He is said to have threatened his physician with summary execution if word of this disgrace got out. But other people apparently also knew. The disease was now affecting his brain, which explained some of his irrational decisions and absurd behavior. Jaeger added that he had heard a rumor about this already years ago, when he was Swiss minister in Vienna. At that time he had not taken the story seriously. If true, he said, it went a long way to explain Hitler's vengeful attitude towards the Jews.

Lutz shrugged his shoulders ruefully. If there was a God of justice, he asked, why couldn't he make the disease strike Hitler now, to free the world of the monster? Why wait?

What followed was one of the most memorable conversations Lutz had ever had with Minister Jaeger. At first, the minister called in two other associates of the legation. There was Anton Kilchmann, the first secretary of the legation. He was a career diplomat in his forties, who had married late in life. He was a nervous, fidgety man, prudent, if not timid. Then there was Harald Feller, the legation's juridical advisor. Feller, thirty-one, was lively, short, and alert. He liked to take chances on any given issue. He had wanted to become an actor, but his father, a renowned university professor, was adamant against it, because as an actor he could not make a living, he said. He forced his son to take up law.

Jaeger explained the dilemma of Consul Lutz to Kilchmann and to Feller, and said that they all needed to be clear about what was happening and what line they were to follow. Hitler had virtually ordered the Hungarian regent to come to Klessheim Castle near Salzburg, because he feared that Hungary was about to betray him, like Italy, a few months earlier. After a shouting match between the Führer and Horthy — during which Hitler doubtless had the louder voice — he made Horthy sign a "joint" declaration that Hungary would keep fighting at Germany's side until final victory. Horthy "joyfully" invited German troops to be stationed on its soil. So much for public eyewash, Jaeger concluded.

Did Minister Jaeger know what additional concessions Horthy had made, apart from agreeing to occupation? Yes, Hungary would have to raise 300,000 additional men for the Soviet front. It would place its economic resources at Germany's disposal, its heavy industry, which was to be run by the German SS, and it would send most of its agricultural supplies to guess who? And, listen to this, Hungary would have to dispatch a labor force of 100,000 to Germany for its war industry. And, as if this were not enough, Hitler made Horthy agree to install a new, fully subservient government. Hitler even named the new prime minister, Döme Sztojay, Hungary's minister to Berlin. He was an admirer of the Nazis, as everyone knew, but of weak character. Moreover, on his return from Klessheim Castle, Horthy was accompanied by the new German minister to Hungary, one Edmund Veesenmayer, who was really meant to be Hitler's proconsul and watchdog. Veesenmayer was an ambitious Nazi and SS man of less than forty, a troublemaker, if there ever was one. He had agitated in Austria and Czechoslovakia in order to prepare for the German takeover. Moreover, he, Jaeger, had heard that Veesenmayer had organized the border incident near Danzig in 1939, which Hitler took as a pretext for his attack on Poland. An utterly undesirable character.

Jaeger fell silent. This was a complete and shameful sellout, Feller finally said. Did Horthy, who always claimed to be such a good patriot, really agree to all this? Horthy, never known for his intelligence, had come to Klessheim Castle unprepared, Jaeger answered, and apparently thought of suicide, as if suicide was a useful strategy. Hitler must have guessed it and said to him that if he did not comply, he would hold his family as hostages. Mephistopheles, that is, Hitler, held the old man in his hands like a lump of clay.

The staff members of the Swiss legation were appalled. The "agreement" of Klessheim Castle was more than a sellout. It was the collapse of Hungarian civilization. Now Horthy sat again in his royal castle, sulking and seeing nobody. Veesenmayer ruled Hungary.

How about the Jews? Lutz asked. Jaeger said he wished he didn't have to answer that question. He continued that after his return from Klessheim Castle Horthy called a crown council, where Hitler's orders were obediently adopted. Already Sztojay, that idiot of a prime minister, went about repeating what he had been told by SS general Kaltenbrunner, a close friend of "Minister" Veesenmayer: "Hungary must in the first place follow the example of its neighboring countries and solve the Jewish question."

Jaeger answered that the consul would have to judge how he could walk the tightrope between helping the people at his doorstep and avoiding becoming a persona non grata. Whatever Lutz decided, he would back him up. About the 8,000 potential émigrés, Jaeger said that the Swiss legation did not have to accept the prohibition for these Jews not to cross the border. He suggested that he and Lutz submit a formal protest to the Hungarian authorities, although he was skeptical about how much good it would do. They would insist that according to international law all new governments were obligated to respect international agreements entered into by their predecessors. "We must not let his pass!" he said.

Jaeger arose. The meeting was over. Casually he added that Veesenmayer had invited him to a reception for diplomats in Budapest. On that occasion he, Jaeger, would seek an appointment for the consul so that he could raise the issue of the 8,000 directly with Hitler's "proconsul."

*　　*　　*

It was late in the afternoon when the black Packard recrossed Pest, perhaps a notch faster than earlier when Szluha had steered the car in the opposite direction. Szluha sensed that the consul was in a more determined mood than when he had driven him to Stefania Street. There were, it was true, few automobiles running about wartime Budapest. The horse-drawn vehicles could of course constitute certain dangers now as dusk was descending over the vast city. No lights were attached to any carriage, horse-drawn or not, because of the increasing air raids. The Packard passed the small Josephtown railway station, and a few minutes later the large Eastern railway station came into view. Szluha reduced speed— there were German and Hungarian soldiers milling about. From this point the troops departed for or returned from the eastern front. The Packard turned left on Rakoczi Avenue. As they passed the Great Synagogue Lutz ordered Szluha to slow down. The consul peered through the dusk at the great, century-old pseudo-Moorish building and at its small garden, where there were some graves from former days. He remembered that there used to be so much pulsing life around the synagogue, even during the week. Now the building stood deserted, like a museum relic detached from its original purpose, except for one or two gendarmes who walked up and down in front of it to keep warm. The Jewish community of Budapest seemed to avoid its central holy place. The gendarmes would note immediately if anyone was foolish enough to try to enter the synagogue. The consul felt the weight of the dark threat that lay over Hungary's Jewry.

The crowd was still waiting when Lutz arrived at the former American legation. They appeared perhaps a trifle more desperate than before. Their fear was comprehensible, because the gendarmes and the green-shirted young Nyilas seemed to be moving closer, as if they were setting their trap. Occasionally, they made nasty calls to their prospective victims. Once night had fully descended, the consul thought, no one knew what these torturers would do. A giant boxer-like figure emerged from among the Nyilas, apparently the leader. He had large peasant hands, and one could easily imagine these tightening around a victim's neck and crushing the bones. Defiantly he sneered at Lutz, as if to say that the game was up for "nice people" like the Swiss consul. Szluha whispered to Lutz that he knew the fellow, a well-known brawler and drunk from the north by the name of Zoltan Bagossy. Some years ago, the authorities had been so desperate, Szluha continued, that they had sent him out of the country. Later, it was said that he had gone to Africa and became the personal bodyguard of Haile Selassie, the emperor of Ethiopia. Now he saw that he was back, Szluha said. He was not surprised seeing Bagossy among the Nyilas. He could never be anything but a street rowdy. "I see, Szluha," Bagossy shouted, "that you have told the consul who I am. Well, we shall not lose sight of each other." He had spoken in Hungarian and Szluha tried to translate for the consul. But Lutz waved with his hand and said he thought he understood. Some of the people shook with fear and cold, and again appealed to Lutz to protect them. The consul asked Szluha if he would be afraid to wait outside for a short moment to keep an eye on things. But he should not let himself be provoked by the "forces of order," least of all by Bagossy. The driver nodded. "You have courage, Szluha!" Lutz said. In these days, Szluha answered, a man had to choose his side. Lutz was astonished at his driver, a man of such discretion and few words. During the two years he had employed Szluha, he had never spoken as much.

Inside the hallway Lutz came across Gertrud. She had, on her own authority, started to take women and their children and some old people inside. They would have died out there, she said to her surprised husband. Besides, one never knew what those fellows would do. She added that she was sure he would approve. The kitchen in the basement was providing warm milk and food. Lutz looked around. There were people sleeping or resting alongside the walls. Gertrud said she had found more space for them in the hallways. She was sure that their presence would not disturb the normal operations of the consulate.

Normal operations, thought Lutz, what were they, when thousands of human beings were threatened by death? He was astonished, though perhaps he shouldn't be, to see his wife doing the obvious, while he and the minister, their colleagues, and probably the whole diplomatic corps in Budapest were debating what acts could be interpreted as interference in the internal affairs of the host country, what exactly constituted extra-territoriality, and how, according to international law, human rights ought — perhaps — to be protected. With her straightforward finesse Gertrud looked people in the eye, acted, and raised legal niceties later. It was as simple as that.

Lutz remembered how some years earlier, after the outbreak of the war in 1939, when he was Swiss consular agent in Palestine, Gertrud had unabashedly called on the British high commissioner in Jerusalem, without telling him, her husband. She, still in her twenties, told the top official for Palestine that she had discovered a concentration camp in Bethlehem, of all places, filled with the Arab wives of German settlers and their children. Their husbands had been drafted into the German army or were prisoners of war of the British. Babies had been born in the camp, and the hygienic conditions were appalling. Meekly, the high commissioner objected that there might be spies among these women. This was why he had them locked up. Nonsense, Gertrud said, what did women know about military things? And how about the babies, were they spies, too? She did not leave the high commissioner's office until he had given her the assurance that the camp would be dissolved. When? she asked. Promptly. A few days later, she turned up in Bethlehem again. The high commissioner had kept his word. The Swiss honorary consul for Palestine, one Jonas Kuebler, was terribly upset, Lutz recalled, when he heard of Gertrud's unauthorized visit to the high commissioner. He said that the British authorities could react badly and move against the consulate and all Swiss economic interests in Palestine, including Kuebler's export-import business. But nothing happened. Gertrud had simply shamed the British high commissioner into doing what was obvious. She made him realize that it was bad taste to arrest these women and their children in the first place. Besides, during her talk with him, she let it drop casually that it would be embarrassing to the British government if the story hit the press. Of course, Lutz knew that the ethics of a British governor were probably different from those of a dyed-in-the-wool Nazi.

Now it was Gertrud's turn to be astonished. Her husband turned on his heels, opened the door wide, and loudly told the waiting crowd to come in. Then he walked out to the outer edges of the crowd — there were perhaps two hundred people — and created a psychological barrier in the face of the astonished gendarmes and the Nyilas, until everyone was inside. He was really looking for Bagossy, but the giant was no longer there.

The secretary came upon the scene when Lutz closed the door behind him. She was perplexed when she saw the crowd. When the vice consul noticed from her facial expression that she neither understood nor really approved, he said to her, almost apologetically, that he had no idea how he would explain this to Minister Jaeger, not to mention the Hungarian authorities and their German friends. The secretary made no comment. She said dryly that Mr. Sampias was still waiting for the vice consul upstairs.

Janos Sampias, indeed. Lutz had forgotten that he had left him hours ago with those American forms. He rushed to the little office in which Rafi had spent the day, intending to apologize. But the young man was asleep, his head resting in the middle of the scattered papers. Lutz noted that some of the passages were erased or crossed out and filled in again. This would never do for Washington. Rafi woke up, shocked to see the consul standing in front of him. He rose to his feet. He looked confused and shook his head. He pointed at the papers. He had to admit the truth, he was not Janos Sampias. He was no American citizen, either, as he had pretended, but a simple Slovak Jew by the name of Rafi Friedl, who was afraid for his life. That's why he had lied. He had bought the passport from someone called Janos Sampias and had replaced the photograph. For two months he had lived in Budapest with this passport, expecting to be caught, because sooner or later the Slovak authorities would inform the Hungarian police about the missing passport. Now that the Germans had come to Hungary, he had no chance to survive anyway. He might as well commit suicide like so many other Jews. Rafi said he had no idea who the father, mother, and grandparents of Sampias were, or where they lived. What he had written on the papers was a pack of lies. He, the consul, would surely have seen it at once. He was experienced with liars like him. Rafi broke down and cried. Could the consul please help him?

For the rest of his life Rafi Friedl would never forget what the Swiss consul answered. Lutz picked up the papers and said not to worry about them. The administrative procedures to verify his identity, even if everything was truthful, would take months and months: "By that time, we might both be dead." He said that he would issue a Swiss protective passport to him, on which it stated that he, Raphael Friedl — not Janos Sampias — was a bona fide American citizen and that he stood under the protection of Switzerland. "However, if we survive this chaos, I must ask you to return this document, which I shall hand you tonight, to me and not to say a word to anyone as long as I am in the service of the Swiss government."

This was a clear case of exceeding his authority, if not of forging false papers. Lutz knew that if Marcel Pilet-Golaz, the foreign minister in Berne, who in 1940 had succeeded Giuseppe Motta, were to hear about this case, he would recall him at once and bring him before an administrative court. Pilet-Golaz was an authoritarian bureaucrat, but unlike Motta, he had no charisma. Even if the story had become public after the war, long after all danger had passed, Lutz could have been fired.

Rafi Friedl survived the war. In 1947 he emigrated to Israel and changed his name to Ben-Shalom. He served his new country as an ambassador to Mali, Cambodia, and Romania. When, in 1961, Swiss diplomat René J. Keller became accredited to Mali as ambassador, he paid an official visit to his Israeli colleague, Ben-Shalom, in order to introduce himself. He sent him a note prior to the visit. "I was astonished at the most cordial reception by Mr. Ben-Shalom," Keller wrote in a letter to a friend. "The Israeli ambassador said: 'When I received your lines, I was moved to tears.' 'What was so heart-rending about my text?' 'It was not the text, but the stamp on it, which was almost identical with the stamp on the protective passport which in Budapest saved the life of a poor Slovak Jew called Rafi Friedl. My life!'"

Luckily, Carl Lutz had retired just a few months earlier.

*   *   *

Starting on March 19, 1944, a series of cudgel blows prepared unsuspecting Hungarian Jewry for its extinction: (1) arrest of all the moderate politicians who had tried to extricate Hungary from its fatal alliance with Nazi Germany and who had protected the Jews; (2) wearing of the yellow star (Jews could thus be easily recognized, molested in public, and arrested without warrant); (3) confiscation of apartments and housing, officially in favor of "Christians," who had lost their homes during Allied air raids; (4) prohibition of travel, no ownership of telephones or radios, suspension of mail service; (5) confiscation of real estate; (6) loss of jobs in industry, banking, commerce, social services and state offices; (7) loss of movable property, bank accounts, jewelry, etc.; (8) house arrest for all Jews, except for two hours each day to make purchases, etc.

From one moment to the next Hungarian Jews not only became paupers. They were beggars.

Within days of March 19, 1944, the age-old Jewish-Christian symbiosis of Hungary broke apart. This symbiosis was, however, a Jewish myth, not shared by the Christians, because there had been persecutions, pogroms, and anti-Jewish legislation throughout Hungarian history. Up to the middle of the nineteenth century the Christian majority had kept the Jews "in their place," by restrictions of every kind. As soon as these restrictions were lifted, the Christian Hungarians found that the centuries of repression had simply made the Jews more adaptable, flexible, learned, and clever than the rest. Now they became free to develop their talents openly and to compete with the Christian majority. The Jews turned out to be more urbane and seemingly more intelligent than the Christians. They knew languages better than anyone else. They had ready-made international connections, and they knew what was going on in the world. As money lenders and then financiers of the rich and powerful, they knew all state secrets. So much so, that there were Christians who imagined that the Jews were plotting to take over the world, no less. Moreover, the Jewish women were more beautiful than ordinary Hungarian women. The Jews, though only 10 percent of the population of seven to eight million, built up Hungary's industries, peopled its universities, shaped law, medicine, and the arts. Others — who were not rich — worked as skilled factory laborers, and they were clever enough to organize workers' unions, often against other Jews, the richer ones. Had it not been for the Jews, Hungary would have remained a backward rural society, governed by reactionary aristocrats and Catholic and Protestant clerics. The Jews were the salt of the earth. But they were also patriots. They fought in World War I and lost tens of thousands of their young men. They shed tears along with the rest, when at the peace treaty of Trianon in 1920 Hungary lost 60 percent of its territory. Even when Horthy killed several thousand Jews during his maneuvers to win power in the 1920s and when the Fascists and the Arrow Cross gained importance in the 1930s, chanting nasty slogans against the Jews, Hungarian Jews believed with a surprising steadfastness that these were nothing but short, if ugly, moments in history. They would soon pass, as they always had before. Even when Adolf Hitler took Hungary under his deadly wings during the late 1930s and made the parliament adopt restrictive legislation, the Jews believed lightheartedly that time would solve that problem, too. The Jews were clever in many ways, but in politics they were not.

2. THE CONFRONTATION

Walzenhausen, where Carl Lutz was born, hangs like an eagle's nest on a steep slope in northeastern Switzerland. In one breathtaking view the villagers behold on clear days the vastness of Lake Constance, the towns on the distant German shore, and the pre-Alpine mountains of western Austria. Centuries earlier, people from the plains had fled here, seeking not only safety from the recurring floods of the Rhine but also relief from burdensome exactions of feudal nobility. The hills mount progressively from one chain to the next, like a series of terraces. They finally rise toward a high mountain range, the Alpstein. The men and women of the Appenzell country, to which Walzenhausen belongs, built up close-knit, self-governing communities of cattlemen and peasants. Repeatedly they fought off the incursions of knights and abbots, who tried to subdue them. During the course of centuries they gained a reputation not only as fierce warriors, but as people endowed with cunning and sharp wit. Their descendants look down from these heights with disdain upon the lesser beings whose misfortune it is to live below in the Flachland, the flat land, as they call it. Their inns and kitchens ring with laughter as they tell each other how their people have put those nitwits in their place. Whenever the Swiss federal government — flatlanders, most of them! — decides to introduce new policies, the first reaction of the Appenzellers is a defiant no. Eventually, after they have carefully weighed the pros and cons and abundantly cursed over those from below, they might fall in line with the rest of the nation. Or they might not. It is not surprising that some of the toughest negotiators the Swiss government has sent to elaborate international agreements have come from the Appenzell hills. Lutz used this shrewdness of generations when he negotiated with the Nazis in Hungary over the lives of thousands of Jews.

He was born on March 30, 1895, the ninth child born to Johannes and Ursula Lutz. Both his father and his mother descended from families whose names are recorded in the church and village annals in Walzenhausen as far back as the fifteenth century. In the communal birth register his name was given as Karl Friedrich. Later, after he had gone to the United States, he called himself Charles F., perhaps because Karl sounded too Germanic. Later, in Palestine, he called himself Carl, the spelling that he retained. Johannes owned a sandstone quarry just below the house, where he and a few workers cut a finely grained sandstone. In later years, Carl Lutz would proudly recall that his father had furnished countless building blocks for the Federal Palace in Berne, which was under construction around the turn of the century.

Ursula taught Sunday school with the Methodists, who were spreading among the "downtrodden and heavyladen," who lived on small farms, and, in order to supplement their meager earnings, pushed shuttles back and forth on their handlooms, day in and day out. It was not only a boring but a badly paid job. Cotton fibers and dust led to lung disease and tuberculosis. The cellars were cold and humid. Young girls and women began coughing and died early. Ursula saw to it that her family prayed at meals, read the Bible, and lived a clean life in an upright puritanical sense. But Ursula did not suffocate her children with religion and moralism. She insisted that they finish school and learn a trade, so that they would not have to depend on others. Reflecting on the poverty of the Appenzell hill country, she would admonish her offspring that it was more important to help those in need than to always run to prayer meetings. Her pietism was combined with a spirit of social protest against the "higher ups," who allowed injustices to subvert what had been a democratic way of life.

The young Carl Lutz soaked up this spirit of pietistic religion combined with a concern for the "neighbor fallen among thieves." Entries in early diaries show that in his youthful enthusiasm he wanted Jesus to guide his life. Once he ran up to the woods in the hills above the house until he was out of earshot and demanded loudly that Jesus make him do something unusual when he grew up, become a missionary or a great scientist. He found school boring and hated his teacher. Ursula knew that, despite or perhaps because of these school problems, Carl really should move on to university. He devoured every book he could lay his hands on. But where would she find the money? When Carl was fifteen, the torture of school ended, and Ursula found him a job as a commercial apprentice in a textile mill at St. Margrethen, the nearest village in the valley below.

In 1909, when Carl was fourteen, Johannes died of tuberculosis. The fine sand from the stone quarry had settled in his lungs. Hours before he died Johannes took a walking stick and climbed through the grassy slopes to a nearby hilltop lookout called Meldegg. Not far from the overgrown remains of a medieval castle he sat on a bench, and all day his eyes rested on the valleys and mountains he knew so well. He absorbed the view until cold began to creep up his legs. Johannes rose, walked home, lay down on his bed, and half an hour later he was dead. The people of the Appenzell hill country never made much fuss over their end.

Throughout his life, his son Carl kept returning to Meldegg and meditating on the very bench on which his father had spent his last hours. "To the left, the eye glides across Lake Constance to the German shore, to Bregenz and the Pfänder mountain," he once wrote. "To the right it follows the Rhine valley as far as the peaks of the Grisons. It is said that this is the only spot in Switzerland from where more than thirty villages and towns with their church belfries are seen." The longer Lutz stayed abroad, the more Meldegg and the landscape seen from that spot became the epitome for the lost paradise, the distant homeland, and perfection, all in one. "Meldegg was the place," he wrote, "to where my thoughts flew from America, from distant Palestine and from Budapest. Even when the bombs made our air raid cellar tremble, Meldegg appeared in my phantasies, along with the desire to be there." Was it this curious discord between his desire for perfection and the facts of hard reality that filled this sensitive human being with such extraordinary force?

Later, in Budapest, Lutz's recollections of Meldegg led to a curious encounter: "One day I sauntered along a road, and to my surprise I noticed a sign on the door of a distinguished-looking house which bore the name of Baron Reichling von Meldegg. My curiosity was awakened, and I finally introduced myself to this 'lord of Meldegg'. My visit surprised him no little. The baron told me that he himself had never been to Switzerland, but that he was told that somewhere near the borders of eastern Switzerland there once had been a castle by the name of Meldegg, inhabited by knights of the same name. He himself descended from these."

In 1913, at the age of eighteen, Carl Lutz decided to emigrate to the United States. Ursula — with a sad heart — encouraged him to go, because she knew that a mere commercial certificate would never allow her son to be more than an office employee. America at that time was the great hope for countless young Europeans, who wanted to break through rigid social structures and who feared losing their lives in Europe's multiple wars.

But for young Carl, like many other immigrants without money or education, America was not the paradise he had expected. He obtained badly paid jobs as factory worker and office employee in Granite City, Illinois, a desolate industrial town across the Mississippi from St. Louis. Overwhelmed by his situation, he suffered extremes between high elation and depression. He had not yet been confronted with the kind of challenge that would make him live up to his potential.

When America mobilized for war in 1917, Carl Lutz refused to be drafted. For three months he hastened furtively throughout Kentucky, Tennessee, Louisiana, Arkansas, and Oklahoma, always a step ahead of recruiting agents. Carl Lutz knew that, if caught, he could be accused of draft evasion, with serious consequences. But America's bellicose fervor subsided as quickly as it had arisen. In his biographical recollections Lutz significantly did not mention this traumatic period. But he wrote later that when he looked into the faces of Budapest Jews nearly thirty years later, he knew what it meant to be trapped.

Traumatic as this period was, the experience prompted him to break out of the rut into which he had fallen. In 1918 he packed his bags and took the train to central Missouri, where he registered at Central Wesleyan College in Warrenton as a liberal arts student and began to study Latin and theology. This was a small-town Midwestern college which the

Methodists had built in the nineteenth century, in order to teach religion and culture to uneducated frontier people. His intelligence was stimulated, and he quickly absorbed all that his professors taught him. He soon grew beyond the limited scope of the little "prairie college," and its simple religious and cultural outlook bored him. In 1920 he quit the school and joined the staff of the Swiss legation in Washington, D.C.

Lutz was enchanted by America's capital, its wide avenues, splendid public buildings, and the proximity to government power and diplomatic splendor. Upon the advice of his superior, Swiss Minister Marc Peter, he registered for part-time studies at George Washington University, one of the elite schools that trained America's diplomats and best legal minds. Carl Lutz's intelligence and abilities were truly challenged and developed there. Four years later, in 1924, he received the coveted Liberal Arts degree. During his years of study he had developed the casual and self-assured working style that later was so characteristic of him, a free and easy way of interpreting texts and instructions. This work style would in the future often clash with the more strict habits of his superiors at the Swiss foreign ministry in Berne. Above all, he became endowed with both diplomatic finesse and legal knowledge which in Budapest would help him save thousands of human beings. The pietist had changed into a man of the world, if such categories are applicable, though the pietist did not simply disappear but continued to exist under the surface. The descendent of the rebellious Appenzell hill people had become a graduate of an elite American university. In tension together these contradictory strands stimulated his thinking and action.

Carl Lutz was twenty-nine and had come into his own.

Minister Peter did not hesitate to recommend his bright young assistant to his superiors at the Swiss foreign ministry in Berne, which at that time was still ruled by Giuseppe Motta like a private fief. The foreign minister asked that Lutz present himself in person. So after more than ten years in the United States, Carl Lutz sailed the ocean again, in the opposite direction. He passed the "inspection" in Berne, and he pleaded to be given a post in Europe. He no longer wanted to stay in America because he was incurably homesick.

But Motta made Lutz recross the Atlantic, and for ten more years

Lutz served as consular agent, at first — again — in Washington, later in Philadelphia, New York, and St. Louis.

It was there that one day, in early 1934, a young woman by the name of Gertrud Fankhauser came to the consulate. She was good-looking without being a beauty. She had the cheerful spirit of one who always seemed to succeed in whatever she was doing. Although only twenty-three, Gertrud had already been five years in Texas on the ranch of relatives. Her father, who was a cheesemaker near Berne, thought that it was time for her to return home, now that she had seen the world. She had come up from Texas and was slowly traveling across the United States toward New York, where she was going to take the boat. She wondered whether she could be useful at the consulate. Gertrud admitted that she needed the money to pay for her passage and that she didn't want to ask her father. Carl Lutz said that he really did not need anybody. The Swiss foreign ministry had reduced his budget because of the economic crisis. Was Miss Fankhauser a secretary? No, but she could type, two-finger system, she answered cheerfully. Lutz liked her and told her he would think of something. She should come back.

Gertrud promptly turned up at eight o'clock next day. Lutz assigned her to working with the downcast immigrants who filed by the consulate. He noticed that for each she had a word of cheer and often the beginnings of a practical solution. After short conversations she sent them away more encouraged than they had come. Lutz marveled.

One day he asked Gertrud Fankhauser to marry him.

Although he had been in love before, he had never been able to make up his mind, perhaps because, unconsciously, he always seemed to look for perfection. Moreover, he was timid toward women. But time was slipping by, and he was already thirty-nine.

Gertrud hesitated. She thought of the age difference, of the disparities in their character. Moreover, she wanted to go home and stay in Switzerland, while as the wife of a consular agent she would have to follow her husband wherever the Swiss foreign ministry sent him. But he persisted, and she relented. The wedding was set for September 1934. The two families were duly informed. Ursula wrote to say how pleased she was. The cheesemaker and his wife were also happy, all the more as

their future son-in-law promised that he would definitely ask the consular service in Berne to assign him to a post in Europe. Carl sailed home
in July, and Gertrud was to follow a few weeks later.

At this conjuncture a troubling incident occurred. Gertrud, enterpris-
ing as she was, decided to attend the World's Fair in Chicago before returning home. The event took place during the summer of 1934. She was
promptly hired at the Swiss pavilion and was asked to dress up in a traditional Bernese costume and to encourage visitors to buy Swiss goods. A
young Swiss architect from the Grisons, who was travelling in America,
saw Gertrud and fell in love with her. She did not really object to his vehe-
ment courting, though she had a bad conscience, because she took a liking
to him. The young man asked her to marry him and insisted that she break
her engagement to Carl Lutz. Although he was unemployed, like many
young people at that time, Gertrud became unsure and promised that she
would talk to her fiancé as soon as she got to Switzerland.

Carl Lutz was crestfallen when Gertrud broke the news, and her parents shook their heads over their daughter's unsuitable behavior. Despite
the difference in age between Carl and Gertrud, they thought that a consular agent was a better prospect than an unemployed architect. Gertrud
protested that many people were unemployed nowadays and that sooner
or later the young man would find a job. The wedding date was provi-
sionally cancelled, but the debate continued. Lutz fought stubbornly. He
employed his considerable diplomatic skills to win his unfaithful fiancée
back, enlisting the support of his future in-laws. Gertrud had never seen
Carl in such a determined fighting mood. He was no longer the correct
official, who patiently climbed the steps of his consular career. She was
impressed, became unsure, and finally submitted. It was the young architect's turn to be crestfallen. The wedding was reset for the end of January
1935 and took place in Berne. The reception at Hotel Schweizerhof in
Berne was a splendid affair. Even Marc Peter, the Swiss minister to Washington, and his wife attended. It was as if Carl Lutz and his in-laws were
making a determined effort to forget the near disaster.

The Swiss foreign ministry took Carl Lutz's request for reassignment
to Europe seriously and made arrangements to send him as consular
agent to London. But days before the wedding the ministry decided to

send him instead to Jaffa in Palestine, where an emergency had arisen. Thus, on the very evening of their wedding day Carl and Gertrud boarded the train for Venice. From there they sailed for Jaffa.

Carl Lutz did not know that Palestine was to prepare him for Budapest.

Curiously, shortly before they parted, at the end of the wedding reception, Ursula slipped a piece of paper into her son's hand. She was now in her eighties, and her handwriting was becoming shaky. She had written a passage from the prophet Isaiah: "And he shall be a father to the inhabitants of Jerusalem and to the house of Judah." Perhaps his mother had a presentiment.

The Holy Land enchanted the newlyweds. Soon after they were installed in Jaffa they visited Nazareth, because they wanted to see where Jesus had grown up. Hand in hand they walked along Lake Gennesaret, "in his footsteps," as Carl wrote, once again the pietist. They stood before the Wailing Wall in Jerusalem among singing and lamenting bearded Jews, and before their inner eyes rose the glory of Solomon's temple. At Christmas they worshipped at the Church of the Nativity in Bethlehem and waited for the rising sun on Shepherd's Field. They drove and walked along the highways and byways of the entire Holy Land "from Dan to Beersheba" — Carl Lutz with his camera at the ready — and crossed the Jordan to climb Mount Nebo, where Moses had beheld the land of Canaan from afar. The biblical world, so familiar to him since childhood, gained new contours before his eyes. Lutz photographed the age-old pastoral Arab world of Palestine, not knowing that within a decade it would vanish forever. He sent lively travel accounts to Ursula and to the rest of his family. These were not the typical travel reports of a tourist but the writings of one engaged in a spiritual exercise.

The couple traveled in great harmony throughout the length and breadth of the Holy Land. If there was any discord between them later on, it concerned the fact that they had no child, even though both of them loved children. In later years, Carl would say that Gertrud did not want to have children, and Gertrud said the opposite. Why this was so remains a secret known only to them, and they took it to their tomb.

But this near idyllic way of life ended one year after their arrival. In

1936, the Palestinian Arabs revolted against the Jews, who were buying vast tracts of land. The Arabs feared that they would became a proletarian underclass within their own country. Arab fighters attacked Jewish settlements and British military installations at the same time. Colonists were murdered. The Jewish settlers hit back and murdered Arab villagers in turn. It was a confused and desperate fight. And Britain did not know how to extract itself from the consequences of its own contradictory pledges made during the war of 1914-18 to both Arabs and Jews. It stalled, compelled as it was to keep an eye on the storm brewing over Europe.

Carl and Gertrud's own situation became precarious, because in Arab Jaffa, where they lived, they were often taken for Jews. One day, Carl and Gertrud, unable to leave their apartment because of tension in the streets, watched from their window as an excited Arab crowd lynched an unarmed Jewish worker. They had never seen such an incredible sight. They were unable to run out and save the victim, for fear of being lynched themselves. The guilt traumatized them. While Carl Lutz understood why the Arabs fought for their land, he refused to accept that such a struggle justified the lynching of an unarmed person, be he Jewish or not. During the same period Lutz heard tales of Nazi horrors from newly arrived German Jews. Why was the supposedly enlightened twentieth century falling into such unspeakable brutality? His sympathy swung over to the Jews.

Two further developments came in quick succession, both outside Palestine. Throughout 1938 clouds gathered over Europe, announcing the coming storm. In March of that year Hitler annexed Austria and entered Vienna under the acclamation of the populace, the Jews excepted. In late summer a conference took place in Munich, where the western European democracies let Hitler dismember Czechoslovakia. They believed that this sacrifice — of someone else — would at last appease the German dictator. Returning to London from Munich, British prime minister Neville Chamberlain waved a piece of paper as he alighted from his airplane, proclaiming that he had gained "peace for this generation." After all, who was mad enough to want to send the world's young to the slaughterhouse again after an interval of only twenty years? Neither Chamberlain nor anyone else realized that they were dealing with a new kind of politician, a destroyer of civilization, a nihilist. In November, being more sure of themselves, the Nazis organized a vast pogrom against Jews throughout Germany and Austria, which has gone into history under the euphemism of *Reichskristallnacht*, the night of the broken glass. Several thousand Jewish businesses were destroyed, apartments confiscated, and synagogues burned. Thirty thousand Jews went to concentration camps. The western democracies were too weak to stop the lunatic.

In the face of approaching disaster in Europe, the British government tried to engage Arabs and Jews in renewed peace talks. Britain was increasingly worried about its precarious military position not only in Palestine but in the entire Middle East. It had to think of the Suez Canal — the empire's lifeline to India — and of the indispensable oil resources in the region. If in the old days a few gun boats had sufficed to settle such a crisis, the might of the European powers was no longer what it had been before 1914. Arab nationalism was more self-assured. The Jewish settlers were not impressed by threats. Both wanted the last vestiges of colonialism in Palestine to go, but on their own terms. Britain knew that, given the dangerous international constellation, a conflict in Palestine could spark off an explosion in the entire Middle East. German agents stirred up nationalist feelings.

The talks took place in London in February/March 1939, but they predictably led nowhere. The Arabs refused to sit in the same room as the Jews, and even less did they want to consider a division of Palestine. Out of desperation, the British imposed a "diktat," which was spelled out in the so-called Palestine White Book. Among other things, the British government conceded the immigration of not more than 75,000 Jews during five years, from 1939 to 1944, after which there would be no further Jewish immigration without Arab consent. Moreover, the geographical extent of Jewish settlements was severely curtailed. Finally, the British declared that within ten years, in 1949, they would arrange for the creation of a joint Arab-Jewish state. How this feat was to be accomplished was mercifully not spelled out.

There was an outcry on both sides. While pledging to keep an armistice of sorts if a European war broke out, both parties loudly declared that they had ultimately no intention of giving up until the opposite side was defeated. Meanwhile, the British high commissioner for Palestine was instructed to keep tight control over Jewish immigration, which was the most obnoxious element in Arab eyes. The Jewish Agency for Palestine would — under sharp British control — issue immigration permits called Palestine Certificates. In order to be valid, they would have to be countersigned by the British authorities in Palestine and the British consuls in the countries where the immigrant originated. In this way abuses could be avoided.

But it was precisely emigration to Palestine that became the major objective for the threatened European Jewry, especially as the ill-fated international refugee conference of Evian in July 1938 blocked Jewish emigration throughout the world. The Jewish underground, the Chalutzim among them, engaged in undercover warfare against the British and the Arabs. They spirited a large number of Jews out of Europe into Palestine, whether these came inside the British-established quota of 75,000 or not. What mattered was that a "remnant of Israel" survive, and that the ancient homeland be resettled by the "returnees." The Arabs, on the other hand, wanted to keep all immigrants out, in order to keep intact the land inherited from their own ancestors. If they caught clandestine Jewish immigrants, they did not hesitate to murder them on the beaches. They also attacked Jewish settlements at night, which caused the Jews to fall upon Arab villages the next night. Thus, injustice was piled upon injustice, and guilt upon guilt. The shameful international collusion across war fronts and frontiers at the expense of innocents knew no bounds.

At any rate, whatever else it did, the Jewish Agency, the quasi-official government for the Jewish population in Palestine, made full use of the official White Book quota of 75,000. It gave priority to orphaned children and young people, whose parents had been deported and murdered. This policy was endorsed by the British government, which as of 1942 allowed a special quota of 29,000 for children and young people within (!) the overall figure of 75,000. Incredible as it may seem, the Palestine Certificates were usually respected by authorities in Nazi-dominated countries of origin and by the governments of transit countries, such as Hungary, Romania, Bulgaria, or Turkey.

Carl Lutz recorded the entire Palestinian conflict in his reports to the Swiss foreign ministry. Little did he know that this detailed background information would become an indispensable tool for his action in Budapest.

When the war broke out on September 1, 1939, Germany asked Switzerland to handle its interests in Palestine. Carl Lutz was promoted to vice consul. He would retain this modest title up to the end of the war in 1945. Almost singlehandedly he closed down the large German general consulate in Jerusalem and the consulates in Haifa and Jaffa and sent their large staff home. Moreover, he and Gertrud looked after 2,500 Germans interned in nine different camps, administered 25 million pounds sterling worth of real estate, and were in touch with 70,000 Jews who still had German passports, many of whom even received German pensions (!). This physically and mentally exhausting work resulted in a nice letter of congratulation by German foreign minister Joachim von Ribbentrop to Giuseppe Motta. A few weeks later, however, the same Ribbentrop decided to ask Franco-Spain to take over its interests in Palestine. Hitler was preparing his campaign in the West for the spring of 1940, and Switzerland may have been one of the countries he wanted to attack.

In November 1940 Carl Lutz went home for a rest. As travel by ship was no longer possible, he travelled to Switzerland by train via Asia Minor and the Balkans. Gertrud was to follow him shortly. But in April 1941, the German armies attacked Yugoslavia and Greece, and Gertrud was blocked in Palestine. The war spread further. In May and June, the British struck French-held Lebanon and Syria, and Gertrud had to prolong her stay in Palestine. She was not bored during this time, as she explored travel possibilities in a world at war. She had more important things to do than spending her afternoons with the wives of other consuls at tedious sessions of tea, cake, and gossip. The war had upset Palestinian society, and Gertrud was busy comforting abandoned women and children and taking care of prisoners. But this undaunted woman finally collected papers, stamps, and all kinds of authorizations and drove home, somehow finding sufficient gasoline as she went along, arguing her way past dozens of control points. By autumn 1941, she finally reached Switzerland.

After a year of separation caused by the circumstances of war, Carl and Gertrud Lutz were reunited. Less than two months later, at the beginning of January 1942, they went to Budapest.

*　　*　　*

Maximilian Jaeger was not keen to call on Edmund Veesenmayer, Hitler's plenipotentiary in Hungary, who was known to be a professional agitator and troublemaker. But diplomatic courtesy demanded that ministers sur place call on newcomers. A conspicuous swastika flag hung over the entrance to the German legation in the center of old Buda. The main door was guarded by two martial-looking SS men. Veesenmayer was a corpulent and arrogant young man in his late thirties, a well-decorated SS brigadier general in uniform. Whom was he trying to impress? Jaeger wondered. Veesenmayer raised a fleshy hand, and in a pronounced Bavarian accent he shouted, "Heil Hitler." Vigorously he shouted Jaeger's name, which was preceded by a well-enunciated "Doktor," and pumped Jaeger's thin hand. Veesenmayer's academic background was apparently impeccable, although Jaeger had heard rumors that his doctoral examinations and university posts, not to mention his diplomatic career, if it could be called that, had been nicely helped along by connections.

Veesenmayer preceded Jaeger to his office and made him sit on a sofa next to a low table. He ordered a distinguished-looking gentleman in his mid-fifties to serve coffee. Casually he introduced him as Dr. Gerhart Feine, the first legation secretary. Feine, Jaeger thought, did not seem to fit in with the burly plenipotentiary. Once Feine had set down the coffee tray, he retired into the background and remained standing against the wall, ready to be at his master's beck and call.

Loudly, Veesenmayer mused that as a Bavarian he and Jaeger were connected by race, weren't they, since the Bavarians were close blood relations to the Swiss. Jaeger nodded politely and answered that the two peoples doubtless esteemed each other, even across frontiers. He knew that the Nazis loved to talk about race and blood and such stuff, and the quicker one got it over with the better. But he did not need to worry. Veesenmayer soon turned the conversation to the Alps, that admirable mountain range which the two peoples shared, and which he missed so much in flat Hungary. How he loved to climb mountains, he said, and to commune with nature, so much so that he often felt closer to ancestral nature gods than to the Catholic faith, in which he had grown up. He also said that his father was a landscape painter — just like the Führer, before the business of state had absorbed his attention. Didn't this artistic bent give him unusual insights into nature, and into human beings? With such an extraordinary person at the head of state, it was no wonder that he, Veesenmayer, had become a convinced national socialist.

Feine poured more coffee, and Veesenmayer bent forward. His voice lost its jovial sound and became almost conspiratorial. The Führer had sent him to Hungary, he said darkly, because he was concerned about this country, which he loved so much, ordering Veesenmayer expressly to help save it from communism and its evils. Of course, not only Hungary, but all of Europe must be kept from communism. With the permission of Mr. Minister he added that Germany protected even Switzerland from these dark powers, at an enormous sacrifice to the German nation.

Minister Jaeger smiled, but failed to express his gratitude, but then Hitler's plenipotentiary did not really expect him to. Jaeger said that one day, when the war was over, he certainly would love to visit Bavaria, which had such an admirable countryside, as his excellency said. If he did, Veesenmayer interjected, a bit too anxiously, he should be pleased to receive him. Jaeger smiled again, and thought how he would indeed love to pay a call on this fleshy Nazi in prison, be it in Bavaria or anyplace else. With pleasure, he said emphatically.

Then Jaeger congratulated the German minister on his appointment to Hungary and said all the polite things diplomats say to each other on such occasions. There was not much else to talk about. Jaeger looked at his watch and said that he did not want to use up the German minister's precious time. He certainly had to attend to many things. When they got up from the coffee table, Jaeger asked casually, whether it might be possible for the German minister to have a conversation with Consul Lutz, the Swiss representative of foreign interests in Hungary. He had a concern related to his work, especially the emigration of children. To add significance to the request, Jaeger said that the United States and Great Britain

39

were among the countries whose interests the consul represented. No problem, your excellency, Veesenmayer answered, raising his fleshy hand generously, if Jaeger believed that he could be of help. He had heard, in fact, that the consul was doing excellent work. The world needed people like that. Could Mr. Lutz telephone Dr. Feine, over there, in order to make an appointment? He turned to his first secretary, who nodded. Veesenmayer urged Jaeger toward the exit as politely as he could. "Heil Hitler," he shouted again, pressed the Swiss minister's hand till it hurt, and dismissed him. The SS guards saluted. Before Jaeger got into his car, he turned around once more and looked at the German legation, puzzled. Veesenmayer had not even asked what Vice Consul Lutz wanted from him.

*   *   *

On his way back to Stefania Street, Jaeger stopped at Freedom Square. Veesenmayer, the "convinced national socialist," he undiplomatically reported to Lutz, was a son of a bitch, full of Nazi talk. Hitler's plenipotentiary nevertheless appeared eager to be on good terms with the Swiss, for reasons known only to him. He spoke about blood relationship and other nonsense. But Jaeger had been unable to figure out what really made the Bavarian tick. Perhaps Veesenmayer's arrogance served to cover up his growing insecurity. At any rate, Jaeger said, the contact was made. The consul would have to see how he could exploit this little opening and phone Dr. Feine.

Lutz was angry when the minister left. He, Jaeger, could now return to his desk on Stefania Street and write a nice report to Pilet-Golaz, the foreign minister in Berne, who had replaced the long-reigning Giuseppe Motta. But it was he, the representative of foreign interests, the consul, the soldier, whom the generals pushed forward to the front where the bullets flew. As a consul he could not even be properly called a diplomat; he had no real status. No one called him "your excellency." Lutz walked up and down his office, thinking of what he would say to the powerful Nazi minister who decided on life and death. His secretary looked in, but she withdrew when she saw that he seemed to be talking to himself. Lutz remembered the years when he was a student of diplomacy and international law at George Washington University. What he had learned there was fine, but how would his professors advise him to deal with diplomats who represented such a vicious state? They, who had never conceived such a possibility, fully immersed as they were in enlightened Anglo-Saxon law, American version? What did diplomatic rules and regulations say about the frightened asylum seekers who pressed against his consulate? About people who had been expelled from their homes, received draft notes for labor service, were threatened on the street because they wore a yellow star, who would die if no one took care of them? Were they not like Lazarus, the poor man on the steps, and was he not to them like the rich man? They told stories of relatives and friends vanishing, of heart-breaking separations, of shootings at night. Their faces, their cries pursued him into his sleep. They ran to him for help, not to Minister Jaeger.

He could of course say that solving "the Jewish problem" was not part of his job. Foreign interests meant passports, pensions, documents, inheritances, prisoners of war, passing on notes — but not Jews. The Jews did not belong to the category of politically persecuted persons (remember the Geneva Convention) to whom asylum must be granted or on whose behalf Swiss diplomatic services should act. There was no category in international law for the racially persecuted. This is what Pilet-Golaz and his smug advisors, who were worlds removed, would answer, and they did whenever he wrote to Berne for advice. They were of course right. But theirs was not his reality.

Jaeger, it was true, disagreed with Berne and backed Lutz. He said that the Jews must be helped. This was important support. But Jaeger left it to his vice consul to fight it out.

This is the background to Carl Lutz's meeting with Hitler's proconsul.

*   *   *

As he let Szluha drive him over the chain bridge and up the hill of old Buda, the vice consul fully intended to obtain a clear decision from Veesenmayer that the 8,000 children and young people be allowed to leave Hungary. He would appeal to the great man's human tolerance. How insignificant such a number was on the check board of world politics.

Lutz was surprised to see the German minister waiting for him in person at the entry of the legation, right between the saluting SS guards. Veesenmayer acted the part of the impulsive and generous South German, the Bavarian neighbor of the Swiss, supposedly related by special ties of blood across frontiers. He was dressed not in SS uniform this time but in a dark business suit, and instead of raising his right hand and shouting "Heil Hitler," he seized the vice consul's hands vigorously, wishing Herr Konsul a lively and warm welcome, saying how happy he was that his excellency, Minister Jaeger, had suggested that Lutz come to see him. He took Lutz by the arm and led him into his office, where Feine was already setting down the coffee tray. With animation Veesenmayer said that the consul's name was well known in the corridors of the foreign ministry in Berlin. The foreign minister, Joachim von Ribbentrop himself, had cabled that he wished to be remembered to Herr Konsul in person. The vice consul's excellent performance in 1939, when he had taken over the representation of German interests in the Holy Land, was truly well remembered. These were Ribbentrop's own words, Veesenmayer stressed. According to the instructions of the foreign minister, all of the consul's desires were to be met, "within the framework of the possible." Of course.

Lutz was not displeased at these kind words from Berlin. He said to the fat Nazi that he really appreciated that the German foreign minister had not forgotten him. Lutz wanted to strike while the iron was hot. Naturally, he understood that some restrictions were unavoidable, what with the war and so on; nevertheless he was concerned that the decision to close the Hungarian borders had disrupted his travel program for the Jewish children and young people who had fallen under his responsibility as Swiss representative of British interests. This was why he was seeking his excellency's help.

Hitler's proconsul nodded gravely and with understanding, which encouraged Lutz.

The order to close the borders, the consul continued with emphasis, went counter to a formal international agreement into which the Hungarian government had entered. Surely his excellency knew about these commitments co-signed by Hungary, that Jewish children and young people who were in possession of Palestine Certificates were allowed to leave for the Holy Land. They were quasi-citizens of Palestine, which, as his excellency knew, was mandated to Great Britain. As temporary administrator of British interests, he, Lutz, by implication represented Palestine. Hence he was the protector of the émigrés, so to speak. Such immigration was permitted, he said, by the quota of 75,000 in the British White Book for Palestine.

Yes, one could put it that way, Veesenmayer agreed with astonished amusement, impressed by the consul's complex juridical argumentation. Except, of course, that Germany had never recognized the White Book, because it went against Arab interests. The Arabs were Germany's friends. But this was beside the point. He wanted to be of help, certainly. Veesenmayer asked how many children and young people were registered with Herr Konsul. 8,000, Lutz answered. 10,000 had already gone to Palestine during the last two years. But he expected that several thousand more wanted to go. The 8,000 were part of an ongoing process.

The German minister took a few notes and was going to say something to Feine but did not, and turned his attention again to the vice consul. Lutz asked whether his excellency could not bring his influence to bear on the Hungarian authorities to lift the travel restrictions imposed on the 8,000. He wanted to get them under way at an early stage, just as had been planned. The Swiss government would certainly appreciate his help. It might be important, Lutz dared to add, if his excellency could remind the new Hungarian foreign minister that some of these international agreements were legally binding. That gentleman may not yet be acquainted with some of these technicalities.

Hitler's proconsul listened with the benevolent attitude of the powerful whenever they deal with persons of lesser rank. He seemed impressed by the persuasive power of the Swiss consul. He answered that, as far as the 8,000 were concerned, he saw no problem and he could do no other than to agree fully with everything Herr Konsul had said. However, whether the two of them, as foreigners, were in a position to discuss matters concerning a third nation was of course another question. Hungary was, after all, a fully independent state, which decided on its own policy.

The Hungarian authorities would hardly welcome it, if he, a simple minister from another country, would even appear to be trying to tell them what they must do. The decision to close the border had been Hungary's alone. It was the Hungarians who must decide on their own whether they wanted to reopen these borders or not. He could gently raise the question, of course, and he would be prepared to do so. More than that . . . well, Herr Konsul would understand.

The fat Nazi's cynical words were like a cold gust. It did not matter whether Veesenmayer was making fun of the Hungarian government that he himself had put in place or at him, Lutz, who was appealing for his help.

Lutz's mind was racing furiously for a reply.

But the German minister hadn't finished talking. He said that he understood the consul's dilemma and that he desired to facilitate his task. He added a curious phrase, which Lutz reported to his superiors in Berne exactly as he had heard it: "As far as the Germans are concerned, Veesenmayer said, they much prefer that the Hungarian Jews be concentrated, in order to avoid any possibility that they would fall into the back of the fighting troops." The full significance of this sentence escaped Lutz, even though he knew that the Hitler regime had always shut its real or imagined enemies into concentration camps. But he set the thought aside, because his mind was almost exclusively focused on the blocked emigration candidates, all the more as Veesenmayer repeated the number 8,000 several times more. These children and young people, he said, could stay under the consul's care. This was indeed a positive sign, though vague. But curiously, the German minister passed in silence over several further remarks made by Lutz, that more applicants wanted to go to Palestine.

Veesenmayer looked at his watch. He said he would tell his foreign minister in Berlin that he had found this conversation instructive and fruitful, which would doubtless please Mr. Ribbentrop. He said he hoped that they would remain in close touch with each other. Any time Herr Konsul had a concern, he, the German minister, was at his disposal. As they rose, Veesenmayer added that he could only recommend that the consul discuss the exit permits with the competent Hungarian authorities, if indeed he wished to do so.

A good example of double talk, Lutz thought. What was he to do?

As they walked to the door of the minister's office, Veesenmayer shook his head and said, as if to himself, that the Jewish problem was certainly complicated and that he wished he knew more about it. He stopped short and poked his finger at Lutz. He said, as if the idea had just occurred to him, that although the Hungarian authorities of course decided on policy, he would suggest to Herr Konsul that he should go and see one Lieutenant Colonel Eichmann, Adolf Eichmann. He was the head of a special unit that had come to Budapest "the other day" in order to advise Hungarian colleagues on Jewish questions in the technical field, such as transportation, timetables, etc. If anyone was a specialist, it was Eichmann. He could perhaps help the Swiss consul on transportation problems. Startled, Lutz replied that he would like to know more about the lieutenant colonel because Veesenmayer's suggestion seemed interesting, but the minister cut him short, saying that he, Herr Konsul, could find this officer at the Hotel Majestic on Suabian Hill, west of the city.

Perhaps he had underestimated Veesenmayer's readiness to help, Lutz thought. But why did the Hungarian Jews need a specialist on transportation and timetables? Were they going anywhere? But the fat Nazi was decidedly in no mood to wait for further questions. He ordered Feine to phone Eichmann, so that Herr Konsul could obtain an appointment with him without delay.

But Veesenmayer seemed a man of impulsive habits. The big man turned around on his heel, went to a cupboard, and took out a small flask of perfume. Chanel, Lutz read. The German minister smiled. He would like to ask Herr Konsul to pay his respects to Madame in the form of this little gift. He hoped that he would meet Frau Konsul in person some day. He continued to say that during the 1930s he had, among other activities, begun a wholesale enterprise in the perfume branch. The war had imposed other priorities. He nevertheless hoped to pick up this line of business again as soon as "these troubles" were over — as if his present doings were a mere digression from his "real" activities.

Gerhart Feine led Lutz to his own office, where he took up the receiver and dialed Eichmann at the Hotel Majestic, making an appointment for the Swiss consul. It was curious, Lutz thought as he listened, that Feine did not address the officer as lieutenant colonel, but as Herr Obersturmbannführer. This was the SS rank equivalent to lieutenant colonel. Eichmann was an SS officer! Feine smiled, as if he understood the vice consul's puzzlement, and gave him the exact time for his meeting at the hotel. Then he conducted him outside, shook the consul's hand, and said politely that he hoped there would be another occasion for them to meet.

Szluha held the car door open. Exhausted, Lutz fell into the backseat. How long had he been with Veesenmayer? A quarter of an hour? Half an hour? An hour? He did not know. All he knew was that he had entered the German legation with a clear objective and that he came out troubled.

Carl Lutz would have been even more disturbed if he had known that late in the previous year the fat Nazi had travelled incognito throughout Hungary — at the Führer's personal request, no less. Hitler had been shaken by Italy's desertion in September 1943, and he wanted to find out whether Hungary would "betray" him also. His secret services had warned him that something like that was brewing, but he wanted to get an appraisal from someone he could trust more than his own secret agents. He knew that if Hungary changed sides the entire German front in the Balkans would collapse. Upon his return Veesenmayer submitted a highly confidential report to Hitler. He noted that Hungary's leadership was sabotaging German policies systematically and that, among other things, the Hungarian government, with Horthy in the lead, was ignoring all German wishes to "solve" the Jewish problem. Not only was such "disobedience" an insult to the Führer, Veesenmayer stressed, but the Jews constituted an acute military danger. Each of the 1.1 million Hungarian Jews (he exaggerated, there were "only" 750,000 Jews) represented so many spies and saboteurs, who were eager to stab the brave German soldier in the back while he defended Europe against the enemy. Had not the uprising of the Warsaw ghetto in 1943 demonstrated what a small but decided band of desperate Jews could do?

In reality, the peaceful Hungarian Jews were anything but spies and saboteurs. They were in no desperate mood like the Polish Jews, nor did they have any intention of transforming Budapest into another Warsaw, all the more as they did not even live in a ghetto. They only wanted to survive, somehow, and to keep their heads down until the storm blew over, as they had done in times past. At any rate, Hungary, though antisemitic, had no really virulent history of pogroms, at least when compared with Poland, Romania, Ukraine, or Russia. The Nazis, Veesenmayer included, believed in their own phantoms, with tragic consequences.

*   *   *

The Swiss flag also hung above the gate of the former British legation on Verböcsy Street in old Buda, as a sign that this diplomatic post was protected by Consul Lutz, held in trust by Switzerland for the day when it would be returned to its rightful owner. While the vice consul was using the former American legation on Freedom Square in Pest for his administrative office, the British legation on the hill of Buda was his and Gertrud's residence. It was really a manor house, if not a small palace, built in the empire style of the early nineteenth century. This splendid place was indeed a far cry from the wooden homestead in the Appenzell hill country where he was born and raised, or the modest apartment in hostile Jaffa. The gate was wide enough for the Packard to enter from Verböcsy Street; inside, the car was parked in a large courtyard. High-ceilinged rooms were arranged on two floors around the courtyard on all sides. Toward the front, in the main tract — that is, in the direction of the river — there was one large representative reception room, forty yards long and twenty wide, a spacious dining room, and a library, all decorated with chandeliers, gold-framed mirrors, and period paintings. Here, Carl and Gertrud imagined, his excellency, the former British minister to Hungary, used to give his receptions and dinner parties for government ministers or visiting royals who happened to step off the Orient Express or who enjoyed Danube cruises. In his early days in Budapest, when the consul still pursued a more leisurely life, he loved to take pictures of these grandiose interiors, with himself sitting on a sofa with an open book, or at tea with Gertrud. Though a modest man, the high-grade diplomatic residence on Verböcsy Street had doubtless created a certain vanity in him, although Lutz knew that it was merely the vicissitudes of war that had placed him and his wife into such palatial surroundings. Altogether the house had fifty rooms of all shapes and sizes that were interconnected by a maze of hallways and passages. Below the building, cut deep into the rocks of the hill, there were two vast cellar caves, remainders of underground casemates from Turkish times. One could walk from one to the other through a long corridor. Somewhere between the floor of the courtyard and the casemates, there was a smaller cave in which the British minister had stored 3,000 liters of gasoline. It was meant to be a wartime reserve, just in case the oil supplies got cut off. Consul Lutz blessed the foresight of his "predecessor." He would have hated to let Szluha soot up the motor of his precious Packard with charcoal, which was inefficient besides.

In addition to Szluha, Carl and Gertrud Lutz had inherited several other servants and two trustworthy policemen, who kept a check on comings and goings. Of late, more people had been added to the household, including an elderly English language professor called Geoffrey Tier and his wife and a few Jews, picked at random from those who had come to the former American legation. By now, a few days after the German occupation, the little palace served as refuge to about thirty persons. When Tier joined the others, he confessed to the vice consul that he really had stayed on in Budapest after 1941 at the request of the British Secret Services. They wanted him to find out everything about the German Gestapo in Hungary. His profession as a language teacher was a good cover, they thought. Tier thought this proposal ludicrous. How could he, a simple professor, spy on a highly secretive and vicious organization like the Gestapo? Consul Lutz should not hesitate to show him and his wife the door, if he thought his presence endangered his household. The consul smiled at the almost-spy. No problem, he said.

The most magnificent aspect of the former British legation, however, was its site. Verböcsy Street was lined by several other manor houses, belonging to aristocrats or rich merchants. Some houses dated from the seventeenth or eighteenth centuries, when Buda had been rebuilt after the destruction inflicted by the parting Turks. Here the upper classes spent the winter season, "recuperating" from summer life on rural estates. If one strolled northward a minute or two, one came to the

Vienna Gate, just opposite a Lutheran church, where the road made a sharp right turn downwards in the direction of the river. The old carriage road used to take the traveler from this gate to a small town called Obuda on the Danube and follow the mighty river upstream all the way to Vienna. In fact, the Vienna Road, as it was called, between the two capitals, was the major lifeline of the old Habsburg empire, long before World War I broke up the Dual Monarchy.

If one walked in the opposite direction, one came upon historic Mathias Corvinus Church, a large baroque structure, where some of Hungary's ancient kings had been crowned. After this church, along Tarnok Street, rose the imposing palace of the Eszterhazy family, the most important magnates of Hungary. Built atop the ancient fortifications on the Danube-side ran Fishermen's Bastion, a splendid late-nineteenth-century balustrade. This section of the defense works used to be entrusted to Danube fishermen in ancient days. Now it was favored by Sunday strollers and visitors, because from this height the river and all of Pest could be seen in a single breath-taking view. A few steps from there, if one walked along Tarnok Street to nearby Disz Square, the hill of Buda descended slightly in a southerly direction. The buildings and walls of Old Buda receded suddenly and another hill came into view, the entire top of which was occupied by a mammoth structure, a royal castle of gigantic proportions and multiple styles, the official residence of Hungary's disempowered regent, Count Nicholas Horthy. From his legation on Uri Street near Disz Square, Edmund Veesenmayer, Hitler's proconsul, could keep a close eye on the tomb-like, 400-room structure.

The view of the Danube from the former British legation was no less magnificent than the view from Fishermen's Bastion. One could also look across the river to Pest, to the hustle and bustle of the larger and more vulgar part of the Hungarian capital, where riches were won and lost, where the first underground railway in Europe had been built, and where government ministries, churches, synagogues, stock markets, theaters, university buildings, cabarets, and brothels abounded, surrounded by the suburbs of the poor, those who created the wealth of the rich. Budapest, the Queen of the Danube, the Paris of the East! On leisurely Sunday afternoons, before the brutality of modern warfare struck Budapest, the vice consul and his wife used to take tea on the veranda of their residence and take in the sights. Carl Lutz recorded these precious moments in many photographs. Mighty horse chestnut trees shielded the veranda on both sides from intruding eyes, leaving the view toward Pest open. With his field glasses the consul would focus on people strolling on the opposite shore, as they walked all the way from the neo-Gothic House of Parliament to St. Margaret's Island, where a bridge spanned the river. He could observe their smallest gestures and enjoy watching their unruly children. Even wartime could not entirely suppress Budapest's cheerful atmosphere, though few young women were accompanied by boyfriends or husbands. These had gone to the front.

*   *   *

Carl Lutz was exhausted after his visit to Veesenmayer, when Szluha opened the gate that night and drove the Packard into the courtyard.

He ate his dinner in silence, and Gertrud knew she had to wait until he decided to talk. Her husband had said that he did not want anyone else at table tonight. The years in Budapest had brought them closer together, and Gertrud had increasingly become his confidante. Carl knew that his wife kept secrets like a tomb. That fat Nazi, he finally burst out, had promised everything — in principle — pretending what a wonderful job he, Herr Konsul, had done in Palestine on behalf of German interests! Marvelous. But he promised nothing. He only suggested that he, Lutz, should see the Hungarian authorities, because he, Veesenmayer, was not allowed to interfere in Hungarian affairs! Ha! Thanks for the joke and the advice. And then Veesenmayer told him to see an SS officer called Eichmann, a transportation specialist, he said. Of course, one never knew if such a man might not be useful, even if he was an SS officer. The consul drank his coffee in silence. Then he mentioned the first legation secretary, someone by the name of Dr. Gerhart Feine, whom Veesenmayer treated more like a butler than a first legation secretary, even though Feine was older and looked more distinguished than the minister. Lutz shook his head. How had Feine landed at the side of someone like Veesenmayer?

Then he remembered the perfume flask. He reached into his pocket and handed it to Gertrud. His Excellency, he mocked, wished to be remembered to Madame. The fat Nazi had told him he used to be a wholesale perfume dealer before the war, when fate had temporarily thrown him into another profession. By chance, of course. Chanel! Gertrud exclaimed. Carefully she turned the top of the flask, held the opening under her nose, and put a drop of its contents on the back of her left hand. For several seconds she contemplated the marvel and inhaled the scent with gusto. It had been years, she said, since she had smelled such a fragrance. Then she closed the flask again and looked straight at her husband. Didn't Veesenmayer know, she asked grimly, that when Coco Chanel fled to Switzerland in 1940 she had to abandon most of her stock in Paris? Of course he did. Perfume dealers know everything! This story about a wholesale business sounded to her like a clever cover-up of a racket. There were many stories circulating of how top SS officers were getting rich out of all kinds of miserable lootings. This man was doubtless no exception. Gertrud didn't say that Carl should have known better when he accepted the gift, but the implication was there.

The consul became angry in turn. How could he have refused, on what grounds? Didn't Gertrud know that Veesenmayer, as Hitler's proconsul in Hungary, could make or break him? Was a perfume flask worth risking Veesenmayer's revenge? It was not the perfume flask, it was the principle, Gertrud insisted. Besides, what kind of favors had the big Nazi promised that must be protected even at the cost of one's honor? Hadn't Carl just said that his visit had led to nothing?

Gertrud rose from the table and opened a window looking out on the terrace. With all her might she threw the flask out into the night. When it hit the terrace wall, it broke into a thousand pieces.

3. THE EMIGRATION DEPARTMENT
OF THE SWISS LEGATION

Neither Carl nor Gertrud Lutz knew that Veesenmayer at this very moment was raising the curtain to the final act of the most gruesome danse macabre in Europe's bloody history. They had front row seats without quite understanding the plot. When Lutz was seeking an open border for his 8,000 protégés in late March 1944, five million Jews, perhaps six, were already dead. So were half a million Gypsies, and millions of Poles and Soviet prisoners of war. They were *Untermenschen* — in the jargon of the Nazi state, subhuman beings — who deserved to be eliminated, or at best to be used as slave labor. If Hitler won the war, this would be the new European order of the master race. By means of a conspiracy of silence, threats, and propaganda the Nazi state had up to now managed to hide its monstrous crime from the world. But this smoke screen would not have sufficed if sheer unbelief had not reinforced it. Whenever someone escaped from the Nazi domain and told the truth, he was considered mentally deranged. Germany — the nation of Kant, Goethe, Hegel, Mendelssohn, and Beethoven, the land of great philosphers and scientists, the people who had produced Hildegard von Bingen, Meister Eckhardt, Luther, Melanchthon, Francke, and other great thinkers, the land that had given the world some of its best writers of hymns and literature — couldn't do that. The idea was preposterous. Thus, when in 1942 Gerhart Riegner, the Geneva representative of the World Jewish Congress, dispatched the first reliable information to Allied governments on death camps, his news was simply ignored. No one realized that underneath Germany's glittering surface new cultural forces had, in the course of two generations, infused deadly poisons: Romanticism had turned into nationalism; theological antisemitism had been transformed into racism; and science, Germany's glory, had become the whore of militarism. Four years of trench warfare had made the roof of civilization cave in, fusing these elements into deadly combustion. The experience of World War I had transformed a frontline soldier by the name of Adolf Hitler, reared in the Catholic faith, into an unprincipled nihilist. He whipped up the frenzy of a frustrated and confused people and channelled its energies in destructive directions. The rest of Europe followed, half resentfully, half willingly, and shared in the sin. When the world woke up, it was too late.

Through his diplomatic service, Carl Lutz was doubtless better informed than most people about the true nature of the Nazi regime. But even he had at first been duped by the incredible sequence of events. Lutz thought Hitler's Germany to be "extremist," and he knew of course that it persecuted Jews and others. But he thought that the excitement would pass, that the persecutions would run their course, just as they had before, and that this war was a conflict like any other. He had heard rumors about death camps, and he knew about the atrocities committed by the Hungarian army in 1941 and 1942, aided by the German SS. However, when years later a journalist asked Gertrud Lutz — Carl was already dead — at what moment she and her husband had learned the truth about the systematic killing of Jews, she admitted in all honesty that it was not until 1944 that both she and her husband realized the full extent of the disaster.

*   *   *

When the Germans occupied Hungary on March 19, 1944, the SS made its headquarters at the Hotel Astoria in Pest. But within days the thirty-eight-year-old Obersturmbannführer Eichmann and his *Sonderkommando*, special command, of 150 men moved out and took up residence at the Hotel Majestic at Svabhegy, the Suabian Hill. The forest-covered height was a few miles west of old Buda. Before the war a cogwheel train used to heave tourists and other holiday seekers to the hilltop, where the air was said to be healthier and the view over the lowland glorious. Originally the forests and valleys of Suabian Hill were settled by industrious South German artisans and small farmers; hence its name. But since the late nineteenth century the rich of Budapest had built villas on its slopes or spent weekends at one of several fine hostels, Hotel Majestic among them. Eichmann moved there to gain independence from the rest of the SS structure. He had the Hotel Majestic, once a symbol of easy-going old world life-style, transformed into a high security tract. It was surrounded by three rings of barbed wire. From well-placed towers sentries kept incessant watch on everything that moved. Other guards made frequent rounds, accompanied by German shepherd dogs. It was in these once fabulous surroundings that the deportation of Hungary's Jews was planned. From here the directives would go out to concentrate and deport them.

Planning proceeded rapidly. Inside the hotel, Eichmann was physically close to Laszlo Baky, the head of the Hungarian State Security Police, who had his office one flight up, and with whom he struck up a close friendship. Baky had been a Jew-hater since the days when he had helped Horthy to gain power twenty years earlier. Eichmann and Baky were in turn in close touch with Colonel Laszlo Ferenczy, a sinister figure of German Suabian background (he had Magyarized his name), who was in charge of the anti-Jewish operations of the Gendarmerie and who commanded 3,000 to 5,000 men set aside for this purpose. Unlike the ordinary police, the Gendarmerie was a centrally organized paramilitary force with a clear political profile. Many of its members were of German-Hungarian origin, and nearly all had a rural background. Eichmann was Baky's and Ferenczy's "technical advisor." Together the three commanded one single formidable killing machine in the midst of an antisemite or at least indifferent "Christian" society. To Eichmann, both the political and the technical framework were ideal.

Nevertheless, Eichmann lived in mute tension with those top German SS officers who together with the German army had come to Hungary like scavengers, in order to appropriate the large Jewish-owned industries for the SS or for themselves personally. He knew that the academically trained "Doktor" Veesenmayer considered him scum. Eichmann felt that these clever higher-ups stood in his way and had never let him rise above the rank of lieutenant colonel. He thoroughly admired the Führer, even though he had never read Hitler's *Mein Kampf,* the ideological party program. Hadn't the Führer, once the inmate of a homeless men's shelter, risen to be chief of state of Germany and master of Europe? Hitler's word was law to him. The Führer's biography resembled his own. Like Hitler, Eichmann had come from the dregs of society. He fully shared the feelings of this class, the frustrated petite bourgeoisie, from which the National Socialists recruited their foot troops. Apart from that, Eichmann was curiously a man without convictions. He was not even against the Jews, and for a while he even enjoyed a Jewish mistress, which was strictly against Nazi racial laws. He organized the transportation of Jews to the death camps because this was the will of the Führer. He needed no justification other than that.

Adolf Eichmann was born in Solingen in northwest Germany in 1906, but his family moved to Linz in Austria when he was only a child, not far from Braunau, where Hitler was born. His father was an accountant and a member of the consistory of the local Reformed parish. Adolf Eichmann was an indifferent pupil, who neither finished school nor completed an apprenticeship as a mechanic, and he never worked hard. He became a salesman, lost his job, and lived off his father's meager income.

In 1932 the unemployed and dispirited young Eichmann joined the National Socialist party. There was no reason why he shouldn't. He had no other prospects. When Hitler's takeover in Germany occurred a year later, he even joined the SS, the *Schutzstaffel.* With the help of this unit, composed of mindless thugs, the Führer had fought his way to power. Eichmann liked the martial spirit, the songs, and the uniforms of this smart paramilitary corps, which had become the center of the German military security establishment. Above all, he now had a salary without having to work hard, and he was able to get away from home. The SS also provided Eichmann with an identity. He was connected with a unit, which was imbued with a purpose, and this purpose had a name, Adolf Hitler, the Führer, the leader. Where the Führer would lead him, he did not know it wasn't really important. He simply obeyed and didn't have to think.

Eichmann was assigned to Himmler's newly established national security services, which the Nazis had placed within the SS. In 1935 he was assigned to a department that dealt with "Jewish questions." Then, in 1938, he was ordered to set in motion the expulsion of Austria's Jews. His superiors noted that he was a good organizer and let him become an officer. When the war broke out in 1939 his assignment became more sinister. He became responsible for organizing train transports of Jews from Germany and other occupied territories to the East. He was in charge of round-ups, procuring cattle wagons and engines, negotiating timetables, and reserving space at recipient camps. What happened there was not his responsibility. Eichmann disliked seeing executions and blood.

One of the specialities in which Eichmann excelled was the setting up of *Judenräte*, Jewish councils. He would move into the area or the country that had been selected to become *judenrein*, cleansed of Jews, contact Jewish leadership, and associate these unsuspecting people with his destructive purpose. Although the Jews obviously distrusted the Nazis, a thorough censorship of the media kept them from learning the full truth. Moreover, Eichmann became very good at pretending a folksy simplicity and managed to persuade the Jewish leadership that their community was about to be sent to wonderful pioneer settlements in the east, where they would manage their own affairs and be left in peace. After all these anxious years, this was a message that the Jewish leaders gladly received. Eichmann pretended to be interested in Jewish history, had learned a few words of Hebrew, and had a smattering of Yiddish. He thus gained their confidence and made them issue orders to their communities on his behalf. He made the Jewish councils give him lists and addresses of Jewish families, and with the help of local authorities and police forces concentrated them at convenient rail heads, turning over their belongings to the SS and their local collaborators, who would hold everything "in trust." The Jews could not imagine that a highly cultured nation like Germany was capable of the evils of which clear-sighted spirits warned them. Once their community had been deported, the Judenräte followed them to their death. Thus, Europe's Jews cooperated almost willingly in their own destruction, partly out of sheer ignorance, but partly also out of fear that any "wrongdoing" on their part could make matters worse. When the Jews realized what was happening to them, it was too late. The fact of this quasi willing cooperation — instead of outright opposition — has been troubling Jewish survivors and their descendents in no small measure. Of course, Jews resisted, and Christian friends occasionally helped them to resist. But these were the exceptions. The fact is that wherever the Jews fought back or wherever they were protected by their host nation or by courageous individuals, they stood a better chance of survival. The 1943 uprising of the Warsaw ghetto and the actions of the Danish and Bulgarian peoples during that same year serve as an example.

*   *   *

Consul Lutz dutifully drove up to the heights of Suabian Hill, in order to meet the Obersturmbannführer, who, as Minister Veesenmayer had said, would help him with transportation problems. Lutz was surprised to see the extreme security measures as he came near the hotel. Several times Szluha had to slow down, whenever he was waved down by SS guards or Hungarian gendarmes, in order to let the consul show papers and explain the purpose of the visit.

As Lutz entered Eichmann's office at the Hotel Majestic, the Obersturmbannführer was just ordering an aide to collect large maps and to bring them into another room. This was done a little too hastily, the consul thought.

Eichmann appeared sure of himself. He was of medium size, thin, an ordinary person, someone who would be overlooked in a crowd or easily forgotten. Today the Obersturmbannführer was working for the SS, but tomorrow he could equally well be running a general store, asking the customer in a bored voice how he could help. There was a photograph of his wife and children on the desk. They, too, had dull faces. When Hannah Arendt wrote of the Eichmann process of Jerusalem in 1960 and 1961, she coined the phrase, "The banality of evil."

He asked Herr Konsul to sit down and make himself comfortable. Before the vice consul could formulate his question, Eichmann said he already knew from Dr. Feine about the 8,000 whom the consul wanted to bring out of Hungary. He understood the concern of Herr Konsul, of course, and he wanted to be helpful in every way possible. Lutz thought he had heard that phrase before.

It was evident to Lutz that Eichmann was not enthusiastic about his visit, but then he probably wasn't enthusiastic about anything in his life. Nevertheless, the consul knew or thought he knew that the Obersturm-bannführer might be in a position to help. Lutz was desperate for a positive decision. He said he would be happy if he and the Obersturmbann-führer could discuss together departure dates and train schedules for the 8,000, because most of the children and young people had their papers and were ready to depart. If the German armed forces could help provide transportation, the Hungarian exit permits could be obtained without difficulty. This had never been a problem in the past. All the more as his excellency, Minister Veesenmayer, had said to him in person that he would put in a good word with the Hungarian authorities. The minister had been quite understanding.

This was a daring proposal, Lutz thought. Who had ever heard of the German military security transporting Jews to freedom?

Eichmann leaned back in his chair, put his hands behind his head, and smiled. The suggestion certainly seemed odd to him also. Dear Herr Konsul, he said, this was all well and good, and he would do exactly as the consul wished. But Herr Konsul would have to understand that there was one problem. He paused with a smirk of satisfaction, while Lutz tried not to appear anxious, and said that he had not yet been instructed to this ef-fect by his superiors in Berlin. Lutz was going to object that Minister Veesenmayer had himself said he would cable to Berlin for instructions. On second thought he recalled that Veesenmayer had not really promised that, had he? Eichmann continued by saying that under these circum-stances he probably could not help Herr Konsul as quickly as he himself would like to. Before he, Eichmann, could act, he had to await a specific and written authorization from the chief of the SS, Heinrich Himmler, the authority on which he depended. Parallel to this Dr. Veesenmayer needed similar approval from his own superior in Berlin, Foreign Minister Ribbentrop. The consul had to understand that he, Eichmann, and Veesenmayer were subject to these two lines of command, and that instruc-tions from the two had to coincide. He had not yet heard from his excel-lency, Minister Veesenmayer, whether he had received such an order about the 8,000.

Lutz forced himself to suppress his anger over such bureaucratic doubletalk. It was the same wooden language as Veesenmayer's, except that the obstruction was now stated in a more brutal manner. Couldn't the Obersturmbannführer cable Berlin requesting such an authorization? he asked. Eichmann got up and offered the vice consul a cigarette. When Lutz refused, he took one himself and deliberately wasted time lighting it. If there was one thing he had learned in many years of military service, he said, it was that one did not suggest orders to one's superiors. Lutz interrupted him impatiently. He could cable that the Swiss consul had come to him, requesting help with the transportation of the 8,000. How else would they know about it in Berlin? Besides, his name was well known at the foreign ministry, as former representative of German interests in Palestine.

This did not impress Eichmann, who said his line of command was the chief of the SS, Himmler, not the foreign ministry. The question was tossed back and forth until Eichmann said that he would reflect on it and let Herr Konsul know whether he would cable Himmler, but the answer would doubtless take time. Patience was needed. Lutz nervously leaned back in his chair and listened to Eichmann philosophize about the fate of a soldier under orders. His comrades were fighting against the red tide in Russia, and he was fighting the same battle right from this desk. His job, as per orders from Berlin, was to concentrate and observe the Jews, in order to protect the rear of the fighting troops. The Jews were all spies and enemies of Germany and of the Führer's new Europe. If given a chance they would put a knife in the back of every brave German soldier who was fighting to protect Europe from the invading red hordes. If his superiors in Berlin — as they might well do — hesitated to approve the request of Herr Konsul, this was the reason why. Nevertheless, if Berlin decided to be lenient, who was he, Eichmann, to object? If Himmler ordered him to leave Budapest today and to go fight at the front, he would do so without a moment's hesitation. It was anyway better to be an honest soldier, Eichmann pretended, than to sit behind a desk, as he did now.

Lutz listened politely, and Eichmann seemed to realize that this kind of talk could hardly be of interest to his visitor. The Obersturmbann-führer smiled and said that an idea crossed his mind. It was of course possible, perhaps even likely, that a telegram from Berlin would land on his desk, ordering him to cooperate with the Swiss legation on the transportation of the 8,000, he said. If so, it might be a good idea to prepare for this eventuality. In order not to lose time when that moment came, he would suggest to Herr Konsul that he give him a list of the names and addresses of these children and young people. Lutz was astonished. Was he to be glad over this sudden readiness to help? Why did the Obersturmbannführer want the addresses? he asked. So that they can be found easily, when the time comes for boarding the train. Eight thousand people was a large number. Lutz said he appreciated the interest of the Obersturmbannführer. But might it not be better to await the order from Berlin? When it arrived he and his team would prepare the address list of the 8,000 overnight, so that they could be found without delay. As the consul wished, Eichmann answered, with some disappointment.

As he left the Hotel Majestic and was driven back to Budapest, Lutz wondered over Eichmann's curious request for those addresses. He decided to send a cable to the Swiss foreign ministry in Berne, asking that the legation in Berlin request Ribbentrop to instruct Veesenmayer to let the 8,000 children and young people go. When the coded message went off he felt like Moses pleading before the Pharaoh on behalf of oppressed Israel.

But the foreign ministry in Berne, Marcel Pilet-Golaz, did not appreciate such initiatives, and the request was not transmitted to Berlin. The Swiss foreign minister and his leading advisors thought that Lutz was really overstepping his jurisdiction. After all, Lutz was a mere neutral consul and not a plenipotentiary negotiator of ambassadorial rank. Pilet-Golaz was very touchy when it came to diplomatic protocol. The foreign minister and his advisors even considered recalling this undisciplined troublemaker. He might cause further embarrassment to Switzerland. In the end, Pilet-Golaz agreed that one of the secretaries of state — by no means the foreign minister himself, who would not address a mere consul — send Lutz a sharp reminder that Jews were not political refugees. To render assistance to them meant in fact interference in the internal affairs of the host country. Would the consul please abstain from such meddling in the future and restrict himself to his official assignment as neutral representative of foreign interests? The message was sent via diplomatic courier, not by cable, and it took several days to reach Budapest. This was one of the ways by which the powerful superiors added sting to the message, reminding the consul that he was not a ranking diplomat.

This settled the matter, as far as Berne was concerned. In his eagerness to put Consul Lutz in his place, Pilet-Golaz seemed to have forgotten that he himself had passed on countless British instructions to Lutz to help Jewish children and young people to reach Palestine and that the 8,000 were simply the remainder of those who possessed valid Palestine Certificates. For the last two years, the foreign ministry had regularly received lists of Jewish children and young people from the British government and transmitted them to the consul in Budapest. Even from the formal angle, it was quite legitimate for Lutz to request an intervention in Berlin so that he could get on with his job. Even now, as this exchange was taking place, the Swiss foreign ministry kept receiving these names from the British Foreign Office, which it thoughtlessly continued to pass on to Lutz, apparently still not knowing what it was doing. At his office on Freedom Square the consul shook his head over the mindless reply. His superiors in Berne used the same wooden language as Veesenmayer and Eichmann, and the end effect was just as deadly. He had to face his enemies alone.

Carl Lutz mulled again over Eichmann's request to give him a list of names and addresses of the 8,000. He felt that there was something sinister behind the man's uncouth bonhomie. If Eichmann was an honest man, he would have offered to help transport the 8,000 without the required list. At this moment the consul knew that atrocious events were taking place, with which the SS was somehow connected, though he could not comprehend their depth. But he was a fair-minded person and wanted to be careful about believing all and sundry tales of *Kriegsgreuel*, war horror stories, imputed to the "Huns," the Germans, such as had been spread by an excited Anglo-Saxon yellow press during the previous war. Joseph Goebbels, the Nazi propaganda minister, kept rubbing this embarrassing fact in the nose of the Allies, and used it as a smoke screen to hide the truth about the Holocaust, now that the horrors were true beyond imagination. However, even

61

though Lutz had not yet fathomed the depth of the Jewish tragedy, he was approaching the edge of the abyss.

As events unfolded, Lutz knew that his prudence with regard to Eichmann was justified. On March 22, 1944, only three days after the occupation, the Hungarian government of Prime Minister Döme Sztojay, "counselled" by Veesenmayer, ordered the confiscation of 18,000 Jewish businesses. More astute than the Germans during the "night of broken glass" of November 1938, the opportunistic Hungarians did not break the windows of Jewish stores or destroy the interiors. They simply went in and took them over. The morning after, smiling "Christian" men or women stood where the "Jews" used to stand, enticing customers. They were like jackals. Few of the new owners had business experience or disciplined working habits, and most of the stolen businesses went bankrupt. The Jews not only became destitute. Each family became isolated. They were no longer in any position to help each other or to offer resistance as a community. Nor could they communicate with sympathizing Christian friends. Even Jewish converts to Christianity suffered from this persecution.

These orders which pauperized the Jews were published in the press and broadcast over the radio and thereby became known abroad. Within days, the western Allies subjected Budapest to several aerial bombardments, which caused a few hundred dead and several dozen buildings destroyed. The Hungarian official propaganda called the raids "acts of terrorism" and threatened revenge. The Jews were said to be the "cause" of these misfortunes, and several thousands were thrown out of their apartments and houses. These homes were then filled with "Christians," who, it was said as before, had been bombed out.

*   *   *

March turned into April 1944, and one evening shortly after one of these bombing raids there were quick knocks at the gate of the former British legation. Szluha opened the gate. He had been washing the vice consul's Packard, as he did every evening. He took special pride that his master's vehicle appear as impressive as possible to the people of Budapest. At the gate was Dr. Feine from the German legation, which was no small surprise, because Swiss diplomats kept their social contacts with the personnel of that legation to a strict minimum. The visitor looked furtively up and down Verböcsy Street and entered quickly.

Feine said to the astonished consul that perhaps he recalled him saying that they would surely meet again. He was sorry that he came without any previous announcement, but he hoped that Herr Konsul would understand that it was impossible to telephone him from the German legation or to send a note. All staff was closely surveyed. Could they converse in private?

Lutz led the guest to the library, which was adjacent to the great hall. He realized that Dr. Feine surely came with an important message. Feine looked around and seemed impressed by the splendid surroundings. The consul offered him a chair, but the visitor remained standing and refused to accept any refreshment. Feine appeared to be choosing his words with care. He said that he had of course overheard the conversation between the consul and his excellency, Minister Veesenmayer. Also Obersturmbannführer Eichmann had informed him of the consul's visit. He hesitated. Herr Konsul should understand that what he was about to say was highly confidential. If his superior, Veesenmayer, or anyone else at the German legation learned that he had gone to Verböcsy Street in order to talk to the Swiss consul, he would not only be suspended, but worse. . . . He moved his right hand across his throat. Could he absolutely trust Herr Konsul?

Lutz gave Feine his hand and said that when he had come back from the German legation he had told his wife that even at first sight the first secretary didn't seem to fit in there, even though they had not exchanged a word.

Feine felt more relaxed. They sat down, and the German visitor said he wouldn't mind a cup of coffee now.

Gertrud brought it. After her husband had introduced her to the visitor, she withdrew discreetly, sensing that her presence was not wanted. Feine sipped the coffee thoughtfully. Then he pulled out a white sheet of paper. Without a word he showed it to Lutz. It was the copy of a cable that Veesenmayer had sent to Berlin. Astonished, the vice consul read that the fat Nazi proposed to Ribbentrop to let the Jews of Budapest "pay" for the air raids. For every dead Hungarian, 100 Jews should be executed. Thus, if the bombs killed 300 or 400 Hungarians, this meant that 30,000 to 40,000 Jews would die. After a few air raids, the entire Jewish population would thus be wiped out. No one could protest, Veesenmayer suggested, because they would be "justly" punished for being the cause of the air raids. Lutz looked at Feine flabbergasted. Hostages! Were they back in the Middle Ages? Had Veesenmayer lost his mind? He got up, walked around, studied the cable again, and repeated the words aloud. Years later, this particular moment remained engraved in Lutz's mind: "I read Veesenmayer's telegram of April 3, 1944, with consternation; I didn't trust my eyes. On the basis of my conversation with Veesenmayer I had believed that he was capable of at least a small measure of human feeling. Now I became convinced that he was not only a convinced Nazi, but a sadist."

Lutz later learned from Feine that Ribbentrop, who certainly had no compunctions about eliminating Jews, had decided not to answer the cable. It would be devastating, he thought, if the Jews were killed in public, because the Holocaust was to be kept a secret from the world. Four years later Judge Maguire confronted Veesenmayer with the text of this cable before the International Military Court at Nuremberg. He asked whether the executions had taken place. Veesenmayer's reply revealed his complete cynicism: "No, thank God, they didn't, thanks to the United States Air Force, because for once it interrupted its attacks. There was not a single execution. We did not even publish our menace. The disaster fortunately passed."

Feine said that he, too, as a German, was deeply shocked about what his government was doing in the name of the German people. He was moreover terribly disturbed about his own involvement with Veesenmayer and Eichmann. Feine told Lutz the story of his life, and it sounded like a confession. His father had been an honorable and renowned professor of theology. If he knew what his son was doing, he would turn over in his grave. A jurist specializing in international law, Feine used to be the private secretary to Gustav Stresemann, that high-minded and cultured German statesman of the Weimar Republic, and he had risen to become secretary of state in the foreign ministry. When the Nazis took power in 1933, he wanted to quit. He talked to his wife. After much heart searching he decided to swear fealty to the Führer, fully expecting that Hitler would fall after a few months. Had he refused, the Nazis would not only have blocked his professional future, but they might have thrown him into a concentration camp and threatened his family. Moreover, he needed an income. He had thought of emigration, of course, but what could a middle-aged expert on international law do in another country? Hitler did not fall and Feine was caught, like so many others. The German war machine was rebuilt. It brought disaster on most of Europe. And with every passing year, he, Feine, got more entangled in the terrible system. There he was, at the German legation in occupied Hungary, and he had to play along with two brutes like Veesenmayer and Eichmann, to mention only them; and he was officially responsible for "Jewish affairs," as if everything else was not enough. The Nazis knew exactly how to needle someone like him who didn't shout hurrah every five minutes. Against his Christian convictions and flouting his academic upbringing, he had become inextricably tangled with the Nazis and hated himself for it.

Carl Lutz was appalled. What if he had been caught in such a dilemma? It was bad enough to have one's hands tied by diplomatic considerations. He remembered how the pietists, among whom he had been raised, loved to speak about sin and forgiveness. It had all sounded so simple. These sins were really ridiculous personal infractions of rules. Forgiveness, it was said, meant that the sins could be washed off by "the blood," kneeling at the foot of the cross — until the next trespass. But what about the sin caused by a government system involving wholesale murder with the help of modern technology? How, within such an anonymous conglomerate, could an individual refuse to participate in such an unimaginable collective sin, except perhaps by committing suicide, which in itself was a sin and an escape from responsibility, or by making one's family suffer want and humiliation? Where, within this generalized hell, could "the blood" wash off what sin and what guilt and whose? Or should one stay on and try to do one's best within the evil system, at the cost of one's integrity, knowing that such a sacrifice made little difference? And why was God, who supposedly loved all creatures and hated sin, silent in the face of such unspeakable collective evil?

For a long while they sat together without saying a word.

The German diplomat finally said that it was time for him to go, and he rose. But he hesitated, as if lost in thought. There was one more thing, he began, but he stopped and shook his head. It was as if he begged not to have to say anything more. It was surely enough, he seemed to say, that he had impressed upon Herr Konsul that both Veesenmayer and Eichmann were not only liars, but dangerous men. He shook his head and breathed deeply and nervously.

Lutz accompanied his guest to the gate. Once again, Feine turned toward him, but hesitated. He walked away quickly, his head down, as if in shame.

*   *   *

During the first few days after the German occupation of Hungary, the actions of Consul Lutz to save Jews had been sporadic responses to specific circumstances. After his encounters with the three Germans he knew that he had to act more decisively. He undertook two actions immediately, with breathtaking speed and boldness.

First, he gave asylum to the Budapest office of the Jewish Agency for Palestine. He gave Swiss protective passports to its president, Otto Komoly, the former army officer, to its vice president, Reszö Kasztner, the young lawyer from Transylvania, and to its executive director, Moshe Krausz, so that they could move freely about Budapest, formally on his behalf, in semi-official capacity, but in reality for the "illegal" Palestine Office. Second, he changed the name of the Budapest office of the Jewish Agency to the Emigration Department of the Swiss Legation. Backed by his superior, Minister Jaeger, Lutz revisited government contacts in various minstries, who were hanging on to their posts by the skin of their teeth despite the political changes, and brazenly requested recognition of the takeover. The consul pretended that this was merely to assure the continuation of the emigration program, in which he had been involved more than two years. Didn't Hungary wish to respect its international obligations as it had done up to now? He said he fully expected the borders to re-open. In these dealings Carl Lutz was at his best, negotiating brilliantly and trying to persuade his discussion partners to accept the fait accompli. He knew that he was sailing close to the wind and that in reality he was demanding privileges that no diplomat had ever obtained. The consul knew that if he failed, not only could he be declared persona non grata and have to leave the country, but the situation of the 8,000 children and young people would be desperate indeed. He was gambling for high stakes.

Lutz was surprised at how speedily this imaginative coup succeeded. The Hungarian authorities agreed. Henceforth, the Palestine Office enjoyed diplomatic immunity under its new name, the Emigration Department of the Swiss Legation. Boldly, Lutz had a brass plate engraved with the new name and attached to the legation building. Every passing person could see that in the heart of German-occupied Hungary the Swiss legation was offering emigration services to anyone who cared to leave Nazi-dominated Europe! What Lutz did not say to the Hungarian officials was that he also attached the Chalutzim to his new Emigration Department and that he gave them Swiss identity papers. Their new headquarters were located in the basement of the former American legation. These courageous young men — and several young women — became his means of communication with the isolated Jewish community, the consul's eyes and ears. They brought Schutzbriefe discreetly to those who did not dare to visit the consul and brought in new names of those who wanted to be protected. The Schutzbriefe were impressive-looking documents. There was a Swiss cross at the top of each protective letter. Then there were some empty lines, which were filled in with the name of the bearer, who — as the German and Hungarian text explained — was registered with the Swiss legation for emigration to Palestine. He or she enjoyed the full protection of Switzerland. The Hungarian authorities were requested by the Swiss legation to accord all possible protection to this potential emigrant.

Veesenmayer and Eichmann took the creation of the Department of Emigration of the Swiss Legation as a personal insult. Had they not outsmarted the bespectacled consul, who had approached them like a humble petitioner for his 8,000 protégés? Now it was he who without troops and guns had made the might of Greater Germany look ridiculous. The

Hungarian officials whom Veesenmayer took to task for their gullible tolerance blandly answered that they could find no formal reason for rejecting the consul's request. What was the problem? The lower echelons of the Hungarian administration, now that the shock of the German occupation had given way to mute resentment, were gaining expertise in applying passive resistance. For the first time Veesenmayer felt that he was reaching the limits of his power. Furiously, he thought of having the SS storm the American and British legation buildings. But Feine quietly explained to his bumbling superior that this would not only constitute a very serious breach of international law but would also make Switzerland stop all arms deliveries to Germany and deny access to its banks. In the end it would be Germany which took the raps. Veesenmayer's fat fist banged violently on his desk; he mumbled about tricky lawyers and wondered how to explain his failures to Berlin. In the closet, the perfume bottles rattled, and for the first time Hitler's plenipotentiary to Hungary was afraid. What would the Führer do to him if he failed?

There remained Marcel Pilet-Golaz and his prudent secretaries of state. At this time, Maximilian Jaeger was recalled to Berne "for consultation." This was the cautious diplomatic method the Swiss government used to protest against the German occupation of Hungary, without breaking off official relationships. When the storm blew over, the minister would quietly slip back to his post, as if nothing had happened. Jaeger's journey home saved Lutz from another nerve-racking exchange of correspondence with his superiors. Jaeger quietly explained to Pilet-Golaz that the consul's move to establish an emigration department was the logical consequence of his previous engagement to help Jewish children and young people emigrate to Palestine. After all, the Swiss foreign ministry had requested him to do this work, at the demand of the British government. It wasn't he who had started it on his own initiative. This was true, Pilet-Golaz had to admit, but didn't Lutz go much too far, was he not too anxious to help? Perhaps, Jaeger replied, but unusual situations demanded unusual responses. The consul had to fulfill his task in the midst of violent upheavals, and it was he who had to look into the faces that were distorted by fear, day after day.

*   *   *

The Jews of Budapest were relieved when they learned that the Swiss legation was giving out papers to anyone who felt his life was in danger. But it would be a mistake to think that during the two hours allotted to them each day they flocked to Freedom Square in untold masses. The western Allies had landed south of Rome and were fighting hard at Monte Cassino. As soon as Rome fell, Italy was virtually conquered, they thought, and when that happened the western Allies stood practically at the gates of Hungary. Surely it was a matter of weeks, if not days. In the east, the Red Army pushed into Romania and was driving the Germans before it toward the eastern slopes of the Carpathian mountains. The Soviets, it was rumored, might even be on Tartar Pass, the ancient eastern gateway to the plains of Hungary. Everything seemed to be moving fast. If the Almighty — blessed be his name — was merciful, he would see to it that the western Allies rolled into Budapest ahead of the Red Army. The nightmare would end as quickly as it had begun.

For the time being, however, daily reality remained brutal for the Jews. They were insulted when they hurried out of their homes, trying to buy food. There were those who never returned. Gendarmes broke into the apartments of Jewish families at midnight and stole whatever they could lay their hands on. They did not hesitate to rape women and school-age girls before they left.

One of those who was scared was beautiful Magda Grausz née Csanyi, a young woman in her early thirties. She lived in a mansion on Bathori Street in the center of Pest, not far from the American legation building. Her husband, Sandor (Alexander) Grausz, was a wealthy dealer at the grain stock market — until March 19, when he lost his position. Magda had come from Baja in southern Hungary, where she had spent a happy youth, being courted by numerous young men. She was inevitably drawn to the capital, and she completed an apprenticeship at Klara Rothschild's prestigious haute couture store on Vaci Street as a high quality seamstress. It was there that she caught the eye of Sandor. They were married in 1937.

Magda Grausz rushed over to Freedom Square one day in early April in order to ask Vice Consul Lutz for help. With her was her six-year-old daughter, Agnes, a lively, blue-eyed girl with long, dark blonde curls, bound together with a bright red ribbon. With her bearing and her immaculate clothes, Magda had no difficulty passing the long queues of people lining up in front of the desks of the Emigration Department to find her way to the consul on the second floor. Immediately, Carl Lutz gave the visitor his full attention, astonished that such elegance could still be found in a city ravaged by years of wartime scarcity, where clothes had become ever more shabby.

Magda's story was quickly told. Sensing the coming danger, Sandor Grausz had in early 1938 arranged to send his young wife to London, where she gave birth to their new baby. This made the child automatically a British subject, which — who knew? — could become useful one day. They had even baptized her into the Church of England. Could Herr Konsul, Magda pleaded, find a way of protecting her English-born daughter? Lutz took a moment to chat with Agnes and to admire her curls. The consul had always been fond of little girls, perhaps because he and Gertrud didn't have children of their own. For a moment he forgot all other urgent demands and focused his attention on Agnes. Minutes passed in chatting.

The consul finally lifted his eyes to her attractive mother and said he thought there would be no problem helping the child. But what about her, the mother? Mrs. Grausz surely wouldn't want to be separated from Agnes? (He didn't realize that he was stammering a little, when he spoke to Magda). Of course not, Magda replied; what did Herr Konsul have in mind? Lutz said pensively that he wanted to talk to his wife about it. She always found good solutions. Could Mrs. Grausz come back in a couple of days? Magda sighed with relief. With tears in her eyes at so much generosity, she took both of the vice consul's hands into her own and pressed them. They felt soft and warm, Lutz thought.

Gertrud Lutz thought that this woman and her small daughter were indeed a special case. Perhaps they could join the thirty or so people who had already found refuge in their residence on Verböcsy Street. So, shortly thereafter Magda and Agnes Grausz moved to the former British legation in Buda. They were given a small, two-room apartment on the ground floor. If anyone asked, it was said that Mrs. Grausz was hired as a housekeeper in charge of a section of the building and that she occasionally set tables. Her daughter just happened to have come along. At any rate, the girl was a British subject and could legitimately claim protection from the representative of British interests in Hungary. Years later Gertrud Lutz remembered what a beautiful and lively girl Agnes had been and how much she cheered up those living in the vast house on the hill of Buda, back in 1944.

Carl and Gertrud had saved Magda and Agnes from an almost certain death.

4. THE TERRIBLE SECRET

Ominous developments are often heralded by apparently unrelated signs long before they take place. One, selected at random, was the seemingly impertinent announcement of German philosopher Friedrich Nietzsche shortly before the dawn of the twentieth century, that God was dead. Another, also selected at random, was poison gas warfare on the western front in 1917. These two very dissimilar occurrences bear no direct relationship with each other. But seen in historical perspective, they gave a frightening indication of what the twentieth century would be like. Liberation from religious belief in conjunction with scientific advances did not produce human progress as that generation expected, but incredible disaster. Nietzsche's cold, if passionate, analysis told him that science and modern industry were making the idea of God redundant and that ethics based on traditional religion was dissolving. If society was to be built afresh, he thought, rule must belong to the courageous and to the mighty. As if to prove the truth of these insights, the war of 1914–18 suddenly erupted, profoundly shocking Western civilization. Its pivotal event was the use of poison gas. The new combination of science and industry exploded all previous restraints.

The devastating effects of gas warfare were observed by a young Austrian lance corporal by the name of Adolf Hitler who was fighting within German ranks. In the mind of this fairly uneducated man the two above-mentioned elements fused. The four years of pitiless warfare had destroyed the small measure of civilization and religion with which he had

72

been brought up. Hitler probably had never read Nietzsche, but like Nietzsche he believed that Europe had to be rebuilt on new foundations. One master race must dominate the rest, and God or the idea of God must simply disappear. This led to the next step in his mind. Could not poison gas, which he had seen to function so efficiently at war, be a suitable means for disposing of real or imaginary enemies?

If Europe's civilization had not gone bankrupt after World War I, Adolf Hitler would have been locked up in a lunatic asylum. As it was, he communicated his dangerous notions to a confused and angry people and was heard. The masses believed that he was the God-appointed messenger who would fill the spiritual and cultural vacuum. Humanity cannot be without hope.

World War II and the Holocaust were the result of this delusion turning into crime, the logical consequences of the already existing cultural disaster.

During the autumn of 1941, as Hitler's armies became stuck in the mud and the snow of his over-extended eastern front, he realized that the campaign against the Soviet Union was lost and that he could not win the war. Ultimate defeat was just a question of time, even though in his speeches he kept proclaiming the *Endsieg*, the final victory. If the one major enemy, the Bolsheviks — who had a rival project for the reconstruction of Europe and the world — could not be defeated, he thought that at least the Jews must be eliminated before defeat came. The Jews were to Hitler the symbol of all the detestable peoples who stood in the way of the master race. They were different, more intelligent. They constituted a permanent subversive conspiracy against the Germanic master race, as the Führer repeated in his harangues. With each new military disaster, his personal pessimism grew, and he became convinced that he would not live long. He began to talk of a *Götterdämmerung*, the twilight of the gods, which was the ancient Germanic notion that at the end of times the gods would destroy themselves. His favorite composer, Richard Wagner, had set this theme to music. During the last four years of the war, when the German *Wehrmacht* (armed forces) went from defeat to defeat, Hitler convinced himself in his beclouded mind that not even his own people understood his designs, that the military was betraying him and therefore merited doom.

It was at this moment of growing gloom that Hitler recalled what he had seen at the front in 1917. No written directives exist. But in 1941 he seems to have issued a verbal order to his security forces that research into efficient killing methods must be undertaken, with a view to using poison gas. Such gasses would be applied to selected population groups, such as the mentally insane, Slavic peoples, Gypsies, and above all the Jews. When someone in the Führer's entourage expressed fear that the world would cry out against such destruction, he answered that the world had not cried out when the Turks had slaughtered the Armenians in 1915. It would not cry out now when the Jews were killed.

In January 1942 the feared chief of German secret services, Reinhard Heydrich, a Nazi devoid of human feeling, called together thirty representatives of all government and military branches to a one-day meeting at a lakeside villa at Wannsee near Berlin. The recording secretary was a little known SS officer called Adolf Eichmann. Heydrich handed out statistics on European Jewry. The outline for the "final solution," as he called it, was revealed over lunch. The Jews would be systematically collected in temporary camps, loaded on trains, and dispatched eastward. The aim was to make Europe judenfrei, free of Jews. The Führer wished that these trains be given priority over military transports. If anyone in this gathering was opposed to the plan or even entertained misgivings, he wisely kept his thoughts to himself. Questions from participants were limited to the technical aspects: time limits, transportation methods, division of labor, administrative questions. Over coffee the vocabulary rules were fixed. No one was ever to speak of deportation or killing. The code word was "resettlement in the east." This did not mean that qualified Jews would not be used as skilled workers in the arms industry, including in the making of airplanes. But as soon as they lost their usefulness, they, too, would be "resettled." Moreover, Heydrich warned that to divulge the murderous program was equivalent to high treason, which would be punished accordingly, regardless of rank and standing.

Rumors began to circulate in the autumn of 1942 about systematic Nazi atrocities. Not only Jews but also Gypsies and nationals from various Slav countries were gathered up and deported. Slowly the world began to perceive that the final destination of these unfortunates was some mysterious death camps and that a Europe-wide kingdom of the "master race" was being set up. Most victims came from the ancient pale in Poland, western Russia, and Lithuania, where in old days the tsars had forced the Jews of their domain to settle. But the rumors seemed so absurd and irrational that they were not really believed. Morever, German propaganda kept insisting that any such talk was enemy-inspired propaganda, which intended to bring discredit upon the honorable German people. But the rumors did not stop, even though they were not precise. This vagueness comforted the Allies, because it relieved them of any obligation to deal with the matter seriously.

*   *   *

The curtain of deliberate ignorance was finally torn apart by two young Slovak Jews, Walter Rosenberg and Alfred Wetzler, who were later known as Rudolf Vrba and Josef Lanik. Incredible as it may seem, they succeeded in escaping from the largest Nazi death camp, Auschwitz, located in Upper Silesia, not far from Cracow. At least eighty escape attempts were made, but only five prisoners got out, the others being Jerzy Tabau from the Polish underground, and Czeslaw Mordowicz and Arnost Rosin, two Polish Jews. The rest were executed on the spot. Vrba and Lanik did not simply want to stay alive; they wanted to tell the gruesome story of Auschwitz to the world, in order to have this industrial death machine stopped. They had been in the camp since 1942 and survived only because they were given administrative jobs and had relative freedom of movement. Knowing that they, too, would eventually be killed, the two young men kept their eyes open, learned as much as possible about the deadly mechanisms of Auschwitz, and planned their escape.

On April 7, 1944, Vrba and Lanik set out for freedom, and miraculously succeeded in crossing the two chains of watch towers that surrounded the vast camp. They found their way across electrically charged barbed wire, evading search patrols and vicious dogs. They walked across the surrounding high security zone and passed into German-occupied Polish territory, whose population was known to be generally hostile to Jews. After countless close calls, the two young men crossed the border into Slovakia on April 21 and immediately got in touch with the stunned Jewish leadership of Zilina and later the leaders of Bratislava. For several days they were thoroughly interrogated. Both Vrba and Lanik were engineers by profession and could give precise information in — presumably — unemotional language. Their account was later supplemented by statements from the other three escapees, Tabau, Mordowicz, and Rosin.

Two paragraphs from Rudolf Vrba's part of the testimony are selected to give the tenor of the sixty-page document that came to be known as the Auschwitz Protocol, one of the most frightful texts of the twentieth century.

During my first night shift (after arrival in 1942) I had the opportunity of directly observing how the arriving transports were handled. There was this transport of Polish Jews. In their cattle wagons there was no water, and when they arrived, 100 of them were dead. The doors of the wagons were opened, and with much shouting we drove these utterly exhausted Jews out of the wagons. They came out quickly, because SS men came in after us and beat them up. Then they were lined up in rows of five. It was our job to clear the dead, half-dead and the prisoners' personal luggage out of the wagons. The dead were carried to a collection point and thrown onto a heap. Those unable to walk unaided were considered dead. The luggage was thrown onto a different pile. After this the wagons were thoroughly cleaned. No trace was to be left behind from the transport. A commission from the political section of the camp arrived in order to select about 10% of the men and 5% of the women, who were led away to the barracks. The rest were loaded on trucks and brought to the birch forest (Birkenau), where they were gassed. The dead, and the half-dead among them, were also loaded on trucks. They were burned directly in the birch forest. Often, small children who were still alive, were thrown on top of the dead lying on the trucks. The luggage was also loaded on trucks and brought to the stores, where its contents were sorted out.

Vrba and Lanik proceeded to describe the exact killing method:

In February 1943 the newly built crematoria and the gas chambers in Birkenau began to operate. At present four crematoria are in function. The crematoria consist each of three parts: (a) fire ovens, (b) shower room, (c) gas chamber. In the middle of the fire ovens rises a high chimney, around which are constructed nine ovens with four openings each. Each opening can normally take in four normal-sized bodies, which are burned to ashes in one and a half hours. The daily capacity of the ovens is 2000 bodies. Next to them is a large reception hall, which is built in such a way as to give the impression that it leads to a shower room. This hall can receive 2000 persons at the same time. Below them there are presumably other reception halls of equal size. From there — the reception hall — a door leads to a very long and narrow gas chamber, a few steps lower. Along the wall make-believe shower fixtures are attached. The whole seems like one gigantic shower room. From the gas chamber to the fire oven a railway track leads into this hall. On the flat roof of this chamber there is a window, which is hermetically closed by three valves. The victims are led into the reception hall, where they are told they would take a shower. They are ordered to take their clothes off, and, to have them believe what they are told, each prisoner receives a hand towel and a soap bar. Then the prisoners are driven into the gas chamber. The doors are hermetically shut. The three valves at the window above are then opened. From above, SS men pour a powder-like substance out of tin cans through the open valves into the chamber. On the tin cans it says Zyklon zur Schädlingsbekämpfung (Cyclone for Pest Control), and they bear the brand name of a factory in Hamburg. This is probably a cyanide substance, which at a certain given temperature turns into lethal gas. The three valves are closed. After three minutes everyone is dead. Afterwards, a special command brings the bodies to the fire ovens. The four crematoria can gas and burn 6000 persons each day. On the opening day of the first crematorium in March 1943, 8000 Jews from Cracow were annihilated. Prominent guests arrived from

Berlin for the day. They were extremely impressed by the capacity of the destructive apparatus, and they looked personally through the peepholes.

Horrified, the Jewish leadership of Slovakia, all of whom had lost family members and seen entire communities disappear, asked the two escapees how many Jews had gone to their death at Auschwitz. Once again, Vrba and Lanik had precise information, because they had compiled statistics. The victims, they said, had come from the following countries:

Poland (arriving on trucks)	300,000
Poland (by railway)	600,000
Holland	100,000
Greece	45,000
France	150,000
Belgium	50,000
Germany	60,000
Yugoslavia, Italy, Norway	50,000
Lithuania	50,000
Bohemia, Moravia, and Austria	30,000
Slovakia	30,000
Foreign Jews from Polish concentration camps	300,000
Total	1,765,000

Despite this unspeakable experience under the shadow of death, Rudolf Vrba had not lost his sense of humor. In his book, *I Cannot Forgive*, in which he retold this somber story, he wrote that after his cross-examination by Slovak Jewish leadership — followed by a similar investigation by a papal envoy — he decided to leave his hideout in order to visit his mother, who lived in Trnava. Even though he carried false papers, the risk was great that he would be recognized and betrayed. When he met his mother, she didn't recognize him at first. Her son had gone to Auschwitz at seventeen. Now he was nineteen and had seen nearly two million people die. The two years in hell had left their mark. When his mother did recognize her son, she took a step back and looked him up and down, just as in the days when he had returned home with dirty knees or was late for the evening meal. He, Rudi, was really a naughty boy, she finally said. Not once in two years had he written. He had not even left an address. Rudolf apologized. Times had been difficult, he said. Besides, he had been very busy. "That's all right," his mother answered, "I knew that you would come back this summer." More than two years he surely would not stay away from home. She wanted to know where he had been. Did he work? Did anyone make his bed, wash his clothes? Where did he get that suit he wore?

Rudolf Vrba embraced his mother, who was wiping a tear from her cheek. "Sit down, Mama," he said, "I have to tell you something."

*   *   *

Oscar Krasnansky, a young Slovak chemical engineer and leading Zionist, put Vrba's and Lanik's Auschwitz Protocol together and had it translated from the original Slovak into German. On April 26, 1944, less than a week after they had crossed the Slovak border from Poland, the document was ready. The two young men pleaded desperately that the world must know about the death camp and that the Hungarian Jews had to be warned without delay. The installations were set up in order to kill 12,000 human beings per day!

Krasnansky and the Slovak Jewish leadership decided to dispatch copies immediately through confidential channels to key contacts: the Jewish Agency offices in Istanbul and Geneva, the papal delegate in Bratislava for transmission to the Vatican. The chief rabbi of Bratislava, Michael Dov Weissmandel, prepared a Yiddish translation and sent it to the orthodox Jewish community in Switzerland and elsewhere. No efforts were spared to spread the news and to pass on the plea: "Auschwitz must be stopped!" Dr. Reszö Kasztner, who seemed to have the special confidence of the Slovak Jewish leadership, was alerted. He was able to travel freely, a rare thing for a Jew in those days, since he still possessed a regular Hungarian passport in addition to Swiss papers. He arrived in Bratislava on April 25. He was shocked by what he heard, and before he left on the evening of the 28th, he promised that the Hungarian Jewish leadership would have the Auschwitz Protocol in their hands the next morning.

And then, nothing happened.

Each day Vrba and Lanik tormented Krasnansky and the rest of the Slovak Jewish leadership, asking whether the Hungarian Jews had been informed and what defensive measures they were taking. And each day, the increasingly pained answer was: "Dr. Kasztner has things well in hand!"

It was not that Kasztner had kept the terrible news about the threatening deportation to himself. On the following morning, April 29, overtired as he was, he showed the report of Vrba and Lanik to the top Hungarian Jewish leadership, which met at the headquarters of the Jewish Council of Hungary at Sip utca number 12, just behind the Great Synagogue. The venerable Dr. Samu Stern, the chairman, shook his head and asked whether the described monstrosity was really conceivable. Though a Jew, he was a *Königlicher Hofrat*, a member of the royal privy council of Count Horthy, Hungary's otherwise antisemite regent. Never within that distinguished body, Stern said, had he ever heard of Auschwitz and even less of plans that the Hungarian Jews would be deported there. Was this Auschwitz Protocol, so-called, not the imaginings of two excited young hotheads? Over the last two years, so many wild stories had circulated, each of which had in the end turned out to be little more than a wild fairy tale. Other members of the council raised similar questions. What would happen if they distributed this paper? They would be accused of spreading misinformation, of disturbing the population. They could be arrested. If so, who would take care of the Jewish community? The Jewish Council seemed to have forgotten, or wanted to forget, that Otto Komoly and others had reported long ago the disaster that had befallen the Jews of Poland, and that under the German occupation since March 19 the Hungarian Jews, too, had been unbearably mistreated. Moreover, the Jewish community was isolated from the rest of society. They had no mail services, no telephone, no radio. The Jews could barely leave their homes. Jews had lost their jobs and their properties and were forced to wear the yellow star. They were impoverished, and many were starving. The "Christian" Hungarians, with whom the Jews had lived in harmony for a thousand years, had not lifted a finger in their defense.

The members of the Jewish Council did not admit to themselves that they were mortally afraid. Deep inside they knew that the Auschwitz Protocol was true. They were clutching at any straw. When Adolf Eichmann had visited them recently at Sip utca, he had assured them that he was well disposed toward the Jews. They soaked up his words as if he was their savior. Eagerly they accepted his advice that the Jewish Council should tell their community to keep calm, that all measures were taken for their protection, even if some appeared painful. Anything else was a lie, a horror story spread by the enemy.

They were like the rabbit staring at the serpent and could not think straight. But they kept talking "normally," as if they were participating in the board meeting of a business corporation or a welfare foundation. They agreed with Kasztner that the Auschwitz Protocol must be handled "prudently." There was no need to make the Jewish rank and file excited. The young people, especially the Chalutzim, might otherwise engage in actions for which the entire community would be sorry. As a first step it was decided to make a Hungarian translation of the paper, just in case. This would give the Jewish Council time to reflect further. They knew that a Reformed Church pastor, Joszef Elias, who was secretly sympathetic to the Jewish cause, had a capable and trustworthy secretary by the name of Maria Szekely, who had translated other confidential texts.

When she made the translation this sensitive young woman was extremely disturbed by what she read. She had heard rumors about what was happening to Jews, but never before had she been confronted with such horrific details. She spent a week in late April/early May 1944 in a hidden chamber, translating the Auschwitz Protocol from German into her native Hungarian. "I was extremely struck by the brutal fact," she said in an interview thirty years later, "that there were human beings who had prepared this hellish plan, and who could have fallen that low." She wanted to shout out her fear and her anger, but Pastor Elias admonished her sharply to keep the matter strictly to herself.

While Maria Szekely was doing her translation, Reszö Kasztner kept busy. Not that he informed the Jewish rank and file. Incredible as it may seem, he brought a copy of the Auschwitz Protocol to none other than Adolf Eichmann at the Hotel Majestic. From the available evidence it is not clear whether Kasztner did this on his own initiative or at the request of the Jewish Council. The result was the same. Since early April he had entertained within his agile mind an unusual, if not grandiose, idea, namely, to buy freedom for all Hungarian Jews. Kasztner reasoned that throughout history desperate Jews had sometimes paid money to their persecutors in exchange for their lives. In fact, as late as 1942 and 1943 the Slovak Jews had given a large sum of money to the commander of the SS in their country, Dieter Wisliceny. Half of Slovakia's Jews had thereby survived. This explains why Vrba had found his mother and the Jewish leadership still alive. Part of the money went into Wisliceny's own pocket.

Kasztner had cautiously sounded out Eichmann on a similar deal. The Obersturmbannführer seemed interested and contacted his SS officer colleague Kurt Becher, the man who had come to Budapest to effect the transfer of Hungarian Jewish industrial properties into SS ownership. This was one of the largest thefts undertaken by Nazi Germany, even though Becher was considerate enough to let family members of these wealthy industrialists depart unmolested to Portugal. This concession was reasonable in his eyes, because it avoided sabotage and resistance. Like Wisliceny, Becher used his position to make handsome personal profits. Becher spoke to Heinrich Himmler, the chief of the SS, about Kasztner's idea. He sounded vaguely encouraging, so much so that Becher felt that he was officially backed. It was clear to Himmler and to some other Nazis that the Germans were losing the war, and that a way out had to be found for a future life, if only for themselves privately. They were anxious to correct their image as criminals and killers.

But despite his great power as the top man of the SS, Himmler was mortally afraid of Hitler. He had to be extremely prudent in his answers to Becher. Kasztner, on the other hand, let his project grow by leaps and bounds, because he intended to bank on the growing spirit of corruption and fear within the SS hierarchy. Becher in particular believed that Kasztner had access to the legendary financial and political power of "World Jewry," which had been one of the major features of Nazi antisemite propaganda. This myth of concentrated Jewish power had originated in the ill-famed Protocol of the Elders of Zion, which had been a fabrication of the Russian tsarist secret police at the turn of the century, before the Nazis adopted the story and ended up by believing it themselves. They ascribed to the governors of "World Jewry" extraordinary powers and unlimited financial resources. "World Jewry," they were convinced, controlled the Allied governments, alongside the Communists and the Freemasons.

Playing on these Nazi fancies, Kasztner nonchalantly offered unlimited amounts of U.S. dollars and British pounds. He even agreed to transmit a demand to the "Zionist powers" and/or to the Allies for ten thousand trucks — against the lives of one million Jews. World Jewry and the Allies, he assured his SS partners, would gladly strike such a bargain, because they were anxious to save the last surviving million of his coreligionists. In talking like this, he, Kasztner, became himself convinced that fate had chosen him to become the most important savior ever within Jewish history.

When Kasztner showed Eichmann the Auschwitz Protocol in late April 1944, his "negotiations" with the SS were still in their initial stages. Eichmann leafed through the document. Instead of appearing impressed or angry, as Kasztner had expected, he shook his head, laughed, and handed the document back to his visitor, as if the Auschwitz Protocol were nothing but a collection of nonsensical sheets. Did Herr Doktor really believe this? he asked sarcastically. Without waiting for an answer, he continued by saying that this was a good illustration of the kind of *Greuelmärchen,* tales of horrors, which were spread by the enemy. Then Eichmann took a more threatening tone. If Kasztner wanted to spread this so-called protocol he should know that he would be committing an act of subversion. He, Eichmann, would have him arrested and brought to a military court for spreading slander against Germany. Moreover, all negotiations to save Hungary's Jews would automatically end. Was that clear? He, Herr Doktor Kasztner, would have to think very carefully, because the fate of the Jewish community, the lives of literally hundreds of thousands, now lay in his, Kasztner's, hands.

This was not the kind of honor to which Kasztner had aspired. Eichmann's words made him shudder and Kasztner wondered whether in showing the Auschwitz Protocol to Eichmann he had not made a serious error. Now it was he who became subject to blackmail and not the Nazis. But he decided to continue with his "negotiations." Eichmann, he decided, was an uneducated moron, whom in the end he would outwit. In order not to endanger his scheme, he would keep silent on the Auschwitz Protocol, even to those whose lives were at stake, Hungary's Jews. After all, he was acting for their benefit. If he succeeded, they all would be saved anyway. If he didn't, they would be condemned, and he with them.

*   *   *

When Vrba and Lanik were escaping from Auschwitz and the Jewish Council of Hungary was doubting the reality of the death camp, preparations for the deportation of the Hungarian Jews were already far advanced. Eichmann had hardly arrived on Suabian Hill in March before he and Interior Minister Andor Jaross, his fire-eating secretaries of state, Laszlo Baky and Laszlo Endre, and the equally ferocious commander of the gendarmerie, Laszlo Ferenczy, were meeting daily. These were reliable men, Eichmann thought, the kind he had rarely found elsewhere. They had been with Nicholas Horthy as far back as November 1919, when Horthy had come up to Budapest from Szeged in southern Hungary in order to overthrow that detested "Communist-Jewish" republic of Béla Kun. Horthy had entered the capital riding on a white horse, promising to clean up Hungary from that riffraff and to bring the nation back to God. He wanted to re-create the mystical Magyar kingdom, which had vanished centuries before, and to recover the lost provinces. Horthy proclaimed himself regent of Hungary and pretended that he was holding the kingdom in trust for a future monarch — who never appeared. Few protested when, during the course of the 1919 putsch, Horthy and his rebel officers killed thousands of Communists and Jews. This was necessary, it was said, in order to purify Hungary.

A quarter of a century later, the "Jewish question" was back, thanks to the German Führer. If Horthy had been satisfied killing a few thousand and to enact antisemite legislation, Hitler and his Hungarian fellow travelers wanted to exterminate the Jews altogether. The regent certainly did not like Jews, but he had misgivings about such radicalism. What would the other countries think? Baky, Endre, Ferenczy, and Jaross had distorted minds, Horthy thought. His control over the Magyar "kingdom" had badly slipped, and he realized that its restoration would not take place in his lifetime. Horthy resented being pushed aside by Veesenmayer, but he was really glad that since March 19 he no longer had to assume political responsibility himself. No one could blame him if matters turned out badly.

Horthy's fellow Szeged officers no longer thought much of the old man. He stood in the way of Hitler's new European order. He was a leftover from the nineteenth century, when the Habsburgs, the Hohenzollerns, and the Romanovs had ruled the world. For Jaross, Ferenczy, Baky, and Endre, a new and more vigorous world order was shaping up. The Hungarians, too, wanted to be a master race, dominating the multitude of inferior peoples in the Danube basin. Past glory would be resurrected.

To Eichmann the help of these pitiless Hungarians was indispensable. With his *Sonderkommando* alone, his special command of a mere 150 men, he would never be able to handle the deportation of three quarters of a million Jews. Ferenczy said he could place 4,000 out of his 20,000 gendarmes at Eichmann's disposal. For "administrative" purposes, it was agreed that the deportations should proceed successively on the basis of Hungary's six gendarmerie districts. Jaross, using his influence at the ministerial level, would see to it that the rest of the Hungarian forces, the regular police and the army — most of which was luckily at war and away from home — would not intervene. Eichmann said he would get the necessary railway cars ready. He was backed up by other SS officers of rank, Krumey, Wisliceny, and Hunsche, and a number of high-ranking German army officers. Minister Veesenmayer bore the overall political responsibility, keeping the lines open to Berlin and watching Horthy and the useless nobles around him. A formidable force for the destruction of Hungary's Jews was being lined up.

The concentration and the deportation of Jews would begin in the Carpathians of northern Hungary. Transylvania would be second. These regions would be first for "obvious" reasons, it was said: they would soon

become areas of military operations, and the Jews were of questionable loy-
alty. They had to be removed. Moreover, many of them were *Ostjuden,* eastern Jews, who had originally come down from Galicia and spoke Yiddish.
They were really foreigners. Hungary's Christians disliked them. The country's enlightened Jews did not appreciate the bearded Ostjuden, either.
Thus, few would object to the removal of these strange people. Once they
were gone, Eichmann and his Hungarian cohorts reasoned, the country
would have become accustomed to deportations, and the rest of the Jews
could be made to disappear with relative ease. The local authorities were
ready to cooperate. After the Carpathians and northern Transylvania were
cleared of Jews, it would be the turn of western and southern Hungary and
of the Puszta. The Budapest Jews would be deported last; they were a quarter of a million strong, the largest concentration of all Hungarian Jews. The
entire process would take three months at the most.

This was the timetable that Eichmann and his Hungarian team
elaborated:

Region		Start of systematic deportations	End of concentration
ZONE I	Carpathians	April 16	June 7
ZONE II	Northern Transylvania	May 4	June 7
ZONE III	North of Budapest, between Kosice and German border	June 7	June 17
ZONE IV	East of the Danube without Budapest	June 17	June 30
ZONE V	West of the Danube without Budapest	June 29	July 9
ZONE VI	Budapest	Beginning of July	End of July

The Hungarian Council of Ministers, chaired by Prime Minister
Döme Sztojay, endorsed the deportation plan. Nicholas Horthy, the regent, disempowered as he was, was also informed — and did not object.
Veesenmayer cabled the plan to Foreign Minister Ribbentrop in Berlin,
who was delighted.

In region after region the SS, the Hungarian gendarmes, aided by the local political authorities, transmitted their orders to the condemned Jews through the local Jewish councils to turn over their last belongings, leave their homes, and march to their assembly points. They were told that they would be resettled "in a nice place," where all their needs would be met. If his own religious authorities said so, it must be true, the ordinary Jew felt. Without fuss the victims were assembled in makeshift concentration camps, which were usually located in abandoned factories or brickyards, away from population centers, but conveniently close to railway yards. Surprised as they may have been, the members of the local Jewish councils were ordered to join the others in the queue.

The "final solution" could succeed only if credulity and secrecy were maintained.

When the marchers were herded together at the assembly points, often under great brutality, it would dawn on even the least informed that they and the Jewish councils had been duped and that a terrible fate awaited them. But even then, up to the very end, few could imagine what a death camp was like. Such a monstrosity was beyond human comprehension. If someone objected to having to leave home or if there was resistance, an SS or gendarmerie officer would shoot him or her in the neck in sight of everyone else. The rest would not rebel. News of the deportations was nevertheless often leaked out to the local Christian populations, who could guess what was happening to the Jews. Sometimes people would come out of their houses and watch the marching columns. These Jews were after all their neighbors, bakers, storekeepers, tailors, or innkeepers. They had played together with them as children and had often remained on friendly terms with them, despite antisemitism and name-calling. If individual Christian Hungarians protested, as did happen on occasion, the gendarmes seized them and deported them along with the Jews. The gendarmes even mistreated those Christians whom they caught with tears running down their cheeks.

For days and often weeks on end the deportees were exposed in the makeshift camps to sunshine and rain, heat and cold, with few latrines and barely any food available. They endured these brutal conditions until the day the cattle wagons and the train engines pulled up and the unfortunates were pushed through the narrow doors without mercy.

The first train left Hungary for Auschwitz on May 15, 1944. It arrived two days later, on the 17th. It was composed of over forty sealed cattle wagons with 100 persons in each. On a special railway track these 4,000 human beings stopped directly in front of the gas chambers at Birkenau. They were gassed and burned immediately, except for seventeen men who — by orders of Dr. Mengele — were temporarily allowed to stay alive in order to do the "cleaning up" of the empty wagons. On the next day, May 18, another deportation train arrived with 4,000 persons aboard. This time twenty women were allowed to stay alive and were brought to the barracks. During the first four days 16,000 Hungarian Jews were killed. On May 21 no less than three trains arrived, carrying 12,000 people, of whom only eleven men and seven women were left alive. All the rest lost their lives immediately upon arrival. During the same day deportation trains also arrived from Holland and Belgium. One of these was filled with Gypsies, of whom Nazi Germany murdered several hundreds of thousands. Never before had the death camp of Auschwitz-Birkenau gone into such high gear.

Each day Minister Veesenmayer cabled the numbers of those who had been sent to "labor service." He mentioned Auschwitz as the destination point. Four years later in Nuremberg, before the International Military Tribunal, he pretended that "Auschwitz meant nothing to me. I didn't know what it was. It was a name like any other. When I was in Hungary, I didn't even know where it was located. On the Hungarian maps, if I am not mistaken, it was called Ossowicce, or something like that. . . . I believe it was a Polish town, but I can't really tell." When questioned further, the "convinced national socialist" claimed to have been nothing but an innocent bystander in all this. Horthy, Sztojay, Ribbentrop, or the SS officers in Hungary were those responsible, he said. Not even the telegrams to Berlin were dispatched by him, but by Feine. He, Veesenmayer, simply signed them without quite knowing what they were about.

*　　*　　*

Despite the news blackout Consul Lutz inevitably sensed the growing horror that was engulfing the vast Jewish community of Hungary. He noticed that he himself was coming under increased pressure. The people from

Jaross's Ministry of the Interior kept asking questions about the 8,000 children and young people whom the consul protected. They hinted that their papers were no longer valid, as they could no longer leave for Palestine. They also said that the many people hiding inside the former American legation was a flagrant abuse of diplomatic extra-territoriality. If they did not leave, the gendarmes might come in to clean them out.

Almost daily the consul made the rounds of the government ministries, insisting that Hungary had to respect international treaties. There was no formal reason why the 8,000 children and young people should no longer be under his protection. And the asylum seekers would not have entered the legation compound had they felt secure outside. They were afraid of the Hungarian government, which did not protect its own citizens as it lawfully should. If Hungary rescinded its obligations and violated extra-territoriality, the international community, especially the neutral states, would consider this an extremely unfriendly act. They might withdraw their diplomatic recognition from Hungary, as they had doubts whether the Hungarian government was really an independent state. This was tough language for Hungarian officialdom. The Swiss consul touched a vital nerve of national pride. The argument was effective, and the Hungarians had no answer. They did not wish to admit the obvious, that ever since March 19 Veesenmayer was their ruler. Lutz knew that if he gave way even an inch, the 8,000 would be lost. But he was forced to return to the various government ministries again and again and to keep educating the officials on basic elements of international law.

Carl Lutz began to gamble for higher stakes. He soon issued tens of thousands of Schutzbriefe, letters of protection. In the end there would be at least 80,000 of these. He noted that the authorities were becoming suspicious about whether he and his Emigration Department were really limiting themselves to the 8,000 "agreed upon" letters of protection, but they were unable to prove the contrary. Regardless of how many of these documents Lutz issued and signed, they were always numbered from 1 to 8,000, never beyond. The consul hoped that his enemies would not discover his ruse for a long time. Moreover, in order to provide a better legal guarantee, each letter of protection was entered on a Swiss collective passport, with photographs pasted next to each name. Such collective passports contained one thousand names each. They were deposited in a safe in the consul's own office, to which only he had access.

He was becoming the focal point of a vast operation, which was shaping up in silence, counteracting death and rumors of death. The Chalutzim, who knew where each protected person lived, were busy in seeking ever more safe places for them with courageous Christian families, pastors, priests, orphanages, convents, and monasteries. They maintained contact with the Jews of Budapest. To go beyond the city limits was becoming risky. More than one Hechalutz never returned to the safety of the legation. The consul would discreetly enquire, but he was not always successful. By relating them to his Department of Emigration of the Swiss Legation, the consul had nevertheless placed a unique instrument at their disposal, which also served his ends. Dependence was mutual. The Chalutzim used the department as their base, and through them Lutz was in touch with the Jewish community, despite attempts at isolation by the authorities. Nothing like this existed in any other part of Nazi-dominated Europe. To be sure, Moshe Krausz, the general secretary of the Emigration Department, was a bureaucratic fusspot. He was suspicious of the unruly Chalutzim, who often did not respect his petty prerogatives. Adding to the occasional discord in the department was the obvious authority of Komoly and the sharp-minded political astuteness of Kasztner — at least as long as he maintained his credibility.

Lutz learned to live with such tensions among his associates and their personality and generation clashes. Because he was "neutral" among the various Jewish factions, he gained their respect. He increasingly became the focal point for the maintenance of the one common purpose that bound them together: survival. Infighting came to a stop whenever he reminded them that their situation was dangerous. His quiet nature and precise reasoning — and the fact that the indispensable diplomatic immunity for the entire action depended on his person and his person alone — gave him an all-around authority that grew week by troubling week. Had Lutz been an impulsive activist, the pressure caused by the terrible external events and inside tensions could have blown his team sky-high, ending all hope for saving a Jewish remnant.

Even though part of Hungarian officialdom secretly backed Lutz, the consul could not count on more general support within Hungarian society, insofar as this society still survived. Political resistance barely existed. Even some of the opposition leaders fled to the former American legation and sought his protection. Church leadership, too, was by tradition subservient to the state, and in the absence of clear signals from their hierarchs, the majority of church membership was indifferent to the fate of the Jews. Though a few individual pastors, priests, and nuns quietly exercised charity toward their Jewish fellow citizens, they acted alone. In the midst of daily anti-Jewish propaganda it began to dawn on some Christians that Jesus Christ, the Virgin Mary, and the apostles had also been Jews, and if they were living in present-day Hungary, they too would be persecuted because of their "Jewish blood." It was an astonishing discovery for these Christians to realize how much traditional church dogma and a one-sided reading of Holy Writ had obscured this truth.

Then there were the agnostics and communists, for whom religion was nothing but pie in the sky, but who recalled how Horthy and his fellow officers had cut short the fledgling reforms of the Jew Béla Kun in 1919. They remembered that not all Jews were capitalists and plutocrats, as Nazi propaganda pretended, but that most were ordinary workers, employees, and shopkeepers, who were as poor and downtrodden as most other Hungarians. However filled with courage and human decency such scattered secularized opponents may have been, they were unable to organize any effective resistance network. Such a reading of history, which had no basis in fact, was invented later in postwar Hungary.

*   *   *

In early May, Reszö Kasztner came to the former American legation with a copy of the Auschwitz Protocol. Quietly, Consul Lutz read it, turning page after page. Every once in a while he looked at Kasztner, who nervously smoked cigarettes. Lutz was thunderstruck. When the consul put the paper down, his hands shook. He rose, walked to the window, and looked down on Freedom Square. The chestnut trees were blooming, but he did not see them. Then he walked up and down his office, hands behind his back. Why hadn't he told him? he finally shouted, much against his habit. Who was "he," Kasztner asked, perplexed, wondering if the consul meant him. But Lutz was thinking of Gerhart Feine from the German legation, who a month earlier had secretly revealed to him Veesenmayer's plan to execute 100 Jewish hostages for each Hungarian killed by Allied bombs. He remembered that Feine wanted to say something else, but didn't. He had been afraid to share the Auschwitz secret, perhaps because he had been already too ashamed of his involvement with the Nazi regime. Yet, what would he, Lutz, have done, if Feine had told him about Auschwitz? What was he to do now?

Lutz and Kasztner decided to call in Otto Komoly and Moshe Krausz. They came immediately, sensing that the issue was serious. Komoly said without hesitation that he had heard of Auschwitz, although not in such detail. He had no doubt that what Vrba and Lanik had put on paper was authentic. If the Hungarian Jews were to survive, they would not only have to be informed, but somehow plan their defense. Kasztner objected. The Jews were in no position to organize resistance. Their young men had been cleverly removed to the eastern front, thousands of them, where they served in auxiliary battalions. Should the children, women, and old people fight, facing the SS, the gendarmerie, and a largely antisemite population? They would be murdered like flies. Komoly objected, saying that they would be murdered anyway. Had not Gandhi in India shown what passive resistance could do? Yes, of course, Kasztner answered tensely. Nevertheless it was not the British who occupied Hungary, but the German Nazis, aided by a willing Hungarian government. That was the difference.

Komoly knew that Kasztner was right. But he said that at least the Chalutzim could help the Jews to organize resistance, so that a good proportion could survive, perhaps by crossing the border into Romania. Did not the Jews in Warsaw offer an example of courage the year before and tie down many German troops? He added that the Chalutzim had arms cachés hidden throughout Budapest.

This brought Krausz into the discussion. The Chalutzim, never! he shouted. If they were told about the Auschwitz Protocol, they were likely to engage in untold foolish actions. They would start shooting at German soldiers and have every Jew killed. Besides, what good had the Warsaw uprising done to the Polish Jews? They were all killed in the end. Jewish honor was saved, that was all.

It was then that Reszö Kasztner revealed to his shocked discussion partners that he had taken a copy of the Auschwitz Protocol to Eichmann. This was treason, both Komoly and Krausz answered. They had doubted Kasztner's reliability from the beginning, when he had said that one had to speak with the Germans. Kasztner said he knew that he was trying to do the impossible, to negotiate with the worst enemy the Jews had ever had. But were negotiations not their only realistic chance to escape Auschwitz? Had not this discussion shown that there was no alternative? If there was and if they, Komoly and Krausz, could convince him that there was, he would gladly stop all contacts with Eichmann and with the rest of the SS.

The group fell silent. There was no reply. The burden was heavy, and any decision was likely to be wrong.

It was finally agreed that Kasztner should keep talking with the SS, in order to see whether they would accept money against Jewish lives. But he would have to act strictly on his own. Yes, yes, Kasztner said, he knew he was alone. But he insisted again that the Jewish community must not be informed, nor must resistance be organized. Else, he could not succeed.

After his visitors left, the consul remained at his desk in silence. What was he to do? He wanted to dial the number of the German legation and ask for Legation Councillor Dr. Feine. He must obtain an appointment, during which he would ask Feine when the deportations from Hungary to Auschwitz were to start. But then he realized that even requesting an appointment was dangerous. The Gestapo would listen in on the line, and Veesenmayer would suspect that his associate was revealing top secrets to an outsider, to the Swiss consul, whom he considered a troublemaker. Besides, what could Feine advise? All over Budapest there was surely a growing number of persons who knew, but like him, surely none of them knew how to prevent the disaster. The consul put the receiver down.

He went to the basement, where the Emigration Department was located. He found Moshe Krausz hidden behind piles of papers. Why did he insist on typing every single letter himself? Lutz wondered. He understood why the Chalutzim became impatient over this bureaucrat. He told Krausz that the letters of protection must be vastly increased. Tens of thousands more forms were to be printed, filled out, and signed. Rapidly, Lutz said. He himself would spend the next few days doing nothing but signing them. The consul looked at the piles of paper on Krausz's desk. He must get his staff to help him, he said. This was an emergency. The general secretary of the Emigration Department surely did not have to do every single office job himself. Krausz nodded in agreement, but objected to the increase of protective letters. This couldn't be done, he said, because he no longer had any Palestine Certificates on hand. They had all been used. Lutz lost his temper, which he rarely did. To hell with the Palestine Certificates, he shouted. The Schutzbrief holders would not go to Palestine anyway, not for the time being. He simply wanted to keep them away from Auschwitz, that was all. But this was cheating, Krausz answered stubbornly. What if the Germans found out? Yes, Lutz said, he agreed that he was cheating. But he had decided to cheat the devil. Would he, Krausz, please pass the word to everybody in the Emigration Department to keep their mouths shut about this and get down to work?

Time and space are lacking to give a full account of how the Kasztner-Eichmann-Becher "blood-against-money offer" developed. There is little doubt that Kasztner, ambitious as he was to gain his place in history, thought that he could save not only Hungary's Jews but also the other remaining European Jews. In accord with Eichmann, he sent his representative, Joel Brand, to Istanbul and thence to Palestine, in order to submit the offer of exchanging money and trucks against a million Jews to the suspicious leadership of the Jewish Agency. While Brand talked with agency representatives, the British colonial authorities had him arrested. He was jailed in Cairo, and in the end the Allies rejected the deal outright. Under no circumstances did they want to finance and equip a moribund enemy, so as to prolong the war. Above all, the British shuddered at the thought of having hundreds of thousands of Jews stepping on to Palestinian beaches. The Arabs of the entire Middle East would rise up. Also, the Americans, who were ever ready to give advice to anyone who cared to listen but kept their own borders closed, said they did not want to provoke more antisemitism in their country than they had already. The best way to save the Jews, the Allies repeated in unison, was to win the war. Kasztner had misjudged the readiness of the Allies to come to the rescue of the Jews.

Eichmann, for his part, had no intention of keeping Hungary's Jews from the gas chambers of Auschwitz, regardless of whether Kasztner's envoy, Joel Brand, was successful on his absurd mission or not. He knew the mind of the Führer too well. As often happens with highly gifted people, Kasztner had underestimated Eichmann's intelligence, limited as it may have been. He also had not fathomed the SS man's absolute subservience to Hitler and his determination to kill the Jews, regardless of whether the war was being won or lost. Unlike Wisliceny and Becher, his greedy and calculating SS colleagues, Eichmann could not be bribed. He was indifferent to money.

One tragic fact stands out. The Auschwitz Protocol was kept from the Hungarian Jews largely as a result of Kasztner's multiple miscalculations. The Jews of Hungary lost precious time, and because of their ignorance they did not even make rudimentary plans to hide or to engage in other forms of passive resistance, not to speak of preparing for a Warsaw-like uprising.

Meantime, to those around him Kasztner spread carefully selected words about the mysterious negotiations in which he was involved. He kept raising considerable sums of money from the already impoverished Hungarian Jews and turned them over to the SS as "advance payments." He kept "negotiating" even after the deportations to Auschwitz had begun and the object of the deal had fallen by the wayside. He did not break off the talks even when he must have realized that Eichmann did not intend to honor his end of the bargain. There was a fatal flaw in Kasztner's character: his superb academically trained intelligence stood in the way of seeing the truth, perhaps because he lacked that other type of intelligence which derives more from feeling and psychological sensitivities than from logical deduction. In the process he did obtain the liberation of 1,684 persons of his own choice, including members of his family, while a larger part of Hungary's Jews perished in Auschwitz. The ultimate result of his give-and-take with the enemy seemed pitiful, even if each life saved was of course precious. The 1,684, to state it brutally, were his reward for keeping quiet and letting the majority of Hungary's Jews die. There was a striking similarity between this arrangement and the one Veesenmayer and Eichmann had implicitly proposed to Consul Lutz concerning the 8,000. Lutz could have these lives, they suggested, provided he did not insist on saving more and thereby interfere with the Führer's extermination plans. It was the kind of deal that Lutz refused. Kasztner did not.

Kasztner obsessively kept "negotiating" with the SS, especially with Becher, until almost the end. Not surprisingly, he survived the war in the company of Becher and the SS somewhere in Germany, when they gave themselves up to the invading British armed forces. This was in May 1945.

But for Reszö Kasztner, this wartime collaboration with the enemy — it cannot be named otherwise — was not enough. In Nuremberg he succeeded in persuading the International Military Court that Kurt Becher was not a war criminal. Becher was therefore freed, denazified, and in the postwar Federal Republic of Germany he became a successful businessman, making millions.

It was not until the 1950s that the extent of Kasztner's involvement with the Nazis became public knowledge. By that time he had, as a prominent member of the ruling Mapai (Zionist) party, risen high in Israeli politics. He was brought before court. The public at large was thunderstruck: a Jew, and a well-placed one at that, was accused of collaboration with the worst persecutor in Jewish history. His silence had contributed to the deaths of hundreds of thousands! The process reopened deep wounds in Israeli society and within world Jewry. During the course of two painful trials Kasztner nevertheless managed to restore his (juridical) innocence. But his moral image was tarnished. Before the end of the second trial he was shot dead by a gunman whose identity was never discovered.

5. CAN AUSCHWITZ BE STOPPED?

Thirty-five-year-old Alexander (Sandor) Grossman was a leading Hechalutz in Miskolc. He ran a hardware and toy store in suburban Diosgyör near the end of the streetcar line, and while he was not rich, his income was steady and he did not have to worry financially. He was married to Ilona, a beautiful young woman, and they had a lively four-year-old son, Istvan, who was their pride and joy. His widowed mother lived in the same household. The Grossmans had been established in Hungary for many generations. Among the 180 names of the fallen Jewish soldiers during the war of 1914–18 listed on the stele in front of the synagogue of Miskolc, no less than sixteen bore the name Grossman.

In his youth Alexander had been a member of the Jewish boy scouts, the *Kadima*. As a teenager he joined the Chalutzim, who were a spearhead of the Zionists. He helped to prepare young people so that they could emigrate to Palestine and help build up a kibbutz. In his bones Alexander felt that the persecution of Jews during the first decade of Horthy's rule was a mere forerunner of what might yet be. His misgivings increased when during the late 1930s he saw the undisciplined green-shirted Arrow Cross of Ferenc Szalasi parade through the streets of Miskolc, shouting obscene threats at Jews, just like their mentors, the German National Socialists. His fears were fully confirmed when between 1938 and 1941 Hungary copied the German Nuremberg race laws, even though it was slow in implementing them. Horthy may not have been a clever man, but he realized that without the skilled Jewish businessmen and professionals, Hungary's economy would collapse. Between Hitler breathing down his neck and his nation's economic and social crisis, he preferred to perform a balancing act in order to survive and to recuperate Hungary's lost provinces. Horthy tried to make use of Hitler in reestablishing the old order in the Danube basin. Hitler, more astute and less scrupulous, wanted to exploit the difficulties of the Habsburg successor states to extend his own domination throughout the region. Horthy was to him a useful idiot, to use Lenin's expression. Of course, Alexander thought of emigrating to Palestine himself, but his mother and Ilona did not want to leave their home and live in a tent in the desert amid stones and scorpions, as they said. They felt that their vast network of relatives and friends would somehow protect them, and besides, the Jews had always managed to survive difficult times. This crisis was no exception.

The Grossmans became scared when the Germans came on March 19, and they, like all Jews, were forced to wear the yellow star and suffer all the other humiliations. Soon, their Christian neighbors stopped talking to them, keeping a watch from behind window curtains. Then came the distressing news that in towns and villages further north the Jews were being concentrated in schoolhouses and brickyards. What must they do? In small-town Miskolc, and even more so in Diosgyör, where everybody knew everybody else, the Jews could not hide. Alexander and Ilona agreed that whatever happened, little Istvan must be protected. They talked to a Christian cabinet maker, a factory worker, whom the Grossmans had known for many years, and asked whether they could not take Istvan in, at least until the troubles were over. The cabinet maker and his wife agreed to pretend to outsiders that the small boy was one of their own children. They were simple and reliable people with a good heart; they could be trusted. The trouble was that Istvan, who had never been away from home, was unhappy and cried day and night, sobbing that he wanted to go home. The neighbors heard it and became curious. It was clear that they would guess the story and that before long they would report the cabinet maker and his family to the police. The government had decreed that to hide Jews was a most serious crime. With a heavy heart the cabinet maker brought Istvan back.

Alexander thought it would be better if the whole family disappeared and went to Budapest, despite travel restrictions imposed on Jews. In a big city it would be easier to hide. But once again Ilona and Alexander's mother said no. They had grown up within the Jewish community of Miskolc. If they fled, they would be seen as lacking solidarity. Alexander replied that this meant that they would be deported in solidarity. But the women were adamant. Besides, what real safety was there in Budapest they asked.

Four-year-old Istvan overheard the agitated conversation between the adults, even though he pretended to play with a wooden train. Suddenly, he tugged at his father's arm and said: "Papi, if we are in danger here, let's go to Budapest at once!" He had no idea where Budapest was, but he knew that it was a safe place.

Two days passed in indecision and agony. Early one morning a tall corporal of the gendarmerie knocked at the door of the terrified Grossmans. But he was polite and did not order them out of the house, curse, or steal. He politely asked Alexander whether he could come with him to the town house of Diosgyör. Gendarmerie captain Kalman Horvath wanted to see him. Alexander was relieved. He knew Horvath. He was one of the few gendarmerie officers of good reputation. In fact, he once had kept Grossman from getting arrested when he had ignored a draft order into labor service.

Without further ado, Alexander left his house, accompanied by the gendarmerie corporal. Only once he briefly looked back and saw Ilona, his mother, and Istvan behind the window. The little boy was pressing his nose against the window pane.

When Alexander and the corporal reached the town hall, Horvath asked a favor of the young Jew. The captain, who was in his late thirties, ordered the corporal out of the room and carefully locked the door after him. Then he made Alexander sit across a table from him and spoke in a low voice, almost in a whisper. Horvath said that he was in charge of several labor camps in the region of Miskolc, which housed 2,000 Jewish men, ages twelve to eighty. The secret orders he had received from Ferenczy were clear: he had to work these people to their death, if not to kill them outright. But he was not going to let his conscience be ripped to shreds by this god-forsaken fanatic, even if he risked his life and that of his family. Horvath paused in anger. He wanted to gain time, he said. Each day the people entrusted to him stayed alive was a day won. The war's end was coming closer.

What in the world could he, Alexander Grossman, a simple Jewish merchant do? came the astonished question. The answer was simple, Horvath said. Had he, Grossman, ever heard of Swiss Consul Lutz in Budapest, who had his office at the former American legation? Yes he had, although he did not know him personally. The Chalutzim thought highly of Lutz, because he had helped to send thousands of children and young people to Palestine. Horvath answered that Lutz was apparently issuing Swiss Schutzbriefe, protective letters, to all kinds of people, not just to potential young émigrés. He gave them to adults, even to old people. Moreover, he had persuaded the Hungarian authorities that his government in Berne wanted these papers to be respected, meaning that none of the Schutzbrief holders must be arrested or in any other way molested. And the Hungarian government had said yes, because it desired to maintain good relations with Switzerland, despite the present German occupation. Horvath said that his uncouth superiors among the gendarmerie were furious about paying so much respect to Switzerland. They believed that Switzerland was in the hands of the Zionists. Lutz, in their eyes, was crazy and unreasonable. He stood in the way. Moreover, all the Jewish rabble — if Grossman would excuse the expression used at gendarmerie headquarters — was hiding in the former American legation, protected by the Swiss consul. Ferenczy, Eichmann, and company were at a loss. Even Veesenmayer had requested instructions from Berlin, asking whether they could enter the building and smoke these people out. But he was getting no reply. He, too, was suspecting a sinister game. At any rate, this was how he, Horvath, had learned about what Lutz was doing.

This was astonishing news, Grossman realized. The gendarmerie captain leaned across the table and his voice was barely audible. He said he needed someone he could trust absolutely to go to Budapest and ask the Swiss consul to give him 2,000 blank Schutzbriefe for the men in his camp. He would fill in the names afterwards, as long as the forms were duly signed by the consul. Would he, Alexander Grossman, go to see Lutz and ask him? Grossman became excited. Before he could reply, the captain added that obviously Grossman should use this opportunity and obtain letters of protection for himself and his family as well. The young man answered that the captain knew that he could count on him for whatever assignment he had in mind. Horvath had once helped him out of a tight spot, and for this he was eternally grateful. Alexander had never imagined that he, a Jew, would ever be sent on an official mission on behalf of the gendarmerie. He trembled. A solution to his own desperate situation suddenly seemed possible. Other Jews of Miskolc could be helped as well. Perhaps many.

The conversation between Horvath and Grossman had lasted barely fifteen minutes. Alexander was anxious to go to Budapest. Horvath insisted that the entire matter be treated with absolute discretion. Only the consul must be informed. The SS and the gendarmerie were in an ugly mood, and any leak would be highly dangerous to the two of them.

The understanding was settled with a handshake. Horvath insisted that Grossman go without delay and return the next day. There was a train leaving Miskolc in less than an hour, at ten o'clock. He apologized for rushing. He had heard that the Jews of Miskolc did not have more than four days. Also his own 2,000 were in danger. Grossman was thunderstruck. He wanted to go home and take his family with him. But Horvath said that he had no time. He could make all arrangements tomorrow, as soon as he was back. He, Horvath, would help him.

The captain's request had become an order.

He took off Alexander's yellow star and gave him a letter of safe conduct, on which it said that Alexander Grossman was on official business for the Hungarian gendarmerie. The captain had prepared it beforehand.

Then Horvath called in the corporal, who was waiting outside. Pointing at the corporal's chest, Horvath told him that he was to accompany Mr. Grossman to Budapest immediately. The matter was of great importance. Tomorrow, he would return with Mr. Grossman. Horvath slightly raised his voice. "If anything happens to him, I shall kill you with my own hands! Is that clear?" He patted his pistol. The young man did not blink: "Don't worry, Captain," he said. "I shall execute this order as I have carried out others." Horvath accompanied Grossman to the front entrance of the town house. He wished him good luck and said he would anxiously await his return.

In those days, to travel from Miskolc to Budapest was slow. Desperately slow, Alexander thought. The train stopped at nearly every local station. Troop or freight trains passed. Sometimes there was no evident reason for the delays. Then there were steam engines pulling nothing but empty cattle cars. This was strange, Grossman thought. Where were they headed?

Rafi Friedl chanced to be at the entry of the American legation building on Freedom Square. He had met Grossman at Chalutzim meetings and was happy to see him, but he eyed the gendarme with curiosity, until Alexander signaled to Rafi with a twinkling in his eye that his improbable companion was all right. Alexander said that he had come to Budapest in order to see Consul Lutz. They entered the legation building, and Grossman asked the corporal to wait. What was it about? Friedl asked curiously, when they were out of earshot. It was an urgent matter, Alexander said, but he couldn't talk about it. Did he know, he asked Rafi, that Jews of Miskolc would be deported in four days? How did he know? Rafi exclaimed. There were so many rumors flying about these days. The information was trustworthy, Grossman said. Would he stop asking! He was in a hurry.

Rafi brought his friend to the consul's office. He did not hear the secretary's protest, knocked briefly, and entered into Lutz's sanctum without her permission. He evidently took pleasure in pointedly subverting her protective attitude toward her boss, knowing that she had never forgiven the consul for declaring him an American citizen, when he obviously was not. Alexander heard a muffled conversation through the closed door. The consul suddenly came out. He stretched out his hand, smiled, and welcomed Grossman to the Swiss legation, Department of Foreign Interests. The consul led him into his office, and when Rafi Friedl tried to come in also, he asked him gently to wait in the front room. The secretary smiled triumphantly, and the two glowered at each other in silence.

Lutz led Grossman to a group of sofas and offered him a cup of coffee, which was a rarity in wartime Hungary. Coffee, Grossman knew, fetched astronomical prices on the black market. He declined, explaining that he had come on an urgent matter. He then told Lutz about Captain Horvath's request. The consul was astonished to learn of this gendarmerie officer who was not a hostile brute. When Grossman added that, according to the captain's information, the Jews of Miskolc would be deported in four days, the consul was crestfallen, and it seemed to the visitor as if this thin, austere-looking man was about to burst into tears. Never had Alexander thought that he would meet a diplomat with human feelings. In the films he had seen at the theaters in Miskolc, diplomats were high-nosed snooty characters in dress uniforms decorated with golden tresses and wearing three-cornered hats, forever sipping champagne, dancing under chandeliers, or kissing ladies' hands.

The consul agreed that no time must be lost. He went to the door and asked his secretary to prepare 2,000 letters of protection. She should tell Krausz that he wanted to have these forms immediately and not the week after. At this, Rafi Friedl jumped up and said he would go and shake him up. The secretary was annoyed and shouted after Rafi not to make Krausz angry. After all, he did what he could, in his limited way. When she sat down at her desk again, she said that none of the Chalutzim had any patience with Krausz. They were such hotheads.

Grossman said he was a Hechalutz, too, and that he knew Krausz from Miskolc. Krausz hadn't gone to school much and was always jealous of those who had succeeded better in life than he. Oh, the secretary said, he had his good sides, too. She turned to the consul. Didn't he? Of course, Lutz said, except that Krausz still did not seem to realize that there was an emergency. He was meticulously slow, as he apparently had always been. Except that now Hungary was burning. He should speed up his work and distribute responsibilities. He sighed. The trouble was, he said to Grossman, that Krausz represented one Jewish faction among several and the Chalutzim another. Even in the midst of mortal danger some of these groups, be it for religious, political, or personal reasons, would not stop bickering among themselves. If he removed Krausz, there would be hell to pay. Grossman laughed. He said he sympathized with the consul for trying to hold together this crowd of Jewish individualists, whom he knew well.

Rafi returned within minutes. He had had to find the forms himself, he said in exasperation, while Krausz remained at his desk, scratching away at some lengthy letter and barely mumbling his answers. The consul handed one of the forms to Grossman. He studied it with great respect, looking at the Swiss cross, then at the space reserved for the name of the protégé. Then he loudly read out the text, where it said that he/she was shielded by Switzerland and that the Hungarian authorities were requested to cooperate. At the bottom was the consul's signature. This was a marvelously human document, Alexander thought, unlike the ugly, threatening, and humiliating edicts to which the Jews of this country had been accustomed for years. His eyes moistened. Lutz explained that each paper was numbered and that he would need a list from Captain Horvath of the recipients of the protective papers. The names must all be recorded on a collective Swiss passport, which, if ever there was a question on the part of the Hungarian authorities, functioned as an official proof that he protected the document holders. These collective passports, each of which contained 1,000 names, were so important that they were kept within the consul's personal safe. He was the only person who had access to them.

Rafi Friedl made a package of the Schutzbriefe. He wrapped them in innocuous brown paper, which he tied together with string. In one extra folder were the letters of protection for Alexander, Ilona, Istvan, and his mother, all properly filled out. Then he handed it all to Grossman, who pressed the package close to his chest, as if it were a most precious gift. He profusely thanked the consul and left.

Grossman would have liked to return to Miskolc on the same day. However, there were no late trains. He decided to stay overnight at the apartment of his brother Julius, who was a pious Jew, he explained to the gendarme. Julius didn't like gentiles to stay overnight with him. But this time he would have to make an exception. Grossman hoped that he, the corporal, wouldn't mind Julius's very Jewish habits. The corporal laughed. One had to be tolerant, he answered. If all gendarmes were like him, Grossman thought, Hungary would be a different country.

They left Budapest early next morning. Around noon there was a long stop at Hatvan, where several railway lines crossed. The late spring sun was already hot, and the two travelers were thirsty. A passenger train, coming from Miskolc, pulled up next to them. The car opposite them was filled with young Jewish men who were parting for labor service. They were talking loudly, but some of them looked depressed. One knew Grossman and he shouted: "Hey, Sandor, did you know that the Jews of Miskolc have been deported?" Fear gripped Alexander's heart. How was this possible? Yesterday, when he left, everything had looked quiet. Moreover, Captain Horvath had said that the deportations would not start for four days! What about his family? he asked feebly. The labor-service men in the other car all fell silent and stared back empty-eyed. From somewhere he heard another voice saying that no one was left. If he went near his house, he would be deported, too.

Alexander remembered the fearful words of Istvan: "Papi, if we are in danger here, let's go to Budapest at once!" Where was Istvan now, and Ilona, and his mother? He recalled how they had all stood at the window, including Istvan, wondering where the gendarmerie corporal would take him.

Later, Grossman could not recall what happened next. He turned the package with the Schutzbriefe over to the gendarme and admonished him with a broken voice not to let it out of his hands and not to talk about it to anyone. The package had to be given to Captain Horvath in person and to no one else. Of the others, only one letter of protection was of use, the one made out in his own name. And those destined for little Istvan, Ilona, and his mother? They would remain as painful memories of lives snuffed out.

The corporal did not know what to say. He had observed the excruciating scene in silence and realized that words were useless. He simply pressed Alexander's hands. Grossman probably did not see that there were tears in the gendarme's eyes, while he himself was unable to cry. At least not yet. He wrote a few words for the captain. Would he excuse him if, in the light of circumstances, he did not continue his return journey? He added that the gendarmerie corporal had fulfilled his duty like a personal friend. Then Alexander left the train and boarded one that took him back to Budapest. He never returned to Miskolc.

The next morning Grossman went to the seat of the Jewish Council at Sip utca number 12. He vaguely hoped that Samu Stern would say that the news from Miskolc was an error and that the Jews had not been deported, and that Horvath was right, that they would have four more days of grace, or perhaps three by now. Sadly, Stern and the others shook their heads. It was true, the Jews of Miskolc were gone. They had numbered 13,500. Concentration and deportations were carried out with great cruelty.

Julius was with Samu Stern, too. He wept when he embraced his brother and asked: "Sandor, where is God?" As a pious man he knew the Torah, and he would chant the kaddish for the dead at Dohanyi Street Synagogue as soon as this encounter was over. Julius was shaken when he realized that he had let this question erupt spontaneously, almost angrily, he, who had been raised in the belief that whatever the Almighty — His holy name be blessed — did was just and good.

When Rafi Friedl told Lutz of the tragedy that had befallen the Jews of Miskolc and Alexander Grossman personally, Consul Lutz left the office and went home. He needed to be alone.

Within days, Grossman placed himself at the disposal of the consul. There were many more Istvans, Ilonas, and mothers to be saved, he said. He threw himself into writing names into the empty spaces on letters of protection and bringing them to the consul for his signature. Many more people came to Freedom Square these days, asking for Schutzbriefe, and the former American legation was a beehive of activities, as it probably never had been since it was built twenty years earlier. Sometimes, if the applicants did not dare to come in person, Alexander would deliver the letters himself. This work kept him from losing his mind.

The gendarmerie corporal did hand over the brown package with the 2,000 Schutzbriefe to Captain Kalman Horvath. The officer distributed them among the Jewish labor service men under his orders, and he informed Consul Lutz accordingly. Horvath planned to let them escape to freedom, so that they could join an uprising against the Germans in Slovakia, about whose preparations the captain knew through underground channels. Unfortunately, the second officer in command of Horvath's camp betrayed the scheme. All men would have been murdered if Horvath had not vigorously fought for the recognition of the consul's Schutzbriefe. He thereby saved also his own life. The second in command was transferred to another post, and by and by Horvath let the 2,000 men filter into Budapest, instead of letting them go to Slovakia. In the big city many found protection within those buildings for which Consul Lutz was obtaining extra-territorial status. They all survived.

*　　*　　*

At times, when Carl Lutz was deeply troubled, he withdrew into himself and was not easily accessible to others, not even to those closest to him. This happened during the change of seasons in 1944, when spring turned into summer. The progressive lifting of the terrible secret signified the collapse of basic certainties, which had guided him throughout life. The well-ordered and purposeful universe had vanished, and nothing else was taking its place. In Carl Lutz's pietistic/humanistic worldview, every event, insignificant as it might be, had been part of a meaningful puzzle, a movement of history, which would ultimately complete itself at the end of times, when Jesus Christ returned. One rarely talked about such innermost convictions in sophisticated diplomatic circles, where national and personal power was the objective, although exchanges were always couched in polite language, and the question of God was raised nowhere, even though it was assumed that Divine Providence, whatever it was, kept the whole mess together. Diplomats were after all no theologians. But now Auschwitz had cut a gaping hole into all convictions, superficial as they might be, through which one could look directly into hell.

The mental blow caused by this insight was frightful. As if in a slow motion film, the pieces of what had constituted meaning flew apart and could not be recovered or ever be put together again. Moreover, Auschwitz, that gigantic machine of death, was not run by the devil himself, but by ordinary human beings who — strangely enough — thought they were doing the right thing, creating a new, clean society. Veesenmayer, Eichmann, and their collaborators in Hungary, for instance, did not look like what devils were supposed to look like, with horns and hooves. They talked, ate and drank, probably made love, and went to the toilet. They doubtless loved their wives. Eichmann had a picture of his family on his desk. These men did not carry three-pronged forks, as Lutz used to think as a child, by which one could have recognized devils immediately, like some kind of inverted yellow star. Ridiculous thought. But these men represented hell, and behind them appeared the great Nothing. The consul was troubled that there was little he could do to stop this perversion and to protect a threatened people in its entirety. It was fine to issue letters of protection. He must continue with them; they were a foothold against madness. The papers saved hundreds, even thousands of lives, and he was glad that he did this. But then there were those who vanished, the majority. His actions, important as they might be, were little more effective than the raised hands of King Canute holding back the ocean's tide.

In the evenings after days when particularly disastrous news had overpowered him, the consul would return home to Buda and eat his dinner in silence. Sometimes, he did not eat at all. Gertrud knew enough not to ask questions. She even hushed little Agnes, Magda's daughter, out of the room when the six-year-old greeted Carl with cheerful child's talk. In the weeks after she and her mother Magda had moved into the house, Agnes had taken a keen liking to "Unkie," as she called him, to which he responded in kind. She made him become a different person. He placed the girl on his lap and began to chat and laugh and sing with her and tell her stories. Agnes had a way of chasing away the gloom that threatened his equilibrium. Then, to the girl's amazement, he would put her down abruptly and send her out. At moments he opened himself up and poured out his frustrations and fears to Gertrud about the evil that was engulfing him. She possessed that unusual mental solidity, which made other people want to confide in her. Carl would talk to her all evening, often until the early hours of the next day, until he had emptied himself. In the morning, at six, when the bells rang from the tower of the nearby Lutheran church, Szluha would take him in the black Packard around the sharp bend at the old Vienna Gate and drive him downhill and across the Danube to his office in Pest. Carl Lutz would have the strength to face the incomprehensible world again.

But on the day after Lutz returned home from his second encounter with Alexander Grossman, he was so agitated that he refused all food. He decided to walk out into the falling night, as he sometimes did when he wanted to be alone. Physical exercise was one way of reducing nervous tension. He would walk around the ancient walls of the old city until he found some calm. When he was a boy at Walzenhausen and the teacher had been especially nasty to him, he used to rush up the hill of Meldegg, sit on the bench on which his father had spent his last hours, and look across the Rhine valley. Sometimes he would pray, as his mother Ursula had advised him to do whenever he was troubled. These were simple prayers, cries for help against that teacher, for instance. But how could one pray now, knowing that a four-year-old boy named Istvan, his young mother, and his grandmother were at this very moment riding in a cattle wagon toward that unspeakable place or were already there?

Lutz had barely left his residence when he was accosted by a young man. He was at first taken aback. He thought that the Gestapo or someone from the Ministry of the Interior was trying to play a nasty trick on him. But when the visitor began talking to him in his native Swiss-German he relaxed. The stranger introduced himself as a young medical doctor from the Bernese Oberland, who was on a visit to Hungary. To forestall the consul's curiosity, he said that he certainly had not come as a tourist. His mother was Hungarian, and he had come to settle an inheritance problem in a small town in one of the provinces in northern Hungary. He had planned to visit the consulate the next day for the verification of some papers. But what he had seen that day was troubling him so much that he wanted to talk with the consul right away. He only hoped that Herr Konsul did not find his approaching him in off-hours inopportune. Lutz did not. Whatever the young man had to tell was surely important.

They walked and walked, while the young man poured out his story. They went over to Anjou Bastion, past the high walls of Capistran monastery, to Esztergom Rondell and beyond, along the western ramparts of Buda. Lutz kept his hands behind his back, while the young man gesticulated and talked, always searching the consul's face in the dark, to see whether he believed his unusual story. Indeed, never in his life had Carl Lutz heard an eyewitness account of this kind.

The Swiss doctor said that the evening before he had planned to take a night train to Budapest from his mother's home town, having completed his mission. But the timetable was upset and his train was hours late. When he arrived at the station, he noticed that there were several cattle wagons stationed on a side track. They were hermetically closed and wouldn't have aroused his attention, had not the station master from time to time emerged restlessly from his office, in order to look at the cars across the railway yard. He stood next to the young doctor: "Now they are quiet. But before they sang all the time." "Who?" the doctor asked, astonished. The station master placed a finger on his lips and hastened away. He seemed to act in a peculiar way, the young man thought. Hesitatingly, he walked across the tracks toward the train. What was the problem? But he did not get far. Two Hungarian soldiers came forward and released the safety catches of their rifles. "Get away from here!" they threatened. Only now he saw that the wagons were surrounded by soldiers on all sides. He returned to the station building. The station master looked at him with burning eyes. "Have you seen them?" he asked. "No," the doctor answered. "Who is in the cars?" "Jews," he said. "They were driven together this morning, and as soon as it is entirely dark, the train leaves. There are children and old people among them." He left and returned to his office. The young man remained rooted where he stood and looked back at the cattle wagons as if he were under a spell. On the side boards he noticed small air holes. How many people were inside? The air must be terrible.

The singing began all of a sudden. It started in the last car and continued throughout the others. It was a peculiar tune, more like a cry. It sounded like a question, because it was answered like thunder with many voices. The station master suddenly stood next to the doctor again, as if he wanted to talk. "It went on like this all day long," he whispered. His face was ashen. "They will be shooting right away!" Indeed, the guarding soldiers started to hit the doors with their fists, and when the singing did not stop, they shot through the air holes. There were shouts of pain from inside. The singing lasted about two hours, and the Swiss doctor kept watching the cattle wagons. The guards were becoming bored and sat down, while the shout with the question pierced the darkness and was answered by a multi-voiced thunder. As if someone forced him, the young man turned his head, and at a distance he saw peasants in the dark, as if rooted, in a field across a road. The station master now stood with them. No one uttered a word. The people kept steadily looking at the closed cattle cars, whence the strange singing came. The guards noticed the crowd, became nervous, shouted at the people to go away, and started to walk up and down along the vehicles. The people in the field remained.

The consul and the young doctor kept walking along the western ramparts of old Buda. They did not realize that it had begun to rain. They saw and felt nothing. When they passed Veesenmayer's legation on Uri Street, one of the SS guards nodded at the consul in slight recognition, embarrassed as he saw the rain soaking into the diplomat's suit. Lutz did not even ask himself whether the German minister, or perhaps Feine, might be looking down from behind one of the windowpanes, wondering whether the consul had at last learned the truth. They continued across Disz Square and then climbed up the steps to the Fishermen's Bastion, where the round white towers kept guard over the darkened city. They finally stopped and saw the grey line of the Danube and Pest looking like a city of phantoms. All the while the doctor did not interrupt his account. Air raid sirens sounded the alarm. There was the humming noise of hostile airplanes. Bombs exploded in the distance, somewhere to the south, perhaps amid the industrial complexes of Csepel. Fires reflected on low clouds. A policeman shouted at the two, ordering them to find shelter. They did not hear him, and the policeman did not insist. In their mind they saw only the cattle wagons and heard the strange funeral dirge of the kaddish, chanted by the victims themselves.

When it was completely dark, the young doctor continued, an old engine came steaming along. The cattle cars were shunted back and forth. They were finally arranged together and placed on the track next to the station building. The young Swiss doctor was close to them. He saw one of the guards open a door. He put in a sanitary bucket — if one could call it that — a few loaves of bread, and a bucket of fresh water. In the wagon it was dark, but in the light of the guard's lantern the doctor saw countless dark figures. They stood so closely together that they could barely bend or sit down. The light shone on faces. A newborn baby was among them, held by an eight-year-old girl. Next to them was the terribly pale face of a woman. There were streaks of red across her face. She must have been beaten. Was this the mother? An old man with a white beard had collapsed, but there was no room for him to lie down. His eyes were closed. The other humans remained invisible in the dark. An incredibly foul smell poured from the open door, which made even the guard shudder. He shut the door quickly and rushed to the next wagon. Now it was entirely dark, but they kept on singing. They sang even when the engine got up steam and slowly pulled the train away. They must have known where they were headed.

*   *   *

During the Eichmann trial in Jerusalem in 1960 one of the few surviving Hungarian deportees, Imre Reiner, recalled that the Gestapo had placed two containers in each cattle wagon at the point of departure. One of them was filled with drinking water and the other was empty, to be used for human excrement. Underway, at train stops, they were neither filled afresh nor emptied. As in May and June the weather was becoming warm, many children and sick and old people were not able to bear the congestion, the heat, the lack of air, and the foul smell. They died underway. The Gestapo did not allow the dead to be taken out for burial. They traveled to Auschwitz, standing amid the living.

*   *   *

Consul Lutz asked Minister Jaeger to send a copy of the Auschwitz Protocol to Berne. He thought the document would carry more weight if the top-ranking Swiss diplomat accredited to Hungary forwarded the document. Jaeger added a note to the foreign minister, Marcel Pilet-Golaz, saying that this was for his information and "appropriate action," if so desired. He would not dare to tell his superior what to do.

It must be admitted that Pilet-Golaz was duly shocked when he read it, because he was not an inhuman person. He had heard the same story from different sources, but never with such precision as now. So the wild stories about the death camps seemed true. He knew that the International Committee of the Red Cross in Geneva had been informed by the World Jewish Congress office about it. The British and American lega-

112

tions in Switzerland were also receiving copies. Diplomats, government offices, and private agencies began to know. But Pilet-Golaz put the Auschwitz Protocol in a drawer. It was not that he put no faith in it. But what could he do?

Within days, other neutral and Allied governments also gained knowledge of the Auschwitz Protocol. Shortly before the Hungarian deportations began, a British reconnaissance plane discovered Auschwitz by chance. This was on May 4, 1944. As the plane flew over the region, a sudden gap in the clouds opened up, and the vast complex came into view. The pilot took a picture. The pilot realized that this was the death camp which everybody had been searching for.

But Auschwitz was not a priority, American and British military leaders asserted with vigor, and the politicians succumbed. The war had to be won first! When the war was over, the Jews would be safe. The Allied powers must not deviate men and materials from that primary objective.

The secret lay in the open, at least to a select circle of decision makers, and nothing happened. A curse lay on the Auschwitz Protocol.

Carl Lutz, now that he had been confronted with the awful truth firsthand, informed the other neutral legations. He had been the first to act on behalf of the Jews ever since 1942 and he had confronted Veesenmayer, Eichmann, and the Hungarian government immediately after the German occupation on March 19, 1944, when he wanted the 8,000 to emigrate. Moreover, he often transmitted notes from the Allied governments to the Hungarian leaders, protesting against the progressive restrictions imposed on the Jewish minority. Lutz was the key person in the resistance of the diplomats against this evil.

It was high time, he felt, that the neutrals addressed a joint protest to the Hungarian authorities, even if they could not easily consult with their home governments in advance. Lutz and Minister Jaeger spoke with the papal nuncio, seventy-two-year-old Archbishop Angelo Rotta. As the senior diplomat in Hungary — Rotta had arrived in Hungary in 1930 — the nuncio was indispensable for any such démarche. He also enjoyed great prestige. Rotta was not only a diplomat but also a churchman. He rebelled at the very thought that human beings were wantonly destroyed. Even though he had not been instructed by the Vatican, Rotta had already taken Cardinal Jusztinian Serédi to task for his antisemitism and his silence. Rotta was ably seconded by his young *auditore,* or assistant, Msgr. Gennaro Verolino, who knew how to get secret information out of Hungarians and to formulate communiqués for the nuncio's signature. Rotta readily agreed that the neutral diplomats be assembled. Moreover, Rotta, while heading his tiny two-man legation, inspired individual clergy, women's orders, and laymen to engage in action. To some extent he was able to counteract Hungary's Roman Catholic primate, Cardinal Serédi, who had no intention of troubling himself with the Jews.

The remaining neutral legations in Hungary were a motley crew. Whereas the Swiss represented western Allied interests, sixty-five-year-old Swedish minister Carl Ingvar Danielsson was in charge of Soviet interests in Hungary. This was an assignment that he disliked. Danielsson thought Budapest was a dead-end assignment, career-wise, and he pestered the Swedish foreign ministry to let him either retire or be sent to an easier post. He quite neglected to look after the Soviet war prisoners in Hungary. He neither visited them nor protested when, contrary to international law, these men were shipped to Germany. Many of them died in Auschwitz, along with Jews and Poles. At war's end, the Soviet army commanders took Danielsson sharply to task for this failure, but they did not punish him. Whatever limited action on behalf of the Jews the Swedish legation undertook, it was done mainly by the minister's aides, among these Danielsson's first secretary, Per Anger. Outraged at the legation's lack of concern and the catastrophic non-policies of the International Committee of the Red Cross (its Swiss delegate, the highly motivated Friedrich Born, had not yet established himself), the Swedish Red Cross opened up its own branch in Budapest, which it placed under the capable leadership of Asta Nilsson, the cousin of King Gustav V. Many Hungarian Jewish children were saved through his actions.

The other neutral diplomatic representatives were the chargés d'affaires of Portugal and Spain, Carlos de Liz-Texeira Branqunho and Miguel Sanz-Briz. These countries did not consider Hungary important and had already withdrawn their ministers. Finally there was a counselor from the Turkish legation, Kemal Sayit. These accepted the Rotta invitation out of diplomatic courtesy, rather than conviction.

Carl Lutz at his office, former American Legation
(Courtesy Archives of Contemporary History, ETH, Zurich)

Postage stamp issued by the Swiss government in 1999 in honor of Carl Lutz

Carl Lutz in Washington, D.C., 1923.
(Courtesy Swiss Federal Archives, Berne)

Nicholas Horthy, regent of Hungary
(Hungarian Museum of Contemporary History)

Edmund Veesenmayer
(Hungarian Museum of Contemporary History)

Maximilian Jaeger
(Source: Ringier AG)

Former American Legation in Pest. View from Freedom Square. This building remained undamaged during the siege. (Courtesy Archives of Contemporary History, ETH, Zurich)

Jewish couple wearing yellow stars (Hungarian Museum of Contemporary History)

Jewish applicants for Schutzbriefe (protective letters) at the Glass House on Vadasz Street (Courtesy Museum of Contemporary History, ETH, Zurich)

Jews on the way to the train station, where they will embark for Auschwitz
(Hungarian Museum of Contemporary History)

Bishop Laszlo Ravasz
(Courtesy Hungarian Reformed Church)

Albert Bereczky
(Courtesy Piroska Victor Bereczky)

Gerhart Feine
(Courtesy Archives of the German Foreign Ministry in
Bonn, Inventar-Nr. 3233)

Friedrich Born
(Courtesy Archives of the International Committee of
the Red Cross, Geneva)

Preparing Schutzbriefe (protective letters)

(Hungarian Museum of Contemporary History)

SCHUTZBRIEF

Diese

schweizerischen Staatsangehörigen,

steht unter dem Schutz der unterzeichneten Vertretung
der
SCHWEIZERISCHEN EIDGENOSSENSCHAFT

, den

Der Schweizerische

No.

SVÁJCI KÖVETSÉG
IDEGEN ÉRDEKEK KÉPVISELETE

KIVÁNDORLÁSI OSZTÁLY
V., VADASZ-UTCA 29.

1270/44.h.m.

SCHWEIZERISCHE GESANDTSCHAFT
ABTEILUNG FÜR FREMDE INTERESSEN

ABTEILUNG AUSWANDERUNG
V., VADASZ-UTCA 29.

Muster eines echten "Schutzbriefes".

Die Schweizerische Gesandtschaft, Abteilung fremde Interessen, bescheinigt hiermit,
dass

Frau K A H Á N Miklós
geb. Polgár Legda
im schweizerischen Kollektiv-
pass zur Auswanderung einge-
tragen ist, daher ist der (die)
Betreffende als Besitzer eines
gültigen Reisepasses zu be-
trachten.

Budapest, 25 Oktober 1944

A Svájci Követség, Idegen
Érdekek Képviselete, ezennel
igazolja, hogy

KAHÁN Miklósné
szül. Polgár Legda
a svájci csoportos (collectiv)
utlevélben szerepel és ezért
nevezett érvényes utlevél bir-
tokában levő személynek tekin-
tendő.

Budapest, 1944. október 25.

Two models of Schutzbriefe used

(Courtesy Swiss Federal Archives)

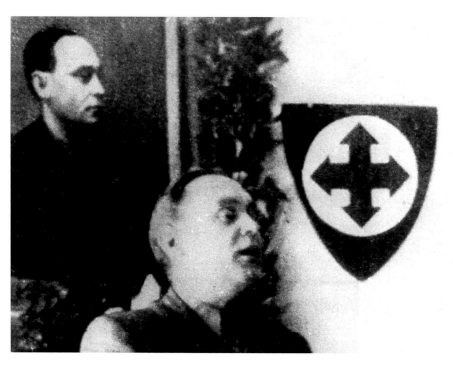

Ferenc Szalasi
(Hungarian Museum of Contemporary History)

Andrus Kun, the Nyilas (Arrow Cross) priest
(Hungarian Museum of Contemporary History)

Peter Zürcher
(Courtesy Swiss Federal Archives, Berne)

Alexander Grossman
(Courtesy Alexander Grossman)

Raoul Wallenberg
(Courtesy Guy von Dardel)

Adolf Eichmann
(Hungarian Museum of Contemporary History)

A Nyilas (Arrow Cross) band on a killing spree
(Hungarian Museum of Contemporary History)

ICRC delegation examines the starved and frozen bodies
of inhabitants of the large ghetto of Pest after liberation
(Hungarian Museum of Contemporary History, Budapest)

The former British legation after the siege. This building was reconstructed.
Today it houses the Hungarian Department of Historic Sites and Monuments.
(Courtesy Archives of Contemporary History, ETH, Zurich)

Carl Lutz amid the ruins of his residence, the former British legation
(Courtesy Archives of Contemporary History, ETH, Zurich)

A sign of hope: Jewish children saved from the Holocaust,
one year after the end of the war
(Courtesy Alexander Grossman)

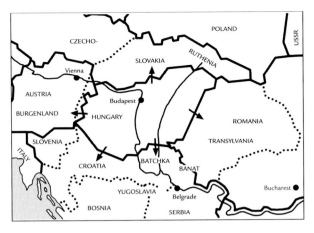

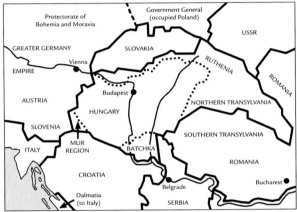

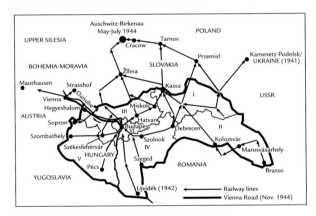

Map 1. The disemembering of Hungary by the Trianon peace treaty

Map 2. Between 1938 and 1941 some of the lost provinces are returned to Hungary

Map 3. According to information from the Jewish Council for Israel in Budapest the following number of Jews were deported from the various Gendarmerie Districts: I. 288,333; II. 50,805; III. 51,829; IV. 40,505; V. 29,556; VI. 24,128

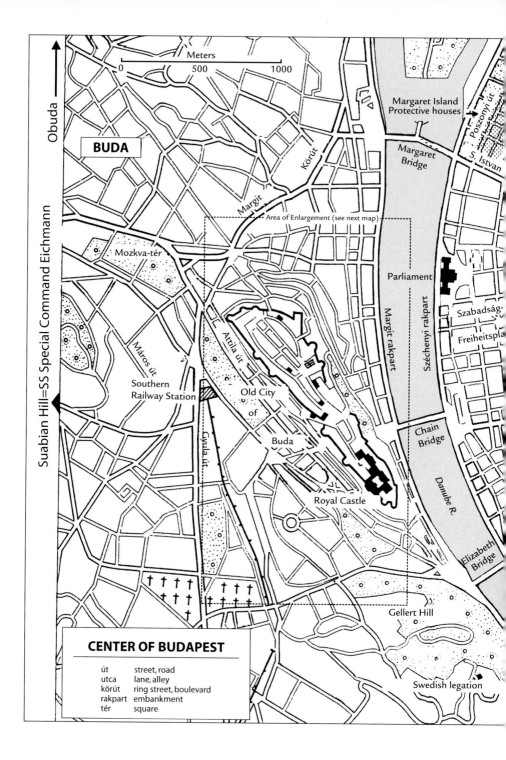

Meters
0   500   1000

Obuda →

Suabian Hill=SS Special Command Eichmann

BUDA

Margit Island Protective houses

Margaret Bridge

Poszony út

S. Istvan

Körút

Margit

Area of Enlargement (see next map)

Mozkva-tér

Parliament

Szabadság

Freiheitspla

Máros út

Attila út

Széchenyi rakpart

Margit rakpart

Southern Railway Station

Old City

of

Buda

Gyula út

Chain Bridge

Danube R.

Royal Castle

Elizabeth Bridge

Gellert Hill

† † † †   † † †
† † †   †† † † † †
†

CENTER OF BUDAPEST

út	street, road
utca	lane, alley
körút	ring street, boulevard
rakpart	embankment
tér	square

Swedish legation

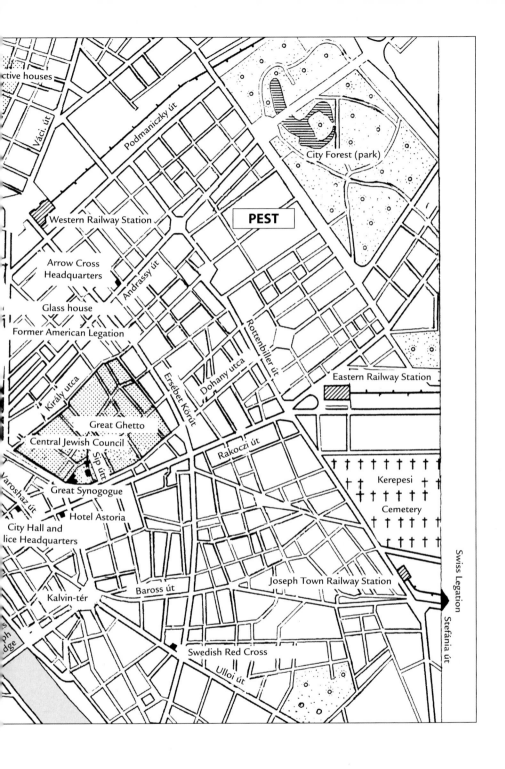

Váci út

ctive houses

Podmaniczky út

City Forest (park)

PEST

Western Railway Station

Andrassy út

Arrow Cross
Headquarters

Rottenbiller út

Glass house

Former American Legation

Eastern Railway Station

Kiraly utca

Ersébet Körút

Dohany utca

Great Ghetto

Central Jewish Council

Rakoczi út

Kerepesi

Varoshaz út

Sip út

Great Synogogue

Cemetery

Hotel Astoria

City Hall and
lice Headquarters

Swiss Legation

Joseph Town Railway Station

Kalvin-tér

Baross út

Stefánia út

s
ph
dge

Swedish Red Cross

Ulloi út

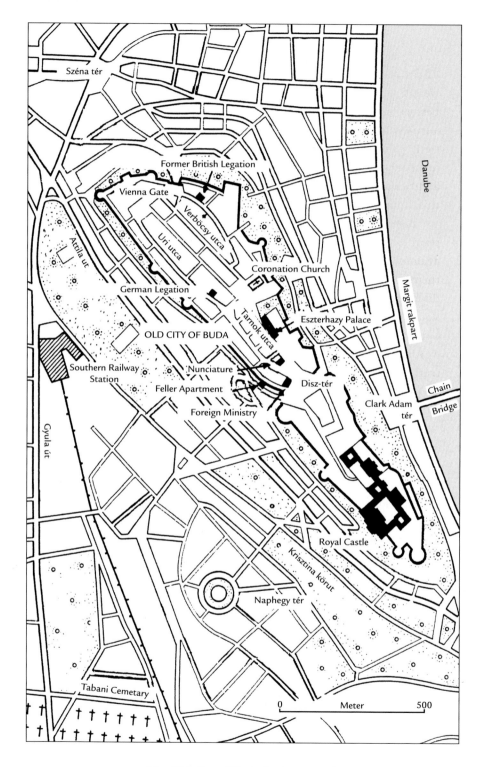

The Old City of Buda (enlargement)

Their governments were military dictatorships. While neutral, they were known for their pro-German sympathies, although they did not persecute Jews. The Spanish were barely involved. It was not before late autumn 1944 that Italian Giorgio Perlasca entered the abandoned legation by the rear door, so to speak, and took the place of Sanz-Briz, who had been ordered back. Through Perlasca, Spain saved several hundred additional Jews. The government in Madrid was not even quite aware of this "intruder's" role.

Being left to their own devices, it took courage for this disparate team of diplomats to get together and to formulate a common protest against the killing machine that was Auschwitz. Although the policies of their home governments toward Nazi Germany varied widely, all of the diplomats were shocked by what they saw and heard in Hungary. With no instructions from home, they no longer worried much about the opinions of their superiors, and they fully supported Rotta's sharply worded accusations that the Hungarian government was hiding the truth:

> It is said that this is no deportation, but an obligatory labor service. One can always talk about words, but reality is something else. When old men of over 70 or even 80 years are carried away, elderly women, children, the sick, one must ask: what kind of labor can these human beings perform? The answer is given (by the government) that this was an opportunity for Jews to take their families along; if this is so, such a departure should be made of one's free will. And how about those old and sick people, who are deported alone, or who have no relatives accompanying them?

The Sztojay government did not know how to respond to these questions. Their pretense that the deportees were sent to work in Germany under government-to-government contract sounded too ridiculous, and the Hungarians were evidently embarrassed. They repeated their lies, and the neutral diplomats met again in order to fight back. This time, the old nuncio spoke like a prophet of old, in a way that no other diplomat could have spoken: "I am tormented by a great fear: because of the injustices committed — against the explicit will of God! — innocent blood is shed without restraint, God's blessings cannot remain upon this country, blessings which are particularly needed at this moment of approaching unknown dangers, which not even the most powerful rulers will be capable of mastering."

If the Sztojay government was on edge over this diplomatic intervention, it was too afraid of Veesenmayer to ask that the deportations be stopped. The German minister rightly told the prime minister that this was the diplomats' personal initiative and that it was not backed up by their governments. In any case, diplomatic protocol forbade them to go public, because that would constitute an interference in the internal affairs of the host country, which automatically signified expulsion. Whatever they said, this was the talk of powerless individuals with no clout.

However, the top church leaders were secretly informed of the protest, and this could have been dangerous to the Sztojay government, if the church leadership had adopted the protest as its own. But all that Cardinal Serédi did was to criticize the authorities gently and confidentially for forcing converted Jews to wear the yellow star. They were thereby compelled, he wrote to Sztojay, to wear the "sign of the devil," meaning the yellow star! This medieval-minded prelate was not interested in the "others." When more open-minded aides asked Serédi to be more concerned about all Jews, threatened as they were by extinction, the cardinal shook his heavy head and answered that if the Holy Father in Rome had said nothing, why should he?

More openness prevailed — but only slightly — on the Protestant side. Laszlo Ravasz, the presiding bishop of the Hungarian Reformed Church, was sick during late spring/early summer 1944 when the deportations began. He was a keen Magyar nationalist, whom the Romanians had expelled from his native Transylvania, and his one fervent objective in life was to regain the lost province. As a member of the upper house of the Parliament he had, in 1938, voted in favor of the anti-Jewish measures. But Ravasz and some other church leaders refused to support further restrictions in 1941, saying that it would be preferable if the Jews left Hungary. Ravasz was a brilliant intellectual, writer, and speaker. He was of austere appearance and many called him the "Protestant Jesuit." His sermons were broadcast weekly over the radio. Hungarian Jews remember that the bishop almost always included an antisemitic statement in his radio sermons, which usually had to do with the "guilt" of the Jews for killing Christ, or with their "refusal" to accept him as their Messiah. Moreover, the bishop broadcast that the Jews were strangers to Hungarian society, and that they dominated the nation's economy and the liberal professions far beyond their true number. There was nothing in all this which was not being said by others. But the radio sermons of Ravasz, which came on the air week after week, year after year, helped to transform ordinary anti-Jewish popular prejudice into theologically and intellectually acceptable antisemitism. His mastery of the Hungarian language was exceptional, and his reasoning was calm but sharp. His opinion carried all the more weight as he was a respected church leader, in whose parish the regent, Horthy, himself was a member. The ultimate effect of his words upon Hungarian society was disastrous. Without realizing it, during the fatal pre-war years Ravasz helped to remove the intellectual barriers against the physical elimination of the Jews. If Ravasz and some of the other church leaders had followed the example of the German Confessing Church and of other religious resistance movements in Nazi-dominated parts of Europe, the record of Hungarian Christianity and perhaps of the Hungarian nation during World War II might have been different.

On his sickbed in the spring of 1944, Ravasz learned that the Hungarian Jews were being deported to Auschwitz. At this moment he must have understood what he had done. He turned his head away from the visitor who brought him the news and began to cry. This was not what he had intended, he said. Repentance came late, but it came. Quickly, he dispatched a note to Cardinal Serédi, asking that they sign a joint protest to the government to stop the deportations. Serédi refused. He was not ready for such ecumenical cooperation, and his inborn antisemitism remained undiminished, though he did write his own letter to the government, asking that the "Jewish problem" be resolved in a more humane way. Desperately, Ravasz prepared his own circular letter, which he intended to be read by every Reformed pastor from the pulpit, in which language the deportations were mildly criticized in baroque church language. Subserviently he submitted the draft to the minister for religion and education for prior approval. The latter realized that even such a subdued protest could have explosive results within the closed Hungarian society, cut off as it was from uncensored information. The minister rejected the circular letter and threatened severe punishment for any clergyman, including Ravasz, who dared to read it from the pulpit. Obediently the presiding bishop dropped the project. Christians might suffer martyrdom for their faith, but not for Jews.

None of this "controversy" became public. Persecution was not what Hungarian Christians desired for themselves, no matter how just the cause. In their eyes, to oppose the government meant weakening the nation, which had gone to war on Germany's side in order to recover the frontiers of Greater Hungary. The Jews paid the price.

Meanwhile, the trains to Auschwitz kept rolling, and each day 12,000 Hungarian Jews were gassed and burned.

Then, on July 8, 1944, a miracle occurred. Horthy, the regent, ordered that the deportations be stopped.

6. JOURNEY TO BISTRITZA

The reader is invited to move nearly fifty years on in time to a day in July 1991.

Shortly before noon on that day, as the Hungarian capital simmered under the heat of summer, a solemn ceremony of unveiling a memorial took place in narrow Dob Street next to the great Dohanyi Street synagogue. The memorial showed a ragged, worn-out person lying on the ground. In his distress the figure reaches out with thin arms for an angel, who is hovering above him. The angel reaches downward, as if bringing salvation. Two hands are about to meet.

This remarkable memorial honored Consul Carl Lutz. The consul had passed away sixteen years earlier, in 1975. This was the first monument ever erected in his memory. Although the commemoration center Yad Vashem in Jerusalem had honored him and his first wife, Gertrud, as Just Ones Among the Nations, Lutz had been conspicuously ignored by Switzerland, by Hungary, and by the world at large. On this July day Budapest at least remembered him. There were speeches by representatives of the authorities, the municipality, the diplomatic corps, and the Jewish community. The Swiss embassy was represented by a minor official, the ambassador himself having left for vacation.

At the edge of the crowd stood a well-dressed elderly gentleman, who had not been invited to the ceremony, but who nevertheless showed up. Nor was he asked to speak. But he listened carefully. Apart from perhaps an alert journalist, none of those present really knew who he was or what connection there was between him and the consul. The gentleman had left Hungary, or more precisely Bistritza, decades before, and now resided in Rome. He was born with the century and had suffered from its absurdities. He had seen the shifting of territories from one state to another and back, watching national allegiances transferred this way and that. He had seen racial persecution and war from close at hand, like thousands and millions of others. But what few of those present at the ceremony knew was that the old gentleman had not accepted this fate without protest. At one moment in mid-life he had even powerfully interfered in high politics, literally forcing Horthy, the regent, to stop deportations in July 1944.

Consul Lutz had been linked to this twisting of the arms of the regent.

The trip to Budapest was the last voyage of George Mandel-Mantello. He wanted to be at the ceremony, because he wanted to remember how his life had accidentally but fatefully crossed that of the Swiss consul. Without that brush with destiny, even the saved remnant of Hungarian Jewry would likely have completely vanished. Strangely, at the time of that momentous event in 1944 George Mandel-Mantello and Carl Lutz had never met in person.

The link between them was a Romanian diplomat in Berne, one Florian Manoliou, who undertook the journey to Bistritza, because this was where the Mandel family had its home. The family had lived there for many generations.

But where was Bistritza?

An early postwar *Encyclopaedia Britannica* has the following entry:

Bistritza, a town of Transylvania, Rumania, yielded to Hungary between 1940 and 1945, capital of the former Rumanian department of Nasaud, on the Sieul river, on the edge of the Carpathians. Pop. (1948), 15,801. A railway runs west to the main system, via Dej; 18 mi. E. of Bistritza (Borgo Bistritza) the line ends, but a motor train runs through the mountains to the watering place of Dornavatra and the Bukovina. Bistritza is a Saxon settlement, center of the old "Nösnerland." There is an interesting Gothic church and arcaded market place.

What the encyclopaedia fails to mention is that up to World War I Bistritza had been part of the Austro-Hungarian empire and that in 1919, along with the rest of Transylvania, it was transferred to Romania. In 1940 Bistritza, along with northern Transylvania, was returned to Hungary. At no point when the power brokers of the day bent over the maps, taking apart and putting together states, did they think of consulting the people directly affected, asking whether they wanted different kings and presidents, other flags and national hymns, new loyalties, school systems, currencies, and languages, even though all this affected their personal lives profoundly. In 1940 Bistritza had well over 20,000 inhabitants. In that year the Jewish population was 2,370 or 11.85% of the total. They went to Auschwitz. By the autumn of 1944, when the tide moved in the opposite direction, it was the turn of the Saxons (ethnic Germans) and Hungarians to flee as the Red Army, aided by Romanian troops, threatened the town. This was bad, of course, but they were not sent to any death camp.

When this second war was over, what had been a prosperous multi-ethnic community was in shambles. Eight-hundred-year-old homesteads were abandoned and rotted away. The saw mills and the flour mills fell to pieces. Once the tough new order became established, the directors of the new state enterprises either lacked interest or did not have the professional skills to make the economy prosper. Decisions on sowing, planting, and harvesting depended on apparatchiks in Bucharest and not on the common sense of the farmer who knows his land. Only the security organs were alert and efficient, but they did not feed the people.

*   *   *

The Jewish tragedy of Bistritza began on May 3, 1944. At five o'clock in the morning the Jews were rounded up by special units composed of civil servants, primary and middle school teachers, gendarmes and policemen, "guided" by the German SS and the Gestapo. They were brought to small enclosed centers and then to temporary ghettos. All communication with the outside world was cut off. All radios were confiscated. At each stage the victims were subjected to barbaric conditions and beatings. The Jews did not know what it meant and offered no resistance. None of them knew that Auschwitz would be their ultimate destination, a place of which they had never heard and whose purpose they could not imagine. The Christian population was indifferent, if not satisfied, and believed what the authorities told them, namely that the front lines had to be protected from the "machinations of the Judeo-Bolsheviks." They were anxious to take over Jewish businesses and other properties and thought they would become rich. Many of them exposed Jews who sought safety by going into hiding. On the evening of May 3 white flags hung from the houses of Bistritza. It meant that the town was judenfrei, free of Jews.

For four weeks the Jews were kept in small ghettos in miserable conditions. They were deported to Auschwitz between May 15 and June 7. Among those who went to their deaths was the distinguished Mandel family. They were Orthodox Jews who owned one of the grain mills and were quite well-to-do. They descended from a long line of rabbis and distinguished Talmudic scholars and remained deeply rooted in Judaism.

Life had been quiet in Bistritza, and no one had ever thought that the Hungarians, Saxons, and Romanians who for centuries had lived together in this small multi-ethnic community would abandon their Jewish minority, let alone attack it. The terrible disaster which befell Bistritza was not immediately known to George in distant Geneva, even though he had been mortally afraid for his family ever since he learned of the German occupation of Hungary on March 19.

*   *   *

George Mandel-Mantello was born in Bistritza in 1901. In 1919, when Transylvania was annexed to Romania, he was no longer a Hungarian citizen but had to swear fealty to King Ferdinand who had his palace in Bucharest. At that time his family name was simply Mandel. He began his independent business career by establishing a textile mill, together with his brother Joseph and a few high-ranking Romanian army officers, among them General Draganescu, an air force officer. Draganescu was a national hero; in 1917, as a simple captain, he had helped to transform a Romanian retreat during the battle of Marasti into a victory over the advancing Germans commanded by Field Marshal Mackensen. Such well-placed partners, astutely chosen, allowed the Mandel brothers to have easy access to those who counted in the new fatherland.

George built up his own fortune. He moved from Bistritza to Koloszvar and later to Bucharest and Budapest. He liked good food and intelligent company and enjoyed the presence of beautiful women. Above all, he was a generous person, who did not withhold friendship and gifts. Although he was a businessman, the studious habits of his family were not lost on him. They enabled him to observe and to analyze the thunder clouds that were building up on the horizon during the 1920s and 1930s. He watched them with alarm. The war of 1914–18, which had been the first industrial war in history, had involved millions of fighters. A mass of disoriented survivors had returned home in anger. In due time they would upset political structures far more than the "peace makers" of Versailles, Trianon, and Sèvres could imagine. The military conflict had cut deep social wounds and the new national frontiers had uprooted millions. Because of this the large powers, while retaining their illusions, had lost their feeling of security — including the victorious western Allies, who had fought the war in order to make the world "safe for democracy." The war of 1914–18 had opened up a Pandora's box out of which flew mean, vengeful spirits that were only waiting for skilled agitators to combine and direct them. The agitators' task was facilitated by the emergence of countless new states, which for the most part were artificial structures, prone to all sorts of political problems. Moreover, Russia, the largest European power, was in the throes of revolution and dictatorship, and in the Far East, Japan's emerging military establishment began to make dangerous moves toward Europe's and America's colonial empires. Capitalist bourgeois society throughout Europe felt threatened from all sides. At least in part, the growth of Fascism and National Socialism can be explained by these multiple fears. As soon as the pyre of despair was built, a single madman sufficed to set the match. The international system, as represented by the League of Nations, was too weak to oppose him.

George Mandel remembered that throughout history Jews had always paid for Europe's crises. They were the scapegoat of Christian civilization. This time, he feared, the danger could become more acute than ever before.

His business caused him to travel widely, far beyond Bistritza and even Romania. He happened to be in Vienna when Hitler annexed Austria in 1938, and he observed the humiliation of Vienna's Jews firsthand. In the spring of 1939 he was in Czechoslovakia when the Germans marched in, ending Czech independence and destroying the famed Jewish community of Prague. Again, in 1941, he witnessed the Nazi invasion of Yugoslavia and saw the beginnings of the atrocities of the Croats against the Serbs and the Jews. One reason for George's presence in these countries at opportune moments was that he had become an honorary consul of El Salvador, the coffee-producing country of Central America. The small country was in the process of establishing a rudimentary diplomatic service in Europe; it was anxious to find new outlets for its one product, since sales had been badly affected by world economic depression. George Mandel had chanced to meet visiting politicians and diplomats from El Salvador, who were making an exploratory tour. They were impressed by his personality, his generosity, and his manifold contacts and asked him to assume "consular responsibility" on behalf of El Salvador for Czechoslovakia, Hungary, and Yugoslavia. Although Mandel had never been to Central America and did not know Spanish, he accepted the offer. Henceforth he added "Mantello" to his family name. To European ears it sounded perhaps Latin, even though it was not a Spanish word.

The main advantage of this appointment consisted of a diplomatic passport that allowed Mandel-Mantello to travel from country to country at a time when visa restrictions and antisemitism were becoming rampant. The Salvadorean "connection" was his insurance policy in case the situation went from bad to worse — as it did.

Romania had tried to stay out of the war in convenient neutrality. The overblown state surely could gain nothing in joining one side or the other. But in 1940 the big powers of the day, Nazi Germany and Stalin's Soviet Union, greedily pounced upon its oil resources and rich agricultural lands and tore it apart. Under the Führer's and Stalin's joint *diktat* Romania "gave back" Moldavia and Bukovina to the Soviet Union and northern Transylvania to Hungary. Southern Transylvania was allowed to stay with Romania. As if these amputations were not enough, Hitler "reorganized" Romania's political structures according to his preferences. He made King Carol abdicate and replaced him with the monarch's teenage son, Michael. The eighteen-year-old became the puppet king of a state "allied" with Hitler and ruled by Marshal Antonescu and his Fascist Iron Guards. The Führer had acquired an advance platform for his ambitious plans of conquest. When in 1941 the German dictator ended his cozy tête-à-tête with his hitherto friend, the mustachioed Georgian Stalin, Antonescu's soldiers marched into the Soviet Union alongside the Führer's troops, in a campaign that they were sure would be a cake walk.

Thus, after twenty-two years with Romania, the people of Bistritza were also "liberated." They were Hungarian citizens once again, without anyone having asked their opinion, and the astonished Romanians fell from their high pedestal and once again became the pariah of Transylvania. The Hungarians, to be sure, accepted the redrafted political border as a gift from heaven. The Saxons felt on top of things, because their powerful mother country had imposed the new order. They were no longer a lost minority in the Carpathians, but the avant-garde of German civilization in the East. Overnight, swastika flags hung from their houses. Parading *Hitlerjugend* bands shouted "Sieg heil."

The Jews did not know what to think of all this. Most spoke Hungarian, and they were inclined to share the patriotic feelings of the Magyars. Moreover, they had always admired all things German and did not really believe all the rumors that had reached them from the Hitler state. But their illusions did not last long, because with the restored Hungarian administration came the anti-Jewish measures that had been adopted in Hungary proper in 1938. Jewish civil servants were dismissed and Jewish students found access to higher education barred; the University of Koloszvar, for instance, accepted only ten Jewish students. The people were told not to buy "Jewish" anymore. More ominously, the local Saxons, seconded by the Hungarians, loudly demanded that the "Jewish problem" be solved.

*   *   *

Questions began to be raised about the Salvadorean honorary consul, who traveled freely from one country to the next; the Nazis suspected him of smuggling Jews. In 1942 George Mandel-Mantello happened to be in occupied Zagreb, Croatia, when the Gestapo at last closed in on him and confiscated his papers. For two months he was held under house arrest at his hotel. Just as he thought there was no way out, his former business partner, Draganescu, asked Captain Vasilescu, a mutual friend, to go to Zagreb and rescue George. The captain appeared in the uniform of a Romanian military pilot, although he really worked for the secret services. In this uniform he was able to cross the tightly controlled frontiers inside Nazi-dominated Europe with ease. Vasilescu brought an extra Romanian air force uniform to the hotel and made George put it on. The two brazenly stepped out of the hotel, passed all controls, and drove to the military airfield where Vasilescu had stationed a small airplane. Together they flew to Milan, Italy. There, George boarded a train for nearby Switzerland. His brother Joseph had fled there a year earlier and was now living in Geneva. Without this daring rescue, George Mandel-Mantello would doubtless have vanished in the jails of the Führer. Unfortunately, his wife and their thirteen-year-old son Imre were left behind in Budapest. Mrs. Irene Mandel-Mantello had not wanted to go along on her husband's risky journey, because she was taking care of her aged parents. Imre, however, managed to join his father soon after.

George Mandel-Mantello's miraculous salvation meant a new life for him. He felt under an obligation to help those who had been less lucky. Upon arrival in Geneva he introduced himself to the consul general of El Salvador, José Arturo Castellanos. He happened to be short of staff and hired the former honorary consul as the consulate's general secretary. George had barely installed himself when he learned that unscrupulous Latin American diplomats were using the desperate plight of Jews by selling citizenship papers at a generous personal profit. The "fees" could run from three hundred to three thousand Swiss francs. These were enormous sums, considering, for instance, that monthly Swiss salaries at that time were rarely higher than two or three hundred francs, fifty to seventy-five U.S. dollars at the exchange rate of the day. This money-for-life commerce enraged George. He remembered what he had seen during his travels. Brutal as this documentary exploitation was, he nevertheless learned that such protective documents did keep the holders from arrest and deportation. His mind started to race.

He met a French-Jewish refugee, Maître Matthieu Muller, a lawyer and former president of the French Agudah, an Orthodox Jewish association. Together with him George created his own Salvadorean citizenship papers for Jews in France, Belgium, and Holland, and wherever cries of distress reached him. The document bore the offical letterhead of the Salvadorean general consulate. The text stated in ponderous old-fashioned Spanish that the holder was a citizen of the Republic of El Salvador in Central America, which extended its protection to him or to her and requested all foreign governments to render all possible help to their compatriot. The government of El Salvador, it said, expressed its profound gratitude to "whomever it may concern" for such consideration. At the bottom George Mandel-Mantello signed in his capacity as the general secretary of the general consulate. The paper looked impressive and terribly official by all accounts. Surely, while few Nazi officials could read the language of Cervantes or knew where El Salvador was, one could almost see these believers in authority stand at attention and raise their right hand in salute. There were additional stamps, each with a signature that certified the correctness of the translations into French and/or into German. Such verifications were utterly devoid of meaning, because they simply stated the obvious. The document, however, gained in official momentousness with each additional signature and stamp. The bogus "passport" was meant to create just this effect. Castellanos, the consul general, was fully aware of the implications of this cat-and-mouse game but gave Mandel-Mantello his personal approval. Castellanos thereby took personal risks, because Fascist and Nazi influence was considerable throughout Central America. For the moment he did not dare to inform his home government.

Numerous appeals reached Geneva from those threatened, because by 1942 the deportation of Jews from occupied territories was beginning in earnest, although no one fully understood the somber nature of their destination. Mandel-Mantello hired university students, and during long hours they filled in the names of the beneficiaries on the life-saving papers. These were given out free of charge. George Mandel-Mantello himself paid the expenses for the entire operation.

Sometimes the documents were sent by the postal mail service, and surprisingly many arrived despite the ever-present censorship. But in most instances mail services between Switzerland and occupied territories were disrupted. Moreover, many potential recipients lived at clandestine addresses and could not be contacted. In such situations communication depended on courageous messengers, who were ready to risk their lives by crossing the Swiss borders and delving into the terrifying night of Nazi-held territories, smuggling the documents to the right addresses. Mandel-Mantello found such people, because a new generation of young men and women was coming of age who wanted to help combat the evil that held Europe in its grip. These messengers used well-organized and skillful resistance networks. To George's relief he learned again and again that the Germans and their subservient occupation authorities respected his papers and that the beneficiaries stayed alive. But it was a limited operation, when compared with the total disaster.

*   *   *

Then came March 19, 1944. George Mandel-Mantello grew nervous about the fate of his parents in Transylvania. Radio broadcasts and papers told of sharply mounting threats to Jews. Like everyone else George had believed that the Jewish community in Hungary was — relatively — safe. Now that defeat loomed, why should Nazi Germany and the Hungarian extremists be foolish enough to murder Hungary's Jews? He was angry with himself that he had not sent Salvadorean papers while there had been time. He, like most other reasonable and decent people, had simply been incapable of understanding the criminal mind of the Führer and of the lunatics around him.

George desperately sought news about what was happening to the Jewish community in Hungary. When he tried to telephone his parents, the long-distance operator answered that the number in question was disrupted. Cablegrams were not delivered. He listened to all kinds of radio stations, Hungarian, BBC, even German. The days were replete with rumors and incoherent news, but nothing concrete. Together with several others, both Jews and Christians, Mandel-Mantello organized a Swiss-Hungarian Aid Committee in order to coordinate information and to seek ways of possible action.

Only much later did George learn that at this moment when he was seeking reliable information, copies of the Auschwitz Protocol had already been filtered into Switzerland by various routes, but he hadn't been shown any of them. Lutz and Jaeger had informed the Swiss foreign ministry under Marcel Pilet-Golaz by diplomatic courier. Berne kept silent. The International Committee of the Red Cross and Jewish organizations had received copies. Silence again. The document went from secret bearer to secret bearer, from diplomats to officials and back. These people did not have the habit of talking, or worse, they did not believe what they read, which was a fine excuse for not having to act. Although Vrba and Lanik had risked their lives so that the truth could be shouted from the rooftops and measures taken in time, momentum got lost. Had not the two young Slovaks said that the deportation of the Hungarian Jews would begin soon?

The vital knowledge was not shared with George Mandel-Mantello, the Hungarian-Jewish refugee who was rising to prominence as one who tried to save people. He would naturally have wanted to know the truth. The fateful pattern already established in Hungary by Reszö Kasztner was repeated in Switzerland. Except that George, like Carl Lutz, knew that something was terribly wrong.

In desperation Mandel-Mantello asked an old friend of his, Dr. Florian Manoliou, the commercial attaché at the Romanian legation in Berne, whether he would not risk going to Bistritza to find out what was happening to his family. Manoliou, in his forties like Mandel-Mantello, had studied economics and had entered the diplomatic services of his country under deposed King Carol. He had never quite approved the German-supported putsch of Marshal Antonescu but remained in government service. During his travels from Switzerland to Romania and back he often carried secret messages between former Romanian foreign minister Gafenco, exiled in Geneva, and former prime minister Maniou in Bucharest.

George suggested that, as an official excuse for the journey, the attaché should pretend that he was going to Bucharest on diplomatic business. He would then step off the train at Bistritza and bring Salvadorean papers to the Mandel family. George also asked Manoliou to take along a thousand signed blank copies, which he was to leave with Consul

Lutz in Budapest on his return journey. Lutz and his staff would be asked to fill in the names and to use the documents in addition to his own Schutzbriefe, as he saw fit. Mandel-Mantello had never met the consul, but he had heard that he was saving many Jews and that, unlike many other diplomats, he was a courageous man. He also knew that El Salvador was negotiating with Switzerland to represent its interests in Hungary. Thus their relationship might become official and quite "legal."

Manoliou set out on his journey to Bistritza on May 22, several days later than planned. The suspicious German legation in Berne was annoyingly slow in giving him permission to cross its territory. War conditions, moreover, made travel from Switzerland to Transylvania hazardous. Allied air bombardments increasingly disrupted rail communications. Far worse, the Gestapo, probably tipped off by its secret agents in Berne, arrested Manoliou during his stopover in Vienna and held him for an entire week. They searched his luggage and brought Manoliou to Berlin for questioning at their headquarters, violating all rules governing the immunity of diplomats. The Germans apparently suspected that the Romanian carried secret messages. They were at that time already on edge over rumors about secret Romanian peace feelers, now that the Red Army stood at the country's eastern borders. Luckily, the Gestapo did not find the papers for the Mandel family or the thousand Salvadorean papers destined for Consul Lutz, because upon arriving in Vienna Manoliou had quickly given them to Romanian consular staff, minutes before he was arrested. In the end, he was allowed to continue his journey, after recovering his papers from the consular staff. He was terribly nervous over the repeated delays. The Gestapo gave him strict orders not to leave the train while traveling through Hungary. Manoliou defied the injunction, but when he got off in Bistritza it was already June 3.

Manoliou came up against a wall of silence and complicity. When he knocked at the address given to him by George, he discovered that "Christians" had moved into the house and, they gleefully told him, the Mandels had gone. Casually they pointed with their thumbs toward the northwest and grinned. These people knew, Manoliou thought. Abruptly, the new "owners" shut the door in his face. Upon some further discreet enquiries the Romanian diplomat learned that the Mandel family had been taken away on May 3, exactly one month earlier. They had been brought to a nearby makeshift concentration camp, where they were exposed to cold and heat and starvation. Finally, on May 15, they had been shoved into the cattle cars and deported. According to the Eichmann plan the Jews of Transylvania were the first to go. If the Mandel family had still been held in their small, local concentration camp when Manoliou came, he could have tried to negotiate their release. Now it was too late.

Downcast, the diplomat continued his train journey across the border into Romania and came to Bucharest. From there he managed to telephone George and give him the bad news. Then he spent time briefing his colleagues at the foreign ministry and seeing family and friends. The spirit in Romania was bad. The city suffered from damage caused by air bombardments. The casualty lists from the front were long and became longer. The victory of the 1914–18 war would not be repeated. Even food in this rich agricultural country was becoming scarce, and everyone feared what was going to happen when the Red Army entered the city. Antonescu's regime was evidently cracking.

On his return journey, on June 19, Florian Manoliou passed through Budapest. If he had failed to save the Mandel family, he still possessed the thousand Salvadorean papers that he had intended to deliver to Consul Lutz.

The consul was distraught when he heard the story of the deportation of the Mandel family. He said that again and again people came to him with similar news about those for whom salvation had come too late. No one really knew what was going on, where the enemy would strike and when. If he had known about the Mandels, he could have gone to Bistritza himself or sent someone reliable with letters of protection. But the deportations were happening at such terrifying speed, and the SS and the Hungarian gendarmes had created an incredibly well-oiled machine of death. And then there was this wall of silence. Lutz added angrily, how easy it would have been for Pilet-Golaz or anyone else at the foreign ministry in Berne to telephone Mr. Mandel-Mantello in Geneva, 100 miles away, after they had read the Auschwitz Protocol, in order to see what rapid political measures must be taken. The document, after all, announced the destruction of Hungary's Jews! Instead, all he, Lutz, ever heard from Berne was to be careful and not to become so involved with "the Jews." He should be a little less emotional, please. The Germans, as the consul knew himself, did not like it if Switzerland became too active in this delicate matter. Neither did the British, really, because of Palestine. The Americans, moreover, showed little enthusiasm for opening their doors to Jewish immigrants. There could be German spies among them! President Roosevelt's government pretended, moreover, that it did not want to arouse the already latent antisemitism in the country. Little Switzerland, according to Pilet-Golaz and his cohorts, must be careful how it dealt with these big powers. This was the refrain of nearly all of the correspondence from his foreign ministry at home. Lutz cursed, quite against his custom. If their Swiss ancestors had always been so considerate with the tender feelings of the big powers of their day, they would never have become independent. These people at the Federal Palace either slept on both of their ears or lacked even a minimum of goodwill or courage. Most likely, they were simply indifferent to human suffering.

The Auschwitz Protocol? Manoliou asked curiously when the consul's anguish had subsided. What was that?

This, Lutz answered, was a terrifying description of the death camp of Auschwitz, apparently the biggest ever established by the Germans. The Auschwitz Protocol, as it came to be called, he said, was written by two young Slovak Jews, who in early April had managed the incredible feat of escaping. Yes, Lutz raised his finger, over two months ago! He described the contents of the document: the deportation trains, the gas chambers, the furnaces. He, Lutz, and Minister Jaeger had sent a copy to Foreign Minister Pilet-Golaz in Berne, as soon as they had received the document, in early May. Moreover, Vrba and Lanik, as the two young authors were called, not only described the camp. They said that ever since January 1944 the death machine was getting into high gear in order to receive Hungary's Jewry, three-quarters of a million human beings. Lutz stopped. His eyes looked feverish, and he repeated the figure. Three-quarters of a million. The paper was translated from Slovak into German and dispatched by underground to various key people in Europe. Lutz said he did not know how it was done, but the Jewish underground seemed to function marvelously well. One copy was brought to Budapest by Dr. Kasztner, where it was translated into Hungarian. Vrba and Lanik had above all insisted that the threatened mass of Hungarian Jews be immediately alerted so that they could get ready to defend themselves. They also wanted to let the neutral and the Allied countries know that they must come and help. No time was to be lost. But what happened? Nothing, absolutely nothing. Dr. Kasztner himself, a Jew, insisted it was best to remain quiet. The Germans might become upset and do "bad things" to the Jews. He persuaded the Hungarian Jewish Council to sit on this vital knowledge. Moreover, Kasztner — was he mad or simply imprudent? — even showed a copy of the Auschwitz Protocol to Eichmann. The SS man pooh-poohed the report as wild imagination. He who organized the deportations, imagine! As soon as he, Lutz, received a copy of the Auschwitz Protocol he asked Minister Jaeger to send it to Pilet-Golaz by diplomatic courier. The foreign minister might accept it more easily if it came from a minister rather than from a simple consul. Did the foreign minister react or send it on to the Allied powers? No. The other neutral ministers did not fare better with their foreign ministers. The silence was resounding. The neutral ministers stationed in Budapest decided to protest to the Hungarian government on their own, without waiting for instructions from home. The papal nuncio, Angelo Rotta, bless his heart, wrote the protest. What was the effect? The Sztojay government denied everything, even though the deportations had already started. The prime minister said that these Jews, old people and children included, were simply sent to labor service in Germany. It was as if a common blindness to evil had befallen the world, which acted like the three legendary monkeys who saw nothing, heard nothing, and said nothing. And therefore did nothing. The consul added that, while his letters of protection were saving many thousands of Jews, he knew that if he went beyond certain limits, he could be declared persona non grata and sent out of the country. If that happened, all his Jewish employees and the thousands whom he was protecting would be condemned. It was a situation to drive one mad.

The consul fell silent. But was he doing everything that could be done? He wondered. Was it right to blame others? He should have reacted immediately when it was clear that Pilet-Golaz would not act. He remembered the time, long past, when he walked from his parents' house in Walzenhausen toward Meldegg, praying that Jesus would make him do something great. Now Jesus had walked by him, offered him greatness, and he had not seized it. He had not even seen Jesus. The consul shook his head. Child's phantasies, he mumbled.

The truth was far worse than Manoliou had imagined. The "labor camp" to which the Mandels had been sent now had a name. It had unspeakable contours. For a long time he said nothing. What would George Mandel-Mantello say?

Could he see the Auschwitz Protocol? he finally asked Lutz. Yes, of course, there was one copy left in the house. Dr. Manoliou could take the extra one back to Switzerland in order to give it to Mr. Mandel-Mantello. He certainly would want to know. It would be of better use there than lying around in his consulate.

The consul went to his safe. There, on top of a pile of his Schutzpässe, the protective passports that contained the names of all Schutzbrief holders in Hungary, lay the ominous document. This description of death rested on top of the books of life, the consul jested. He took it out and hesitated. Under no circumstance must Dr. Manoliou say he received the Auschwitz Protocol from him, Lutz. If the matter leaked out, the German minister to Switzerland, Otto Koecher, would be on Pilet-Golaz's back, saying that the Swiss consul in Budapest had leaked a piece of *Kriegsgreuelpropaganda*, war horror propaganda. Pilet-Golaz might make him return to Switzerland in disgrace, just to please the Nazis. One never knew.

A ruse occurred to Lutz, as it unfailingly did when he tried to get around a problem. He would let Moshe Krausz, who was in charge of his Department of Emigration, give Manoliou the paper in his place. Although Krausz was formally under his jurisdiction and protection, he still represented the Jewish Agency for Palestine in Budapest. In that capacity, he could turn over this key document to someone like Mr. Mandel-Mantello, who was outside the Swiss diplomatic services. No one could accuse him, the consul, of violating formal procedures.

They went down into the basement. On the way they passed a crowd of nervous applicants, who were lining up at the Emigration Department for Schutzbriefe. Near the main entrance, some Chalutzim argued with people who feared that if they went out in the streets, they would run into the arms of the gendarmes, despite their protective letters. This was

134

not so, the Chalutzim replied, the Schutzbriefe were really effective. Perhaps, was the answer, but they only had one life. True, but if this legation was bursting with refugees, the gendarmes and the SS would come in and take everybody out. If so, no one would stay alive.

Everybody's life was hanging on a thin thread, the consul whispered. Manoliou nodded and said that he, the consul, was himself that thin thread. It was better not to think of it, Lutz answered.

As always, Moshe Krausz sat in his office alone, despite the commotion outside his room, amid paper piles that grew by the day, typing on an ancient Remington that had seen better days. He had a secretary but preferred to write all the correspondence himself, sharing no information.

The thin bespectacled man was not keen at the intrusion. The consul introduced the Romanian visitor and summarized Manoliou's trip to Bistritza in the vain effort to save the parents of Mr. Mandel-Mantello. Krausz said he was very sorry to hear that, even though he did not know the Mandel family. But when Lutz explained that he wanted Krausz to turn over the last copy of the Auschwitz Protocol to Dr. Manoliou for Mr. Mandel-Mantello in Geneva, Krausz objected. He said that if he was to contact anyone in Switzerland, the addressee was not Mr. Mandel-Mantello but Dr. Chaim Pozner, the representative of the Jewish Agency of Palestine in Geneva. This was his official counterpart. If the consul wanted to send the Auschwitz Protocol to Mr. Mandel-Mantello through Dr. Manoliou himself, he should by all means do so, but not through him, Krausz. Patiently Lutz explained to Krausz that this might result in difficulties, because if Pilet-Golaz found out that he was passing on confidential documents to non-official, private contacts, he, Lutz, would get into trouble. The foreign minister was a stickler over protocol and procedures. He asked Krausz to be just a little flexible for the sake of an important cause. Surely, Mr. Mandel-Mantello would not object to sharing the report with Dr. Pozner, the consul said. Krausz was adamant. Rules were rules, he replied. Where would the world be, if all the rules were broken? But Lutz argued that if he had stuck to all the rules imposed on him, Krausz would not even be sitting here. Without him breaking all the rules in the book, where would Krausz and his family and all the employees of the former Jewish Agency office be? Krausz relented.

135

They agreed to a compromise. Manoliou would take the Auschwitz Protocol to Pozner. It would be accompanied by a letter from Krausz, in which he would describe the present situation. Whatever happened at the Geneva end and who else would read the letter was no longer his responsibility. Thus, formality and peace were restored.

Lutz returned to his office, and Krausz began to rattle away at his ancient Remington, typing "Dear Dr. Pozner . . . ," while Manoliou waited. The Romanian would have liked to look into the Auschwitz Protocol, but Krausz kept it possessively next to him. He observed Krausz's bureaucratic face. It became softer as he wrote. Sometimes he stopped typing, shook his head and sighed, and typed again. At one point he asked Manoliou what would happen if the Germans stopped and searched him, as they had before. Was he not risking his life this time? He would take the chance, Manoliou said. He would tell the Gestapo the Auschwitz Protocol was no longer a secret, since Eichmann himself had seen it, too! Krausz laughed.

Manoliou took the night train to Vienna, and toward evening of the next day, June 20, he reached Geneva. The Gestapo pretended not to see him. He had hidden the papers somewhere between documents written in Romanian and in the midst of a few Romanian wine bottles. The controllers only checked his diplomatic passport and left his luggage alone. However, as long as he was on Hungarian and German soil Manoliou did not dare to pull out the Auschwitz Protocol and Krausz's letter. What would happen, he imagined, if all of a sudden some unknown person, perhaps a female Gestapo agent, a Mata Hari, sat down opposite him, enticing him in conversation, asking what interesting paper he was reading? One word would lead to another, until he was trapped, perhaps not in bed with her, but in prison, waiting for execution.

He took out the hidden Auschwitz Protocol as soon as he crossed the Swiss border at Buchs. Feverishly he studied it from end to end, and started again, until its letters and words had burned themselves deeply into his brain. He read about preparations at the camp, the arriving trains, the selection of the deportees by medical doctors — how could that distinguished profession stoop so low? — the gas chambers, the fire ovens. In his imagination he saw the ominous chimneys rise above a green countryside, and he accompanied the units of prisoners who threw the ashes into ponds and across fields. He read Krausz's letter and realized that this bureaucrat was capable of emotion. In the letter he had poured out his heart: Up to June 7, 1944, he wrote, over 300,000 Jews had been deported to Auschwitz. All of Hungary's Jewry was condemned to death. He himself did not know how long he would stay alive. He called for help, but did not know what precisely he must ask. This simple, insecure person bore a responsibility far beyond his capacities, under circumstances that would drive stronger men to madness. He was perhaps a bureaucrat, because this had always been his line of defense against the more powerful who tried to push him around. What security indeed was there for him, Krausz, and the other Jewish staff inside the former American legation? The one thin thread indeed . . . the consul. Manoliou shuddered.

He had no eyes for the passing peaceful countryside, the rolling wooded hills of Switzerland and the lakes reflecting the early summer sunshine; he did not hear the chatting and laughing of fellow passengers, who in their pardonable ignorance acted as if the smokestacks of Auschwitz darkened the skies of another planet and not that of their own. He was thinking of other trains, which pulled cattle wagons past different wooded hills and alongside other water courses that reflected the same sun, trains that were speeding toward gas chambers and furnaces. By the time he arrived in Geneva sweat poured from his forehead, and he was shaking as if he had fever.

*   *   *

The moon was already rising over the nearby mountain ranges on that evening of June 20 when the Romanian diplomat knocked at the door of the Salvadorean general consulate in Geneva. George Mandel-Mantello was waiting, sitting on edge. At last, you're here! he shouted, but tears fell from his eyes.

It's important, Manoliou said, for you to read this document. He gave George the Auschwitz Protocol. It explained everything, he said. It was worse than ten thousand crime novels put together. He had received it in Budapest from Consul Lutz, when he had gone to give him the thousand

Salvadorean papers. The document was a sinister and horrible one, written by two young Slovak Jews who had escaped from the death camp. The truth was that the Jews were not sent to German labor camps — this was a big lie spread by both the German and the Hungarian governments — but that they were, without exception, deported, gassed, and burned at Auschwitz. Manoliou wished he didn't have to talk about it. This meant, Mandel-Mantello asked, that his parents had died at Auschwitz? Manoliou nodded. It was a painful story to tell, because it extinguished even the slightest flicker of hope for any rescue action. Manoliou was himself in tears, but he could not wait any longer before telling what he knew.

The Romanian diplomat sat quietly and watched Mandel-Mantello read. George moaned. A wild pain surged up in him. His gentle mother, his good father dead, murdered. They had never done harm to anyone, they had known the Talmud inside out and remembered how the Almighty had unfailingly rushed to rescue the children of Israel whenever they were in danger. Others in the wider family had died, too, an entire active and gifted community, children, old people, those in the best years of their life, whose faces drifted past his inner eye in one painful parade, and whose voices came back to him. How they must have suffered! Had they seen his image in their dying moment? He shook his fist. If he had only done something about it earlier.

It was a night of pain and hatred and despair, which he would never forget. The truth had seized him without mercy.

But George Mandel-Mantello did not lament long. He carefully listened as Manoliou told him the rest of his travel story. He mentioned the bureaucratic complications caused by Moshe Krausz, who had insisted that he, Manoliou, was obliged to turn over the Auschwitz Protocol to Chaim Pozner, the representative of the Jewish Agency for Palestine in Geneva. Krausz had also written a letter to Pozner, not a bad one at that. Krausz had finally agreed that George Mandel-Mantello could see both the Auschwitz Protocol and the letter. This seemed a weird procedure, Manoliou said, but Krausz was a bureaucrat. Even Consul Lutz had complained.

Mandel-Mantello became the efficient business executive again. He said that if Pozner — nothing against him, of course — got the Auschwitz Protocol and Krausz's letter, he would simply pass them on to his superiors in Palestine, who probably had received copies already. At best, precious weeks would go by as before, while the public was kept ignorant and thousands more died. Something drastic needed to be done to shake the world out of its lethargy, even at this late stage.

What did he have in mind? Manoliou asked. George's mind raced. What he was about to propose might not be quite legal, he said, but neither were Consul Lutz's actions quite legal. And the killing of hundreds of thousands of human beings was the least legal of all. George did not spell his plan out. He told his Romanian friend to go to sleep. There was a bed ready for him in the apartment. He had done his job, he had even risked life and career, and he, George, was more than grateful. He wanted to be left alone in order to think.

Feverishly, Mandel-Mantello worked all night. First, he edited the long text of the Auschwitz Protocol to manageable proportions, leaving the essential elements in. No one would read it otherwise. Then he took the letter of Moshe Krausz, replaced Pozner's name with his own as the addressee, and added a triple plea at the end: *Helfet, helfet, helfet!* Help, help, help! He would make his secretary retype the letter the next day. He intended to use the modified letter for publicity purposes.

When morning came, an exhausted Mandel-Mantello told Manoliou to bring the originals to Pozner.

George Mandel-Mantello lost no time, even though the thought of Bistritza made him ache.

First, he alerted the members of the Swiss-Hungarian Aid Committee in Geneva. Second, before noon he was on the train to Zurich, where he met with other members of that committee. The group included Jews and Christians. Among the latter was Reformed pastor Paul Vogt from Walzenhausen. Vogt was the well-known minister to refugees, who had open-minded supporters behind him. The Swiss authorities detested him for his outspoken language. Was it a mere coincidence that he, too, was from the home town of Consul Lutz?

Greatly shocked, the members of the Zurich committee studied the Auschwitz Protocol and the letter of Moshe Krausz. Chief Rabbi Kornfein, himself from Hungary, lamented: "We really should tear our clothes in the face of this disaster, which reminds us of the destruction of

139

the temple of Jerusalem and makes us weep over the countless innocent children, mothers and old people, whom the barbarians are murdering so brutally." The group agreed with George Mandel-Mantello that the wall of silence must be broken down, cost what it may, and that copies of the shortened Auschwitz Protocol and Krausz's letter be sent to the churches, members of parliament, opinion makers, and the public at large. Government officials everywhere be damned! It was midnight when the meeting ended. George Mandel-Mantello was officially charged to take on the world.

On June 22, after only a few hours of rest, he mimeographed a thousand copies of the two documents with the help of Pastor Vogt. They were dispatched immediately. In order to get around Swiss censorship regulations, which forbade the publication of overt "anti-German propaganda" coming out of Switzerland, George adopted another ruse. He added an Istanbul dateline, making believe that the Auschwitz Protocol had originated from there. Turkey was, after all, another neutral country and news from there could not be suspected. If critical publicity had a non-Swiss and especially neutral dateline, it could be published. As it turned out, Swiss censors, afraid of bad German reactions, challenged even this version, because they realized that the supposed neutral origin of the two documents was not authentic. They ordered publication stopped.

This time the newspaper editors rebelled. For four years, they protested, they had been subject to humiliating restrictions imposed by their own government, just to be nice to the Hitler regime. They must submit to such non-democratic measures in order to avoid a German invasion or economic strangling, so they had been told. This threat was wearing thin, and the nation's independence needed to be reasserted. The editors held that the authorities had no right to withhold the awful truth about Auschwitz, whether this pleased the Germans or not. They said they would rather go to jail than obey false orders.

With this rebellion Swiss wartime censorship collapsed, and the country again breathed freely, while the shocking truth about the misdeeds of the Nazi regime, which people had suspected all along, was fully revealed. No less than 200 Swiss papers published the story on their front page.

An appeal for the deportations to stop was published, signed by four well-known theologians: Karl Barth from Basel, Emil Brunner from Zurich, Alfons Koechlin, the president of the Protestant Federation, and W. A. Visser 't Hooft, the Dutch general secretary of the nascent World Council of Churches in Geneva. Mandel-Mantello and Vogt had not even troubled to ask for Barth's permission to put his name down, though he was the best-known of the four. They assumed that he agreed anyway. When the upset censors came to ask the theologian whether he was co-signer to this illegal statement, he at first did not know what it was all about. The censors shoved the text under his nose. He read it and said it was excellent: "Can't you read? Don't you see my name at the bottom?" Then he threw the censors out of his house.

George Mandel-Mantello, the Jewish refugee from Hungary, may not have been fully aware of it at that moment, but his courageous action resulted in a kind of Swiss coup d'état.

Even Marcel Pilet-Golaz, who had really been the indirect cause of this twisted correspondence, regained courage. When Koecher, the arrogant German minister to Switzerland, called on him, protesting against this *Kriegsgreuelpropaganda,* the Swiss foreign minister told him coldly that it was up to the German government to prove that the horror stories were not true. Denials alone were not sufficient. Why not, Pilet-Golaz suggested, invite representatives of the International Committee of the Red Cross to visit Auschwitz? To which the German diplomat replied, more humbly, that he would refer the idea to Ribbentrop. He was most upset that he was losing his clout and that the Alpine republic could no longer be threatened. There was nothing further the German minister could say.

In unison the Swiss press lashed out at their murderous neighbor to the north, making up for four years of imposed silence and humiliation. Local communities took up the protest, and Pastor Vogt rushed from church assembly to church assembly, raising his voice against deportations and the death camps. Resolution after resolution was addressed to the Hungarian government and to the German legation, and Minister Koecher's shock knew no bounds.

But George Mandel-Mantello already thought about the world beyond neutral Switzerland. He saw to it that the Swedish press took up the Auschwitz story. It caused consternation in Sweden, which, though neutral, had, perhaps even more than Switzerland, entertained close commercial and military ties with the Nazi state. Archbishop Söderblom added his weighty voice to the emerging protest and spoke with the nation's authorities.

But this was not enough. On June 23 Mandel-Mantello saw to it that an English version of the Auschwitz Protocol and of the Krausz letter was transmitted abroad. By nightfall he gave a copy to Walter Garrett, the Zurich representative of the British news chain, the Exchange Telegraph Company. Garrett cabled an abbreviated version of the two documents to major British and American papers. He happened to be the son-in-law of British cabinet minister Austin Chamberlain — Neville's brother — and was therefore well connected with the British establishment. The Exchange Telegraph Company, it was said, was a front organization of British Intelligence Services, and its representatives supposedly also had other, parallel functions. It is not astounding, therefore, that Garrett cabled copies of his translations to the governments in London and Washington.

Now all hell broke loose.

The primate of the Church of England, William Temple, went on the radio and denounced the deportations. At St. Patrick's Cathedral in New York, Cardinal Francis Spellman castigated the Hungarian government and called on Catholics in the United States and in Hungary to rise up against the evil of racial persecution. Jewish organizations held protests in Madison Square Garden, and thousands turned up. They demanded that the U.S. government tell the nation what was really happening to Jews in Europe. In Washington, President Roosevelt pricked up his ears. He planned to run for a fourth term the coming November and could not dispense with the Jewish vote. He set up the War Refugee Board, which was to rescue Jews. Unfortunately the president seemed unable to finance it, and, much against their grain, government officials had to approach Jewish organizations to give them money for the operation.

Thus, within a few short days after a tired Florian Manoliou had knocked at the door of the Salvadorean general consulate in Geneva, the world knew, and the spirit released by George Mandel-Mantello could not be squeezed back into the bottle again.

*　　*　　*

A surprised junior diplomat by the name of Imre Tahy at the Hungarian legation in Berne surveyed the disastrous media reports on his country and sent a lengthy report home. He was doubtless unaware of what Pilet-Golaz had said to Minister Koecher, but in his report to Budapest he suggested the same, namely that if the Hungarian government wished to counteract this "misinformation," it had to produce credible proof that the deportations had not taken place. Nothing else would do. Tahy did not receive a reply.

A startled Horthy woke up at last from his stupor. He realized that the international press campaign was serious and that something had to be done. It was not that the regent had been ignorant of what was going on, as he later pretended in his memoirs, because shortly after the German occupation deportation plans had been discussed by the Sztojay government. Horthy was informed and did not object. Even Veesenmayer confirmed Horthy's indifference. He told the judges of the International Military Court at Nuremberg a few years later that the regent used "a very nasty word" when he discussed the "Jewish problem" with him. He wanted to rid Hungary of its Jews, the regent had said, the rich perhaps excepted. Horthy was among the early recipients of the Auschwitz Protocol. Moreover, he had received discreet and respectful remonstrations from church leaders. Now his own family members heard what was going on and became scared and his wife cried. The matter was in the open. Everybody talked about it. Foreign governments ridiculed Hungary's self-designation as a "chivalrous nation." This was intolerable, because Horthy thought of himself as a man of honor who was ruling a nation of honor by the grace of God. Besides, the country was weakening militarily and economically each day the war lasted. How could Hungary justify itself at future peace negotiations? Would it suffice to throw the blame on the Germans? What if the victors brought him to military court like an ordinary war criminal?

On June 25 Angelo Rotta handed to the regent the Holy Father's protest against the deportations. On the following day, June 26, Consul Lutz gave Döme Sztojay, the prime minister, a strongly worded message from

President Roosevelt. It said that all anti-Jewish measures and deportations had to be stopped immediately. Those responsible would be tried after hostilities ended. When he read the letter, Sztojay became pale. Did he have a premonition that within two years he would be tried and executed? He said he would take the matter into consideration. But he also added that no one had the right to interfere in Hungary's internal affairs. Within days Roosevelt's answer arrived in the form of a severe air bombardment. The Americans wanted to make sure that the president's message was properly understood. Finally, on June 30 the king of Sweden wrote a kindly but nevertheless severe missive to his "friend and brother" Horthy, saying that the deportations were really very bad for Hungary's reputation and that they must be stopped.

During the first few days of the unpleasant international publicity, it was a confused and humbled Sztojay who tried to find a response to what he had thought was none of the world's business. At a Council of Ministers meeting, which was presided over by the prime minister, the the minister of the interior, Jaross, refused any softening of deportation procedures. He was the Hungarian mouthpiece of Veesenmayer and Eichmann, who through him exercised political pressure inside the government. Jaross threatened that the "promises" that Hungary had made to the Führer were sacred and binding. There would be serious repercussions if these agreements were broken.

Veesenmayer saw that because of the "Jewish question" Germany's political hold over the Danube state threatened to fall to pieces. Whether the Jews were killed at Auschwitz or not now became secondary. What really counted now was that the Jews had suddenly become a symbol of Hungary's independence vis-à-vis the Nazi state. If the Magyar state decided to rebel over this issue, the vast Balkan front, of which it was the center, would cave in.

On June 26, finally, the regent tried to recover his lost status and took the reins into his own hands. He called a meeting of the Crown Council, a body that was superior in rank to the Council of Ministers. The deportations must stop, he said. If the Germans wanted to continue, let them do so alone, without Hungarian help. It would be interesting to see how the mere 150 German SS would handle the job. Endre and Baky, the fire eaters, were dismissed. They were the principal links to Eichmann, whom people of a better class did not invite into their living room.

Relieved of duty they might have been, but Endre and Baky kept their job, as if Horthy didn't exist. With Eichmann's support, Baky even set in motion a coup against the regent. If it succeeded, the Jews of Budapest would be deported in one swift, gigantic action. One early July day thousands of cock-feathered armed gendarmes marched through the center of Budapest in a show of strength. One last time the old regent rose to the challenge. He ordered the air raid sirens to sound, and the gendarmes disappeared from the streets, afraid of the bombs. A reliable armored regiment drove toward the capital from Esztergom in the north, and an infantry regiment was rushed in from Szeged in the south. They forced the outmaneuvered gendarmes to leave the city.

Then, on July 8, 1944, a miracle occurred. Horthy, the regent, ordered a stop to the deportations.

*   *   *

Less than two weeks after these events, on July 20, Consul Lutz wrote to George Mandel-Mantello via the diplomatic courier:

> I have learned that you were the "spiritus rector" behind the press action, which has made the world aware of the plight of the Jews of Budapest and in the provinces. I have seen copies of Swiss newspapers which contain extensive reports about the horrors committed against the Hungarian Jews. Those who are responsible for these acts are outraged. They are convinced that the news was transmitted through the Swiss diplomatic pouch. Insofar as I know this was not the case. But the way the information was shared is not important. What counted were its results.

This is a curious letter. It was not really addressed to George Mandel-Mantello but to Foreign Minister Pilet-Golaz, who was bound to read and control it before it was forwarded to Geneva. The consul used this innocently worded letter to forestall accusations from government bureaucrats, including from the foreign minister himself, if they suspected that it had been he who was behind the mighty press campaign, in collusion with Mandel-Mantello. This would have been an unauthorized use of the diplomatic courier and a serious breach of diplomatic protocol. No Swiss diplomat abroad was permitted to engage in political agitation at home. It did not matter whether the consul wanted to save thousands of victims from death or had any other reason. Moreover, as long as Pilet-Golaz was in power Lutz sat on an ejectable chair. How easy it would have been for the foreign minister to recall the recalcitrant consul. Lutz's vast operation to save Jews would have collapsed if a proper bureaucrat had replaced Carl Lutz.

There was a belated and unusual epilogue to these events. Moshe Krausz did not care for the consul's pushing him into unbureaucratic "trickery," whatever the reason was. The fact that tens of thousands of his Jewish coreligionists were saved as a result of Mandel-Mantello's intervention, which surely ought to have given him deep satisfaction, did not prevent Krausz from lashing out angrily at him a quarter of a century later. In 1971 he wrote from Jerusalem that what Mandel-Mantello had done with Krausz's letter of June 19, 1944, was illegal and immoral. Mandel-Mantello had not only changed the name of the addressee from Chaim Pozner to himself but had added the words *Helfet, helfet, helfet!* Even in his old age Krausz could not help acting out the unconditional bureaucrat.

Who will deny that Krausz was right? But if such mediocre banality had governed the spirit of Mandel-Mantello, Manoliou, and Lutz, the journey to Bistritza would never have produced the miracle of July 8.

*   *   *

George Mandel-Mantello died in 1992, one year after the ceremony in Budapest.

7. THE FÜHRER'S WISH

The last summer of the war was hot and uncertain. The western Allies had landed in Normandy in June, and in the east the German armies were massively on the retreat, giving up one stronghold and one river bank after the other, leaving dead and debris behind on a shattered land. In Hungary, as elsewhere in Europe, the end of the war was expected at any moment. But the soldiers kept dying, bomb-shattered walls buried more children than ever before, and Jews, Gypsies, and Soviet prisoners were still gassed at Auschwitz, even though the deportation trains from Hungary no longer came. No end to the disaster was in sight. The oppressed shouted "How long, O Lord!" and shook their fists into a sky that the Stukas and Flying Fortresses had swept clear of angels and illusions — and perhaps of faith in God, or God's faith in his own creatures, whom at the dawn of history he had commanded to "replenish the earth."

In Budapest, the rising summer heat coincided with a curious suspense, where no one quite knew what was to happen next, now that Horthy had dared to defy the Führer. It was as if the air stood still. Germany surely no longer frightened others as it had done a short while ago, but it was like a wounded beast, whose next and perhaps last move no one dared to predict.

Veesenmayer, Eichmann, and their master in Berlin, the Führer, were outraged by Horthy's deportation stop of July 8. The regent's determination to assert his independence would doubtless be subjected to harsh tests.

Eichmann was among the first to note that the regent had failed to im-

147

plement his order with further measures. Horthy did not lift any of the restrictions that had been imposed upon the Jews after March 19. They were not allowed to leave the labor and concentration camps. They still bore the yellow star. No stolen property was returned. On July 12, only four days after the regent's order, the Sonderkommando of the Obersturmbannführer, helped by the Hungarian gendarmes, seized the concentration camp at Kistarcsa, twenty kilometers outside Budapest, and heaved its 1,500 inmates onto a train for Auschwitz.

Surprisingly, Eichmann's vicious attack failed. Members of the Jewish Council heard of it and informed the neutral legations and the church leaders. They all alerted the regent, who for once acted speedily. The train was stopped shortly before it crossed into Slovakia, and the 1,500 were returned to Kistarcsa.

But Horthy naively failed to protect the camp with troops loyal to him, and this led to disaster. After two days, Eichmann brazenly restaged the coup. Before he did so, he invited the members of the Jewish Council for "conversation and coffee" at the Hotel Majestic on Suabian Hill and thereby cut off their outside communication. Only after he received a phone call that the train had safely passed the frontier and was beyond recall to Auschwitz did he dismiss the Jewish Council. They afterward realized that they had been duped.

Even though he was shocked, Horthy swallowed the affront. It was as if the impact of the press campaign in Switzerland and elsewhere was already wearing thin. If the regent had any convictions left, this would have been the moment to expel Eichmann and his Sonderkommando and to punish the gendarmes who had taken part in the two Kistarcsa raids. He did nothing of the sort. Unknown to the public he renewed "negotiations" with Veesenmayer about the resumption of the deportations and finally agreed that these be resumed on August 25, 1944.

Budapest would be made judenrein.

The problem was that in July 1944 the checkmated Hitler regime was not ready to die, as some thought that it reasonably should. It refused to repeat the "mistake" of imperial Germany, which, it claimed, had prematurely signed an armistice on November 11, 1918, and had withdrawn the troops from the front undefeated. At any rate, during World War II the Allied formula of "unconditional surrender" excluded all possibility for an early peace. The Führer discouraged any such talk by hinting that he was was about to unleash some terrible secret weapon, which would reverse the course of the war. Not surprisingly, the western Allies met tough resistance in Normandy and in Italy, and the Red Army progressed only slowly up the eastern foothills of the Carpathians. Even when on July 20 the astounding news flashed around the world that German army officers had almost succeeded killing the Führer, the Nazi regime was not broken. The following final nine months turned out to be the most destructive. Between July 1944 and April 1945 half of all the human losses of the entire war occurred; Europe's age-old cultural heritage and industrial structure was destroyed, not to speak of the deep social and psychic wounds and the vast number of refugees the last months created. Hungary lay in the midst of this upheaval.

*   *   *

Consul Lutz heard rumors about the "negotiations" between Veesenmayer and Horthy concerning the resumption of the deportations. He had enough personal contacts among the foreign ministry officials and politicians of the opposition to put bits and pieces of the puzzle together. Even though he knew few details, he sensed the threat. He felt that after Eichmann's double Kistarcsa coup, the relief gained by Horthy's deportation stop was sliding through his fingers like dry sand.

The consul thought that the moment for a countermove had come, in order to send a signal. On July 21 he, in the company of Minister Jaeger, called on Prime Minister Sztojay with a five-point paper. Lutz asked that the Hungarian government confirm formally the protection of the 8,000 children and young people whose emigration to Palestine had been blocked since March. They were not to be arrested or deported. More than that, he requested that they be allowed to go abroad now. In order to make the Hungarian decision effective, would the Sztojay government officially demand unobstructed transit from the Germans for the emigrants to Black Sea ports, where they could embark for Palestine? Would the Hungarian government, finally, place river boats or third-class passenger cars at the disposal of these children? Lutz, seconded by Minister Jaeger, did not fail to add that such an action would create a most positive impression abroad.

Sztojay was more humble and seemed anxious to please. He actually appeared ashamed of having supported the deportation of hundreds of thousands of his Hungarian fellow citizens to Auschwitz. The threat of the Allies to punish him and others for their crimes disturbed him no end. The prime minister agreed to all of the five proposals. He said that he wanted Hungary and Switzerland to remain good friends, as they had always been. He guaranteed that the 8,000 would be safe. He would instruct the grumbly minister of the interior, Jaross, to issue the necessary exit permits, and he himself would request the German government through Minister Veesenmayer to grant transit permits for the 8,000 through German-held territories.

This was an extraordinary triumph, Minister Jaeger said excitedly, as they left the prime minister's residence. The consul answered more soberly that before they celebrated he had one more appointment. Sztojay may have seen the writing on the wall. But had Veesenmayer or Eichmann? Yes, Jaeger commented, with those two sons-of-bitches anything was possible. He agreed that Lutz should see Eichmann first. If he agreed that the 8,000 were allowed to leave Hungary, he, the Swiss minister, would call on his colleague Veesenmayer, in order to make the agreement official. The detour might be worth a few of Veesenmayer's "Heil Hitlers" and some flasks of expensive perfume for Gertrud.

*   *   *

The Hungarian plain was shimmering in the heat as Szluha drove the consul up Suabian Hill to the Hotel Majestic. Eichmann had opened up the collar of his uniform as he received Lutz. He said, mockingly, that he would like to offer his visitor a bottle of Munich Hofbräu beer, which he was keeping on ice, but as the consul was one of the rare diplomats in the world who didn't drink, would a cup of coffee do? That was fine with Lutz. Apart from the heat, everything remained unchanged at the hotel — the guards, the barbed wire, occasional gendarmerie officers. Even the picture with the dull family faces remained on the desk. But the Obersturmbannführer seemed more self-assured. He had, in the meantime, fulfilled the order of his Führer in successfully dispatching over half of Hungary's Jews to their death. Unlike Sztojay, neither Eichmann's conscience nor Allied threats for punishment seemed to trouble him.

Lutz shuddered as he sat opposite the monster who did not look like a monster. He appeared such an ordinary human being, Lutz thought, sipping his coffee. He could be a neighbor with whom one could chat across the garden fence about the best ways of trimming rosebushes, or about hospital operations, or about the children who were growing up. Nothing profound. Lutz thought maybe he should ask Eichmann about his dull-looking brood, whether they missed their father who sacrificed himself in the service of the Führer. He had to pull himself together against any temptation that would reveal his personal aversion. Any such cynical question could turn the family man into a spiteful SS Obersturmbannführer. He had to keep the monster cheerful and unsuspecting and could not afford to gamble away the lives of the 8,000. He had also come to Suabian Hill in order to detect the reality behind the rumors about the planned extinction of the Jews of Budapest, a quarter of a million of them.

The coffee was surprisingly good, not like the usual ersatz chicory brew of Europe at war. The SS evidently had access to black market delicacies that were beyond the reach of most ordinary people.

Eichmann laughed almost discourteously, as he guessed what disturbed the consul's mind, asking how he could help Herr Konsul. Lutz put his coffee cup down. He said he would like to resume the conversation he had had with the Obersturmbannführer after the —, well, after his arrival in Budapest on March 19. He said that he and Minister Jaeger had just come from a very good talk with Prime Minister Sztojay, who agreed that Hungary had no objection whatever to letting the 8,000 children and young people go to Palestine. His Excellency had promised to instruct the various government ministries accordingly. He had also said that he would request from Minister Veesenmayer that German transit permits be given to the émigrés so that they could travel to Black Sea ports and sail to Palestine without further delay.

The consul's host laughed again and joked that to him Herr

Konsul looked like Moses in the Bible who was coming to Pharaoh, wanting the Israelites to be freed. Lutz smiled, but thought the comparison in bad taste. He said he was glad to know that the Obersturmbannführer knew Holy Writ so profoundly. The comparison was well taken. But he, Lutz, had no walking stick that could be turned into a serpent. What did the consul want from him? Eichmann asked. To make the waters of the Red Sea recede? The consul said, like the first time they met, he would like the Obersturmbannführer to lend a hand in the transport of the 8,000.

Eichmann asked why they were talking once again about the same subject as in March. The consul said the answer was simple. The 8,000 were still waiting to go to Palestine. The Obersturmbannführer pretended to reflect, and his right hand smoothed his thinning hair. Then he said that the consul had really come at an opportune moment. If he had not done so, he himself would have visited him at the former American legation. Lutz was all attention. Eichmann continued, his superiors in Berlin had indeed not forgotten the request Herr Konsul had made in the spring concerning the 8,000. But the decision had to be postponed, because everybody had been so terribly busy. He apologized for the delay. However, he wanted to repeat that the German government still remembered the consul's skill and commitment when he represented German interests in Palestine in 1939. Eichmann fully faced the consul, as if he wanted to gain his entire attention. He was now speaking formally on behalf of the German government, which already knew about Prime Minister Sztojay's request to Minister Veesenmayer. His government had decided that it would not object to the emigration of the 8,000. The Obersturmbannführer's voice became solemn. The good news was that the requested transit permits for the 8,000 had been approved by the Führer himself, who had given the order, in appreciation of the consul's work in Palestine.

The SS man paused, in order to let his impressive-sounding words take their effect on his listener. For a moment the consul did not say a word, and almost open-mouthed he stared at Eichmann. This was a historic breakthrough, and perhaps he had misjudged the goodwill of the Obersturmbannführer and, who knew, of Hitler himself. The two men rose. The consul could barely disguise his relief. He said he would of course see Minister Veesenmayer right away in order to complete the formal arrangements. He would also go to the Hungarian authorities, telling them that this transport was at last being made ready, thanks to German cooperation. There was much work to be done, exit papers, transit visas, details of transportation, etc. To move 8,000 persons in wartime was, after all, no small thing.

There was one additional matter that Herr Konsul must take into consideration, Eichmann said casually, and Lutz looked at him in sudden suspicion. While the Führer did concede the 8,000, the consul must under no circumstance try to request additional exceptions, otherwise the 8,000 could no longer be "available" to the consul. All the others would have to be sent to labor service in Germany. Eichmann said he hoped that the consul saw the extent of the Führer's wish. Once the 8,000 were to be sent to Palestine, none of the consul's additional Schutzbriefe would be recognized. But even with such restrictions, was not the Führer's offer generous and unusual?

Lutz felt as if a cudgel had hit him, and he had to hold on to Eichmann's desk. As from far away he heard the words of the Obersturmbannführer, which were dropping from his lips like hard pebbles. It had come to his ears, Eichmann said in his indifferent voice, that the consul, aided by his wild Jewish staff, was giving protection to hundreds of Jews within the former American legation building, and, moreover, that the Gestapo had calculated that several tens of thousands of Schutzbriefe had been distributed left and right, to all kinds of people, thereby subtracting these from labor service. The consul was really damaging Germany's war economy. Eichmann began to threaten. He said that several times he had driven by Freedom Square, and each time an entire swarm of people — mostly Jews — were hanging near the entry of the consul's headquarters. There was coming and going of young Jews and opposition leaders; the activity was incredible. The consul's own office was a mere two floors higher, right above the entry. Had he never noticed what was going on just below his eyes? Of course, Herr Konsul had. Eichmann's voice was vicious. This was a nest of spies he was directing. In the heart of the capital of a country allied with Germany. What the consul was doing was truly intolerable, inimical to

German interests. The Führer was fully informed and he was really very angry, because the consul's activities were not only illegal, but they ran amok of international law. The Führer was nevertheless a merciful and generous person and the offer for the emigration of the 8,000 still stood, despite everything. But only if Herr Konsul complied with the Führer's wish and put his house in order. Thus far, the Führer had refrained from lodging a complaint with the Swiss government, because he did not wish to disturb his good relations with Berne. But he was upset, and the consul must know it.

This was a Faustian offer, Lutz realized, accompanied by a threat. The lives of the 8,000 children and young people, whose security he wanted so badly, weighed against the lives of tens of thousands more. And to "impose order" on Freedom Square.

Lutz was dumbfounded and then angry. Was this really the Führer's wish? he asked pointedly. Yes, Eichmann answered, adding that Herr Konsul should think carefully about the offer and everything else he had just been told. The opportunity would not present itself again.

The consul thanked Eichmann for the coffee and left.

What Consul Lutz did not know at this moment, although he suspected it, was that Eichmann had no authority to make the Faustian offer concerning the lives of the 8,000 against the lives of all of the other Budapest Jews. But the Obersturmbannführer knew Hitler's mind too well to make a mistake. He was certain that the Führer himself would have spoken to the Swiss consul in this way, had the two met in person.

In fact, Sztojay's request for German help with transit permits and transportation had not even been transmitted to Berlin by the time Lutz went to see Eichmann, and no decision could have come down from the Führer. The request was purposely blocked up and down all diplomatic channels. It began with Sztojay himself. Only timidly and after much delay did he pass the Swiss request for the transit visas on to Veesenmayer, who wrote to Ribbentrop at his leisure, who in turn raised the "problem" with Hitler between more urgent issues, and sent the answer to the Hungarian capital when he found the time. When he finally did, he instructed Veesenmayer to deal with the Swiss consul in a "dilatory way," until the 8,000 could be included in the larger "resettlement project."

Rumors were flying around Budapest that Eichmann, Interior Minister Jaross, and the frustrated gendarmes were preparing that larger project and that there would be no exceptions, not even for the 8,000. The second Kistarcsa coup was evidence of what was to come. It was a clear sign that the Horthy deportation stop was nothing more than an empty show in order to make himself a good image abroad. The regent had neither the power nor the will to clean up house. The least that he could have done in his weak position was to call on his people to resist further German encroachment through public disobedience to the orders of the occupying force. But Horthy was more afraid of the Communists than of the Nazis. He did not want to open the sluice gates for the Red Army.

But there were some, including Jews, who fell back into their old illusions and believed that the regent had things well in hand.

Thus, in mid-summer 1944 Budapest hung between hope and despair.

* * *

Consul Lutz had faced up to German power before, and he had no intention of submitting this time. But Eichmann's threat to the former American legation building had to be taken seriously. If the SS came, they would certainly carry away the leaders of the Chalutzim and execute them in some dark corner. Then there was the staff of the Emigration Department, including Moshe Krausz and his family, and the Hungarian opposition leaders who had found refuge with the consul. The attackers would get hold of the address lists of Jews who had received letters of protection. The disaster would be unthinkable. Lutz also remembered having heard from Jaeger about hints from Veesenmayer that the manifold activities in and around the building on Freedom Square were undignified for a diplomatic representation. As if the deportations were more dignified! To make matters worse, even Swiss foreign minister Pilet-Golaz and his advisors had once again sent notes from Berne to the effect that the consul was becoming much too involved in "Jewish questions." Minister Koecher must have come back, complaining, as he always did. The representation of foreign powers, Pilet-Golaz and his advisors wrote, did not mean that he should primarily engage in the protection of Jews. There were plenty of other jobs to be done. The Jews were, after all, national citizens and were juridically speaking out of bounds. Did the consul realize that he was interfering in the internal affairs of a foreign country? True, true, he was. But Pilet-Golaz, the son of a Reformed pastor and a lawyer-politician, who had diligently worked his way up from local into national politics and who knew that confined little world very well, looked at the universe from his oak-panelled chancellery in Berne, from where he could contemplate the snow-covered Alps, a world that was far removed from the horrors of gendarmes breaking into houses at night and pushing people into tightly loaded cattle wagons or shooting them by the roadside. Pilet-Golaz was not a bad man. He was a humanist in the classic sense, like Lutz had been before he had come to Hungary. But the foreign minister did not have to look into the faces of those who ran for their lives.

An attack on the building at Freedom Square was of course conceivable. Eichmann was profoundly resentful, and he considered the Swiss consul to be a major obstacle to his and the Führer's objectives.

Lutz reflected on his dilemma and talked with Minister Jaeger. Then he decided that the Emigration Department must be removed from the American legation building. But it had to remain within easy reach and, above all, it had to be safe. For the sake of outward appearances it was important that the legation building regain its former "dignity," and that the people milling around the entry on Freedom Square did not provide an excuse for an attack. He had to go one step backward, in order to gain two steps forward.

The Chalutzim leaders, Rafi Friedl and Alexander Grossman, found a suitable building in nearby Vadasz Street in the old business section of Pest. The building belonged to a Jewish wholesale glass merchant, Arthur Weisz. Influenced by modern Bauhaus architecture after the war of 1914–18, Weisz had erected the three-story building in this dark little street at number 29. It was almost entirely sheeted with large glass windows, which let in the largest possible amount of light. The glass house, as it came to be called, stood in wholesome contrast to the surrounding heavy fin-de-siècle buildings of downtown Pest. The consul went to see the glass merchant and negotiated a deal with him, whereby the glass house would become an annex to the Swiss legation. Weisz, like all Jews, was out of business, and he and his family were hiding in a small apartment out of view from the street side, trembling and waiting for the knock at the door. He was relieved, because Lutz's offer meant a new lease on life. His house was to have extraterritorial status, and he himself gained a small rental income. Moreover, the consul invited him to work with his Department of Emigration. He and his family were likely to survive.

Then the consul talked with Dénes Csopey, the head of the Political Department of the Hungarian foreign ministry. Over the years he had discovered that this multilingual and intelligent official, who was in charge of drafting diplomatic notes, had the ear of each succeeding foreign minister. Csopey's present superior was Mihaly Arnothy-Jungerth, the deputy foreign minister, who was said to have little sympathy for the government's anti-Jewish measures. He considered these damaging to Hungary's reputation. Both he and Csopey disliked Veesenmayer and Eichmann personally, even though they prudently hid their antipathy. The foreign ministry, contrary to the rightist-dominated ministry of the interior, had always looked with discreet favor upon the activities of the Swiss consul. Lutz was their one link to civilization.

Thus, to the surprise of all Budapest and the entire diplomatic corps, Consul Lutz extended Swiss diplomatic immunity to the glass house on Vadasz Street, and in a swift and well-organized move he transferred employees and files out of the former American legation building. Almost physically the Chalutzim lifted poor Moshe Krausz, who didn't like the change at all, away from Freedom Square to the glass house and installed him with his piles of papers and his Remington typewriter in a new office, where he promptly locked himself in and once again did his own thing. A large brass plaque was attached next to the entry of the glass house, stating in Hungarian and in German: Legation of Switzerland, Department of Emigration. Above the entry hung a large Swiss flag with the white cross in the red field. The glass house, as extra-territorial ground, was out of bounds for military or police, and the shiny building became a beehive of activity. Those who sought letters of protection went there, and if there were Jewish families who felt especially threatened, the Chalutzim let them come in and locked the door firmly behind them, until the glass house was nearly bursting at the seams. Passersby walking along Vadasz Street would see hundreds of faces peering at them from behind the large windows. If quick decisions had to be made, the Chalutzim would rush to the consul on Freedom Square, who thus managed to control his ebullient team of co-workers in a situation of organized permanent near-chaos.

The Chalutzim spread the news of the glass house among the Jews of Budapest. Soon, a permanent cluster of Schutzbrief seekers and of those who desperately sought security hung around Vadasz Street. Pressure increased, so that the consul extended Swiss diplomatic immunity to an adjacent old building at number 31, which to outsiders looked like a ruin. Later, another building was added at nearby Wekerle Street. It is estimated that the glass house and its two dependencies ultimately offered safe housing to 3,000-4,000 persons, even though they lived in extremely cluttered quarters. Moreover, Consul Lutz saw to it that, in addition to formal diplomatic immunity, the glass house was also protected in very concrete ways. A team of strong-muscled Chalutzim kept watch at the main entry day and night, ready to face any ruffians or ill-intentioned gendarmes who might try to force their way in. It was said that weapons were hidden in the cellar, but the consul discouraged all talk of that. Loyalist policemen discreetly kept a permanent eye on comings and goings outside, on both Vadasz and Wekerle Streets. The consul provided generous tips to insure their continuous presence. Finally, an understanding was reached with a reduced army platoon headed by one Lieutenant Pal Fabry, who was stationed nearby. Within minutes of an alarm the platoon would close off both ends of narrow Vadasz Street, in case there was major trouble. Thus the consul could satisfy himself that the diplomatic immunity offered by him had clout. Eichmann and his cohorts would have to think twice before they risked an attack. The Emigration Department of the Swiss legation on Vadasz Street became one of the great legends in the action to save the Jews of Budapest.

The glass house with its huge glass façades miraculously survived the war despite shelling and air bombardments, which during the following winter destroyed one-third of Budapest. Most important, the 3,000-4,000 who took refuge there survived.

*   *   *

Carl Lutz's second move was even more astounding, namely, to extend diplomatic immunity to no less than seventy-two buildings, the *Schutzhäuser,* protective houses, on Poszonyi Road. This, too, was a first in diplomatic history. Nothing on that scale had ever been tried. Poszonyi Road was part of the middle-class Szent-Istvan district in Leopoldstown near St. Margaret Bridge; each house had three or four stories. The road began on St. Istvan Ring and ran northward parallel to the Danube. At its upper end there was a new Reformed parish church, which had been constructed just before the war, and whose young and energetic pastor was Albert Bereczky. This outstanding theologian and preacher had long been at odds with the antisemitic views of his superior, Bishop Ravasz. Bereczky did not hesitate to issue hundreds of baptismal certificates to threatened Jews, which more often than not helped to save them from danger of death, despite Hungary's Nuremberg-like race laws. The pastor was in touch with most of the opposition politicians and with members of the Horthy household, and he informed Consul Lutz of the innermost workings of Hungary's (limited) underground. And, most important, Bereczky kept a constant eye on behalf of the consul on what was happening along Poszonyi Road.

The consul was faced with two problems. First — as already noted — Horthy's suspension of deportations to Auschwitz did not mean that he automatically dropped the government's anti-Jewish measures and that, for instance, the Jews could henceforth return to their homes and resume business and employment. Nothing of the sort took place, because by now, "Christians" had firmly installed themselves in former Jewish apartments, businesses, and jobs. The Jews were now a destabilized, vagrant part of society, ready to be destroyed physically, like the Jews of the province — except that nothing happened for the time being. The consul's Emigration Department established a special housing section, hoping to provide housing for part of these masses. One problem was that the number of well-disposed Christians, local church parishes, and convents ready to accept a certain number of the "illegals" was limited as a result of the still rampant terror exercised by the gendarmes and others. Clandestine hideouts were few. Many homeless Jews, Schutzbrief holders among them, lived in the streets or in the parks or under the Danube bridges. Whenever they succeeded in entering the glass house or the former American legation on Freedom Square, they fought tooth and nail against being put out on the street again, where untold dangers lurked.

But there was a second and perhaps more urgent reason why Consul Lutz, in conversation with the Chalutzim, came up with the idea of creating the protective houses. By mid-summer 1944 rumors were rife throughout Budapest on the supposed agreement between Horthy, Veesenmayer, and Eichmann, which would unleash the Hungarian gendarmerie again in order to round up the Budapest Jews. Few, however, knew that the date for this treacherous attack had been fixed for August 25. It slowly dawned on the surviving Jewish remnant that Horthy's moderate will to resist German intransigence was ebbing away. He lacked fundamental convictions and was unable to challenge and organize the few forces that were still loyal to him. The Budapest Jews would share the fate of the Jews of the provinces. Many fell into a profound depression, and not a few committed suicide.

Most exposed to danger were the so-called "yellow star" houses, in which most Jews were now concentrated. The buildings were each marked with a large yellow star, which gave them their name and made the houses easily identifiable, just like the individual Jews who dared to set foot in the street. Groups of such houses were established in each of the fourteen urban districts; they were usually grouped close together. For all practical purposes the "yellow star" houses were meant to function as small versions of the concentration camps from which the provincial Jews had been deported earlier. The Hungarian authorities naturally denied all deportation plans. They spoke once again about labor service in Germany. They "explained" that the Jews were confined to "yellow star" houses because they were being made to pay for the losses in housing caused to "Christians" by Allied air raids. The Allies were the "friends of the Jews," and both planned to ruin the Magyar nation. It was only just that the Jews be made to suffer for their "perfidious collusion" with the enemy. The transfer to the "yellow star" houses had been effected on June 24. On that day, thousands of Jews were driven through the streets to their new apartments, and the "Christians" went in the opposite direction in order to take hold of the vacated properties. It will be recalled that Eichmann and the Hungarian gendarmes had originally planned to deport the Budapest Jews on July 3. They planned to set a new date for deportation at the first opportunity. Eichmann and his collaborators did not intend to rest until all of Hungary had become judenrein. The purpose of the "yellow star" houses was to help prepare that action.

The problem for the consul was that several thousand Schutzbrief holders were also compelled to live in the "yellow star" houses, which caused him grave worries. How could he exert his effective protection over them once the storm broke loose? Somehow he had to obtain hard and fast assurances that at least the Schutzbrief holders would be kept alive.

In desperation Lutz went to see Dénes Csopey again. The consul said to the foreign ministry official that he would like to protect all Budapest Jews from being deported, but if this was impossible, he at least wanted to fulfill his formal obligation toward those who had entrusted their lives to him, that is, those who had his Schutzbriefe. He was calling on the Hungarian authorities to support him.

Csopey dilly-dallied. To the consul's surprise he said that according to Veesenmayer and Eichmann, Lutz had a "right" to only 8,000. This was also the figure officially accepted by the Hungarian government. It was nevertheless known that the consul had exceeded this figure by far, by tens of thousands. How did he justify this? Lutz became upset. Didn't Hungarian officialdom have any backbone? he thought. He answered that, after the deportation of hundreds of thousands to Auschwitz, to talk like this was immoral. Of course what Mr. Csopey said was true, from the very official point of view. But to limit the Schutzbriefe to 8,000 was outright criminal. He himself had rejected the idea of a deal from the start. He looked sternly at Csopey and said he hoped that the Hungarian government was not once again falling into the trap offered by the "Führer's wish." Unfortunately, those who had gone to their death could not be brought back to life. But there were hundreds of thousands whose lives were in acute danger now and whom he wanted to rescue. There was talk about deportations again, and the foreign ministry was certainly aware of it. How could such danger be met? Did the Hungarian authorities care?

Csopey said he agreed with the consul, but he simply wanted to know how the consul would answer when challenged. He himself was trying to collect arguments to protect the consul, because he himself was bound to have nasty encounters with colleagues within the government on the subject of protecting Jews. He, too, was running great personal risks. Then he asked how many Schutzbriefe Lutz had really issued. The consul pretended that he did not remember and Csopey dropped the subject.

The upshot of this uneasy conversation was that the consul and Csopey agreed to establish some kind of Swiss "yellow star" houses for approximately 15,000 persons. They talked of sixty buildings, but Lutz said he needed more, and they arrived at seventy-two. These Schutzhäuser, protective houses, were to be entirely controlled by the Swiss legation, analogous to the glass house, and would enjoy extra-territorial status. No gendarme or policeman would be allowed to enter, except on specific invitation of the consul himself. Lutz and Csopey selected the houses on Poszonyi Road. This was already a heavily Jewish section, and the apartments were spacious.

The seventy-two buildings were turned over to the administration of the consul. Christian families who were expelled received comparable living space elsewhere and were promised that they could return as soon as the war ended. That kind of promise had never been given to Jews when they were driven from their homes. The arrangement was — once again — officially approved by the Hungarian foreign ministry.

The Chalutzim were jubilant. In their eyes, the Swiss consul was becoming a hero, one of the few whom the Hungarian government could not resist. Who had ever heard of seventy-two buildings being made extra-territorial? The housing section of the Emigration Department of the Swiss legation went to work and selected 15,000 persons, above all Schutzbrief holders from the "yellow star" houses and those who lived in precarious illegitimacy. Those chosen lived henceforth in security, but quarters were terribly cramped. Two hundred persons were squeezed into each building, fifty or more on each floor. Fortunately, the consul received financial help, bedding, and food through Saly Mayer, the Swiss representative of the Joint Distribution Committee, the relief organization of American Jews. Each building was managed by a Hechalutz, who had a direct telephone line to either the glass house or the consul directly. The Emigration Department organized a special transport unit with several small vehicles. They were manned by the Chalutzim and moved refugees, staff, and material supplies. Each vehicle had a diplomatic license plate — another concession Lutz had extracted from Csopey — and on the side of the vehicles were the words: Swiss Legation to Hungary, Department of Emigration. They, too, had extra-territorial status. All this involved an incredible amount of skillful negotiation and the working out of administrative details, and the consul's staff increased from 30 to 150.

Here, too, the consul secured the services of trustworthy policemen, who would regularly patrol Poszonyi Road. He was fully aware that this concentration of Schutzhäuser would otherwise be an open invitation to his adversaries, who could swoop down on them in one terrible night raid, carrying the 15,000 to their deaths. Years later, Carl Lutz confessed with a shudder that the invisible wall of diplomatic immunity and extraterritoriality made all the difference between the Swiss Schutzhäuser and the "yellow star" houses. But he had to make sure that this invisible wall was a solid obstacle and kept out evildoers. Almost daily, sometimes in Gertrud's company, he would drive along Poszonyi Road in his Packard, looking into this building and that, reassuring the thousands of refugees that they were safe in his hands. Sometimes he came at night, when danger was more accute, chatting with the Chalutzim who kept watch, because these young people, too, needed to be reassured, all the more as most of them had lost family members at Auschwitz.

Obviously unhappy over the protective houses were Eichmann and his friends at the ministry of the interior. Veesenmayer called the extension of diplomatic immunity to an entire city street absurd. Crude as he may have been, he understood that the arrangement set limits to his power. Moreover, each Jew subtracted from deportation was a personal threat, because Hitler could call both Veesenmayer and Eichmann back for non-compliance with orders and have them executed. For once, however, the shaky Hungarian authorities stood firm. The creation of the Schutzhäuser on Poszonyi Road was like a strip of blue sky amid mounting storm clouds.

Carl Lutz now felt reasonably sure that if the deportations were resumed he could defend his vast network, as long as he himself kept his own self-confidence intact. By August 1944 well over 20,000 threatened human beings stood under his direct protection, not counting the Schutzbrief holders who lived on their own. They hid in secret apartments, in the cellars of churches or in convents, or with well-disposed individual Christian families, unless they were still out in the open. Bishop Ravasz had gone through a conversion experience and he now passed on the word to his Reformed faithful that Christians had a duty to help the persecuted Jews. He remained very discreet, to be sure, but at least he did this. A small but growing minority of Hungarian Christians, both Reformed and Catholic, decided that on the basis of their faith it was better to obey God rather than the devil of opportunism. If Cardinal Serédi still remained lukewarm toward helping Hungary's Jews, many Catholics let themselves become inspired by the aged papal nuncio, Angelo Rotta. The representative of the Vatican was impressed by the initiative taken by the Swiss consul, and he also requested a number of protective houses on Poszonyi Road, adjacent to those of the Swiss Schutzhäuser. He provided security for 2,000 of his protégés, mainly converted Jews, who were persecuted like the others. Then there was the energetic forty-year-old Friedrich Born, the new Swiss representative of the International Committee of the Red Cross, who also imitated the procedures established by Lutz. Born used to be a businessman in Hungary and knew the language. He coldly disregarded the anxious appeals from his superiors in Geneva to be prudent and to stick to his written mandate, which certainly did not include protecting Hungarian nationals, meaning the Jews. Born lost no time in placing Jewish schools, old people's homes, and hospitals under the protection of the International Committee of the Red Cross, declaring them extraterritorial, even though neither he nor the International Committee of the Red Cross possessed full diplomatic status. He filled the buildings to the brim with orphaned Jewish children, whose parents had been deported. Soon, there were 6,000 under his care. Born was so successful in his efforts that one morning at breakfast in late summer 1944, an exasperated Horthy, when studying the growing list of extra-territorial buildings, exclaimed that between Lutz and Born Budapest was becoming a Swiss colony. Consul Lutz was no longer alone. More protective letters were needed, and he pushed his Eemigration Department to print thousands of additional Schutzbrief forms.

*   *   *

Notwithstanding the grumblings in Hungarian high places and German vengefulness, Lutz was evidently not satisfied with merely protecting 20,000 human beings. More and more Jews wanted to enter the protective houses, which were already filled to the brim. He told Csopey that each day more desperate applicants were showing up. Even if he thought that the flow of applicants had slowed down, he realized that only a fraction of those who were threatened were being helped, despite the flanking measures of Rotta and Born. Time was running out and other approaches were needed.

It happened that one day the diplomatic courier from Berne placed a confidential British report on the state of Palestinian Jewish immigration on the consul's desk. The document stated that while the British White Book of 1939 permitted the entry of 75,000 Jews during the five-year period until 1944 — a small enough figure in the face of the European Jewish tragedy, which affected millions — only 35,000 had entered Palestine up to the summer of 1944. This meant that over half of the quota, 40,000, remained unused. The five-year period would end on December 31 of that year, less than five months hence. This figure struck the consul like a thunderbolt, because it meant that 40,000 human beings could be saved, if only they were allowed to emigrate.

Lutz's imagination was set afire, and his unique capacity for legal reasoning went into high gear. Granted, he reasoned, on the one hand the British government, as the mandatory power over Palestine, had to be prudent for reasons of state and therefore wanted to slow Jewish immigration down. It was afraid of Arab reactions, which, if they became violent, could upset the indispensable petroleum supplies to Britain from the Middle East. On the other hand, the British people were not inhuman. They had an innate sympathy for the Jews based on a profound popular knowledge of the Bible. Ever since George Mandel-Mantello's press campaign they knew of the desperate plight of the Jews of Hungary. Most important, the unused quota of 40,000 would not have to be renegotiated from scratch, not even with the Arabs. The Allies may have rejected the Kasztner deal of one million Jews against ten thousand trucks, which had been an absurd plan from the start. But what he, Lutz, now proposed was reasonable, legal, and small.

The unused quota of the British White Book must under no circumstances go to waste.

Dénes Csopey was flabbergasted at the consul's new proposal. When were the Swiss ever satisfied? From the start, the consul had refused to "exchange" the 8,000 against the deportation of the rest. Then he had made the Hungarian government accept the diplomatic immunity of the glass house, and then of the seventy-two buildings on Poszonyi Road. Moreover, he knew no bounds when it came to issuing letters of protection, which the impertinent Chalutzim transported all over Budapest on foot, on bicycles, or in vehicles that bore the mark of the Swiss legation. But Lutz argued quietly, coherently. From one legal point he went to the next, and to the next, and Csopey had no choice but to nod again and again, because the consul knew each word and comma of international law and could substantiate every claim he made. In the end, the emigration of the 40,000 Jews to the Holy Land was the most logical thing to do; it would benefit Hungary and increase its standing in the world. Csopey could barely hide his astonishment. Herr Konsul was talking like Moses before the Pharaoh, he exclaimed. Others were making this comparison all the time, Lutz answered. If only it were true.

Both agreed that rather than mentioning the unfilled quota of the British White Book, it would be better to begin by referring to the 8,000. This, to Hungary and to Germany, was a fixed and officially accepted figure. They must say that this figure really referred to family units. Or, in other words, to "approximately" 40,000 individuals. This was a cockeyed argument, they both agreed. The consul would have preferred to talk openly about the British White Book, which would have been more credible. But Csopey thought that to follow the roundabout way from families to individuals would have a better chance of being accepted by his superiors, who in any case had to deal with the Germans, who must provide transit visas. If 40,000 Jews could finally be saved it didn't matter how they reached the desired result.

On Csopey's advice, Consul Lutz, accompanied by Minister Jaeger, called on Prime Minister Sztojay again. Sztojay seemed tired. He was evidently looking for a way out of the mess into which he himself had helped to maneuver his country. To save 40,000 Jews was a good idea, he replied without hesitation. Obviously, the visitors thought, the man meant to restore his damaged reputation. The prime minister noted the figure down on a piece of paper, and he promised that he would give orders to his government to allow 40,000 Jews to go to Palestine, just as Herr Minister Jaeger and Herr Konsul Lutz desired.

*   *   *

It was during this time of negotiation on the 40,000 that a Swedish diplomat turned up in Freedom Square. His name was Raoul Wallenberg and he was a vigorous young man of thirty-two. Like Lutz, Wallenberg, who was an architect by profession, had been to the United States and to Palestine. There, at Haifa, he had encountered Jewish refugees from Germany and had begun to take an interest in their fate. But unlike Lutz, who had a modest social background, Wallenberg was related to a highly influential Swedish banking family. He himself had visited Hungary several times before in connection with family business.

The young man said that by reason of a complicated story, in which family business and Swedish and American politics were all muddled together, he found himself in diplomatic service. He was now the third secretary of the Swedish legation, but had an office at the Swedish Red Cross, directed by Asta Nielsson, the king's cousin. He was supposed to help Jews and had brought with him a list of Jewish businessmen and their families, some of whom had connections with the Wallenberg clan, in order to bring them out to Sweden. He confided that the Americans had criticized the vast Germans interests of his banking family and threatened to seize the Wallenberg holdings in the United States unless the family disinvested in the Nazi state. Upon the advice — so it seemed — of the family's influential American lawyer, John Foster Dulles, the Wallenbergs felt it would be a nice gesture if, in order to appease the Americans, they did something on behalf of the Jews, now that everybody had got so excited about the deportations. It would help counteract the negative image of the family and of Sweden on the other side of the Atlantic. It happened that this fuss with the Americans coincided with a personal need of his, Raoul's, to strike out on his own, and to seek an objective in life that went beyond mere money-making.

When his uncle Jacob, in conjunction with the Swedish authorities, including the king himself, asked that he go to Hungary, he readily agreed. His job would be to bring 300 to 400 Jewish businessmen with their families out to Sweden. It might lead to a larger, more permanent life vocation, the young Wallenberg mused.

Lutz was pleased that the young man spoke so freely. He said he had always felt that a country like Sweden ought to be far more engaged in helping Hungarian Jews than it had been. He wished that Switzerland, which had similar problems with the Allied powers, would also make a well-publicized gesture of the kind. For instance, they could give public support to his efforts to rescue Jews, instead of raising obstacles at every turn.

Wallenberg showed him the list of the businessmen, and the consul said he thought that some of these people had already received Swiss Schutzbriefe, but if Mr. Wallenberg got them out to Sweden, all the better.

But the young visitor looked disturbed. He said that this was not really why he had come to see the Swiss consul. What had looked good and reasonable back in Stockholm seemed very different in Budapest. Wallenberg said that at home he was made to believe that the Horthy order of July 8 had made life for the remaining Jews safe, and that all he had to do was to walk in and take his businessmen and their families away. Now he realized that this was not so. Only now after he had arrived in Budapest had he become fully aware of the vast tragedy that had befallen the Hungarian Jews. He had arrived too late to help stop the deportation of the Jews of the provinces. But how about the new threats that aimed at the Budapest Jews? His limited mandate troubled him. He even said that his instructions from home were next to useless. How did a few hundred businessmen compare with the quarter of a million who faced extinction?

The young man paused. He said that since his arrival he had gone all over the city, seen friends, diplomats, government people, and the Jewish Council. Everywhere the name of the Swiss consul had come up as the one who knew exactly what he was doing and who had set up an effective structure to help Jews. He hoped the Swedish legation could share in this effort. Lutz answered with feeling that he himself was desperate, because in the face of the quarter of a million threatened Jews his own options were far too limited.

The consul was impressed by the eagerness of his visitor. Few had shown the same anxiety and seen the whole problem as had this young man, coming straight out of Sweden where he had been living such a protected life.

Lutz explained to Wallenberg how he tried to help Jews to survive. The Schutzbriefe, letters of protection, were his basic instrument. He explained how he had used them, ever since 1942, to provide legal protection to children and young people who were on the point of emigrating to Palestine. Most had been brought by the Chalutzim to Budapest from all over Europe, after their parents had been deported. Until the German occupation of March 19, 1944, everything had worked very well. After that he had encountered nothing but obstacles. He explained how each letter of protection had originally been based on a British-endorsed Palestine Certificate made out by the Jewish Agency for Palestine, but that he had long ago given up that legal pretense. The Palestine Certificates had been quickly exhausted, but the petitioners kept coming. But would Mr. Wallenberg please keep this a secret? He told him about the Emigration Department on Vadasz Street, formerly the Budapest office of the Jewish Agency, which he had taken under the wing of the Swiss legation, giving it a new name. He explained how he had placed Schutzbrief holders into seventy-two protective houses on Poszonyi Road, all covered by diplomatic immunity. Over 20,000 persons, perhaps double that number, had found a safe haven with him, not counting those Schutzbrief holders who survived elsewhere, and the number was mounting. Finally, he explained how much he depended on the Jewish Chalutzim, those courageous young men and women who provided communication between him and the Jewish community at large and transported protective letters, mail, and food. Without their help his operation would be very limited, he said with emphasis. If Mr. Wallenberg wanted to set up a similar operation based at the Swedish legation, he, Lutz, would ask some of the Chalutzim to be assigned to the Swedes. The young man eagerly accepted the offer. Lutz continued that his latest measure was to gain exit visas for 40,000 émigrés to go to Palestine as part of the British White Book arrangement. He felt that as the official representative of British and Palestinian interests in Hungary he must explore this possibility, too.

Forty thousand? Wallenberg exclaimed in astonishment. He said he too would have to think within such categories, going far beyond the 300 or 400. What would they say in Stockholm, Lutz asked, if he went beyond his assignment? He asked this question, he said, because his superiors in Berne continued to subject him to cold and hot showers on the question of Jews, as if he were a prisoner in a Turkish bath. Raoul Wallenberg apparently did not want to remain a papa's boy, now that he had confronted the terror of Budapest. The Swede seemed ready to disregard the very limited mandate he had brought from home and to do something much larger. He would have problems, too, as soon as the Swedish foreign ministry and the Wallenbergs realized what Raoul was up to.

He didn't know, the young Swede answered. It was not really important what Stockholm thought.

Not long after this conversation with Carl Lutz, Raoul Wallenberg obtained thirty-two Schutzhäuser on behalf of Sweden, which were located adjacent to the seventy-two "Swiss" houses. A smaller number of buildings were also turned over to the papal nuncio, Angelo Rotta, and to Jorge Perlasca, who represented the Spanish legation, as well as to the Portuguese.

*   *   *

Within minutes after Lutz and Jaeger had left Sztojay's office, the unusual deal between the Hungarian government and the Swiss consul about the 40,000 Jews became the talk of the town, despite official secrecy and censorship. Furiously, Hitler's proconsul, Veesenmayer, stormed into the prime minister's office, asking whether he was out of his mind making a promise of that kind to the Swiss consul? Germany had never agreed to more than 8,000 to go to Palestine, and this only under certain conditions, which that mule-headed consul had never accepted. Did the prime minister know what such a massive influx into Palestine would mean to the Arabs, who were Germany's and Hungary's best friends in the Middle East? Rotta and Born might come tomorrow, requesting the emigration of thousands more. A young Swede by the name of Wallenberg had also come to

170

town to save Jews; it seemed as if he, too, would make demands of his own. Before they knew it, all of the Budapest Jews would have vanished into thin air. Did the prime minister realize how the Führer would react?

Sztojay looked at his notes and protested weakly that as far as he knew the 8,000 had meant families from the start, hadn't they, which amounted to 40,000 individuals. Nonsense, Veesenmayer replied arrogantly, thinking that Sztojay was becoming senile, nothing of the sort had ever been under discussion. The Swiss consul had tricked the prime minister, and it was not the first time. Lutz appeared a quiet, professorial type, who couldn't harm a fly. But inside he was full of cunning. Well, Sztojay said, confused, perhaps his pencil had slipped when he had written his notes.

Sadly, Csopey informed the consul that he had received counter-orders. The deal was off. He said he was glad that he himself had not been fired or arrested, even though the number of his enemies increased. He had to be more careful. Csopey looked annoyed, and Lutz did not know whether it was because of the 40,000 lives lost or because the consul had made him a laughingstock within the foreign ministry. These officials were all career-minded cynics, the consul thought. They were worried about their own fat skin, and nothing else.

It took a while before the diplomatic courier from London, coming via Berne, caught up with this case. Lutz had informed the British Foreign Office that he was trying to propose a deal for the unused White Book quota of 40,000 and that for convenience' sake he was using the argument that 8,000 families represented 40,000 individuals to make the request more palatable. Visibly upset over the idea, a British Foreign Office functionary answered the consul severely that he was exceeding his authority and that his suggestion was out of order. The official did not refer to what was said in the British White Book for Palestine. Neither did he care that over half of the quota was still unfilled. The top figure, according to this official, which the consul was henceforth allowed to discuss with the Hungarian government was 5,000. He did not even mention the 8,000, whose names the British government had itself sent to the consul as acceptable immigrants just prior to March 19, 1944, and whom Hitler was willing to concede. The Foreign Office official in London sternly spelled the figure out, as if Consul

Lutz did not know how to read. He wrote "5000 = five thousand individuals, not families (!)" and underlined the entire sentence twice and the word "not" three times.

This came as a shock to the lonely consul in Budapest. He no longer knew who his enemies were. The Germans and the British may be at war with each other, he thought, but against the Jews they happily joined forces. His own superiors in Berne had no problems with the remarks coming out of London.

Then he blew his top. On August 22 he wrote a letter to his superiors in Berne, saying that, according to all information he received, the Budapest Jews were now again acutely threatened. Switzerland should do something about this menace that meant the extinction of an entire people. Could the Swiss government at least send an urgent formal initiative to the German government, demanding that all deportations cease forthwith? Lutz thought that as Pilet-Golaz no longer had to fear German repercussions now that the Allies were winning on all fronts, he could engage in some courageous action.

The consul was right about his hunch on the renewal of deportations. Pastor Bereczky and others had sent him several warnings. Veesenmayer and Horthy were aiming for August 25, 1944, and Eichmann had alerted his Sonderkommando and the gendarmes. The final act was about to begin.

But Pilet-Golaz did not call on the German minister, Koecher, with urgency, demanding that the Führer stop deportations once and for all. He was a man without strong convictions, and it was Switzerland's fate to have a foreign minister like him during the war years. Pilet-Golaz considered the Lutz request a nuisance, but it could not be ignored. He chose the bureaucratic way as he always did whenever he wanted to postpone difficult decisions, which happened often. He wrote to the Swiss minister in Berlin, Hans Frölicher, to sound out the German authorities. Weeks of silence followed. Not once did Pilet-Golaz remind the Swiss minister in Berlin that the Lutz request was urgent. In November 1944, finally, Minister Frölicher replied that his contacts at the German office had been highly indignant over the Swiss request. Just what deportations did the Swiss government have in mind? they asked. Did the Swiss not know that there had never been any deportations? Hungary had long ago entered into an internationally valid contract with Germany for sending Hungarian labor to Germany. This was legitimate, and neither Germany nor Hungary had to give an account of this. If anybody was permitted a complaint, it was Germany, whose authorities were upset over the obnoxious activities of the Swiss consul in Budapest, who continuously interfered with matters that were none of his business, namely, by interjecting all kinds of obstacles to the Hungarian labor force leaving for Germany. He was upsetting formal Hungarian-German agreements. Would the Swiss authorities please call their consul to order? Minister Frölicher added that he quite understood the peeved reactions of the German government. Ever since the end of World War II in 1945 historians have wondered whether Minister Frölicher was pro-Nazi or simply naive. Whichever it was, the end effect was the same.

To Consul Lutz in Budapest these delays and distortions between Berne and Berlin made no impression. He expected no miracle. He simply wanted a small measure of goodwill on the part of Pilet-Golaz. The miracle occurred elsewhere. On August 23, 1944, two days before the fatal blow to Budapest Jews was planned to occur, Romania switched sides. The southeastern German front wavered, and suddenly the Red Army stood in the Hungarian lowlands near Debrecen. Eichmann's cattle wagons were hastily withdrawn, and Himmler gave orders that Auschwitz be dismantled.

*   *   *

It was at this time of momentous upheavals that Carl Lutz realized he was in love with Magda Csanyi. He did not know whether this was in compensation to the great blow he had just received, when the emigration of the 40,000 was turned down, or for other reasons. The manifold anxieties caused by a war and the cynicism it generates often cause more imbalances to the human psyche than normal peacetime conditions. Loyalties and structures of faith break up more quickly when hatred and destruction send out shock waves. Perhaps Carl had fallen in love with Magda the moment she had set foot in his office, when she came to plead for little Agnes and for herself. Who can fathom the depths of the human heart? Gertrud sensed immediately that she had let a rival come under their roof, because she felt that her husband seemed affected by the woman whenever she came near. She noted the uncertainties in his eyes when Magda talked with him and made him feel her vibrating sensuality. Such uncertainties can of course occur any time when a man glances at a beautiful woman or she at him. Gertrud thought Magda responded in kind, and these instances became certainty as spring turned into summer. Why did she have to hang around her husband so often, chatting to Herr Konsul about this or that? Just so he would notice her, as if he didn't do so already? During the next phase awareness would turn into outright desire. But up to mid-summer 1944 Gertrud thought that she had matters well in hand.

Then, in July and August, when the consul was engaged in his nerve-wracking negotiations with Csopey and Sztojay, Gertrud's mother in Switzerland fell ill and Gertrud felt it her duty to go back and look after her. Gertrud spent four weeks at home. Then she cabled to her husband that she was returning to Budapest. To her surprise he answered that because of the "difficult situation" she should not come. At first she thought that this had to do with the war. Weren't the Soviets entering Hungary? If the war was getting close to Budapest, it would all the more be her duty to be at her husband's side. Gertrud had a stubborn sense of duty, even to the point of harshness.

But as she contemplated Carl's cable, an intuition arose in her that the "difficult situation" perhaps did not simply refer to the war, and she returned. No sooner had Szluha driven her into the court of the former British legation on Verböcsy Street, she knew. Those who welcomed the lady of the house whispered that Herr Konsul and Frau Magda, you know. . . .

*　　*　　*

Six weeks later, on October 15, 1944, the Horthy regime fell and all hell broke loose in Budapest.

174

8. ARROW CROSS TERROR

On Sunday, October 15, the sun rose into a beautiful crisp autumn day. Its rays were not shadowed by a single cloud. Although the nights were already chilly, it was as if the sun wanted to renew the warmth of summer one last time before the onset of winter.

What was unusual on that day was that the Sunday walkers on Fishermen's Bastion or on Gellert Hill placed their hands to their ears and looked toward the plains east of Pest. The noise they heard was certainly not from a late summer thunderstorm; it came from distant Soviet guns, which were pounding the receding German-Hungarian front. Would the nightmare of the German occupation end soon? If so, should one welcome the Red Army as Hungary's liberator, or would it bring new horrors? Poor Hungary was always at the mercy of its powerful neighbors. It was said that the Germans had been defeated during a great tank battle near Debrecen. They were beaten because their tanks had run out of fuel and ammunition. Rumors had it that the Red Army under Marshal Malinovsky was already near Mohacs and might soon cross the Danube. If they maintained their present speed, the Soviets could well be knocking at the gates of Budapest within days. Stalin wouldn't mind celebrating the twenty-seventh anniversary of the October Revolution by announcing a great victory.

This was a moment of unusual expectation, coupled with fear. Jittery Budapesters paid small fortunes to soothsayers.

Years later Alexander Grossman recalled that on that Sunday morning he and Rafi Friedl had gone to a secret meeting of Chalutzim leaders. They had discussed the launching of a military uprising, in the hope that they would thereby entice the more reluctant Christian young people to join the Jews. Not only would this help speed up the advance of the Red Army, but it might stop any last ferocious onslaught of the German SS and their Hungarian cohorts upon the Jews. They knew that the certainty of coming defeat made them more dangerous than ever.

On their way back to the glass house in early afternoon, Grossman and Friedl noticed that the walkers whom they passed seemed to be unusually excited and happy. They wondered what it was all about and asked. "Oh, don't you know yet?" was the astonished answer. "The regent, Horthy, has just spoken on the radio, announcing that Hungary is suing the Soviet Union for peace. He said he is breaking off the alliance with Germany and that the Jews will receive all their rights back." Alexander and Rafi looked at each other and began to laugh, a laughter that freed them from the constant tension that had lain upon them like a heavy burden. But Alexander's laughter soon turned into tears. He thought of Ilona, Istvan, and his mother. Even good news could not bring them back to life. The event was nevertheless astounding. Excitedly they kept talking. Surely, this time, unlike March 19, the regent must have taken precautions, in order not to be caught again with his pants down. And surely Marshal Malinovsky would seize the opportunity and march straight toward the Hungarian capital. Church bells began to ring, and the two young Jews felt the wind of history.

However, by mid-afternoon the weather changed. A cold wind blew down the Danube and the sky became overcast. The sun disappeared. A gloomy, cold atmosphere settled over the vast expanse of the city. The church bells, which had rung continuously, stopped one by one.

At the same moment, Carl and Gertrud Lutz, Magda Csanyi and Agnes were taking afternoon tea on the terrace of the former British legation, as they often did on Sundays. This sign of normality was necessary to them, in order to help them defy a world that had become absurd. They, too, heard the distant thunder of artillery rolling across the plains and commented on it. They were eventually joined by Geoffrey Tier and his wife, who had sought the safety of the former British legation. Tier, a former teacher of English language and literature at the University of Budapest whom the British Secret Services had wanted to spy on the gestapo, knew some Hungarian and a little German and had a smattering of Russian. Despite his poor secret service record, Tier liked to boast with hints about mysterious inside knowledge. Today, he claimed, the German defense capacities had been so badly damaged that the Red Army would enter Budapest within four days, five at the most. When the consul asked him how he knew, Tier raised both his hands and his eyebrows, saying enigmatically that he couldn't reveal his sources.

Then they listened to Horthy on the radio, and the consul telephoned Minister Jaeger asking what he knew about the armistice, but the minister did not know anything more than they. Tier got excited and said, hadn't he just told them? When the first gust of wind blew up, the group on the terrace of the former British legation felt cold. They rose and were about to enter the house. Suddenly rifle shots were heard from across the river. They stayed rooted where they were, turned, and peered in the direction of the sound. They saw people running back and forth on the opposite shore. Lutz rushed into the house and came back with a pair of binoculars, which he directed at Pest. There were more shots. The consul put the binoculars down and looked flabbergasted. He said that armed men were shooting at people from close range on the embankment of the river. They were placed in such a way that they fell directly into the water. Gertrud grasped the binoculars from her husband. She shook her head and said she saw nothing, except that there were some objects floating down the river. Were they the bodies of those who had been shot?

For a while, despite the wind, the binoculars were passed from hand to hand. The group filed into the main hall, and the consul turned on the radio. They heard a speech by Ferenc Szalasi, the head of the Arrow Cross party, the *Nyilaskeresztes Part*, in Hungarian. His language was uncouth, the words of a poorly educated, primitive person, one who had emerged from the frustrated small bourgeoisie, whom the economic depression and the war had pushed into an abyss, and who now took his revenge on the aristocrats and the pluto capitalists, meaning the Jews. This was a

177

great day in Hungary's history, Szalasi said, because those who had planned the nation's death had been overthrown. The traitor Horthy and his clique were disempowered. A new Hungarian nation, purified of all undesirable elements and led by the Arrow Cross party, would march forward to victory, side by side with an ever-faithful Germany and its Führer, Adolf Hitler, the world's greatest genius.

*　　*　　*

After Romania had changed sides on August 23, Horthy replaced Sztojay by a loyalist general, Géza Lakatos. The regent felt that the moment was opportune to get Hungary out of the dreadful war, and he ordered his new prime minister to open secret peace negotiations with the Soviet Union. But because he hated and mistrusted the communists, negotiations dragged on. To the exasperation of the Soviets, he posed condition after condition. The golden opportunity was lost. Veesenmayer's spies learned of everything. The regent's secret approaches to Moscow were the last straw for Berlin, and Hitler ordered his plenipotentiary in Budapest to solve the "Horthy problem" once and for all. While Horthy annoyed his Soviet negotiation partners by raising ever-fresh obstacles, wasting precious time, Veesenmayer negotiated with Ferenc Szalasi and his Arrow Cross. These violent extremists awaited his signal to take power.

The Arrow Cross was a rightist and racist political group that was so extreme that not even Horthy — who had rightist and racist inclinations himself — had anything to do with them. The Hungarian far right was the child of Hungary's defeat of 1918. It took shape in the midst of political and social confusion and the economic depression of the 1920s and 1930s, when it was led by an absurd personality by the name of Gyula (Julius) Gömbös. The Arrow Cross party itself was founded in 1937 by Ferenc Szalasi, a former army officer, after Gömbös's untimely death. As a fervent admirer of Mussolini, then of Hitler, Szalasi wanted to become Hungary's Duce/Führer and restore the nation's lost grandeur. He hoped to (re-)build a mystical, vaguely Christian kingdom of true ethnic Hungarians, which was to be purified of all undesirable minorities. Their irrational hatred of the Jews was such that the Arrow Cross attracted antisemite clergy into its ranks, such as one Father Andras Kun, a young Roman Catholic priest — later defrocked — who became a Nyilas group chieftain. It is said that he used to execute Jews at close range, pronouncing the words: "I kill you in the name of Jesus Christ!" The Arrow Cross were not simply a foreign body grafted on to Hungary's body politic by the Italian Fascists or the German Nazis. They reflected political and cultural traditions shared in various degree by most Hungarians, except that, heightened by Gömbös, with the Arrow Cross they took an extreme form. Apart from a few individuals, the churches never took a decided stand against the semi-religious and nationalistic aberrations of what Szalasi called Hungarism. On the contrary, they themselves shared in various degrees of nationalism and antisemitism in their own "theological" outlook. Against its murderous consequences, they were defenseless.

Ferenc Szalasi had a cloudy mind. He loved great phrases and instead of "governing" he preferred to withdraw to his farm in western Hungary, where he spent his time writing grandiose political pamphlets about the great future of the restored and purified nation. Veesenmayer had long hesitated to replace Horthy by a man of such weak character. But Szalasi was surrounded by tough-minded career seekers, discarded army officers, and marginalized journalists who were anxious for power and money. Veesenmayer would have to rely on them. Moreover, the Arrow Cross had built up a body of 3,000-4,000 young thugs, the Arrow Cross bands, popularly called the Nyilas. They had come from the dregs of Hungarian society and they adored their leader. Their members were mostly aged from fourteen to eighteen. Szalasi had given them identity, a green uniform, and rifles. They swore fidelity to a flag which flew a cross composed of two arrows, and which was a poor imitation of the Nazi swastika. And they, the young Nyilas, no longer had to starve and look for work. They received military training from a few days to two weeks. They were utterly useless in fighting against a professional army, such as the oncoming Soviets. But they were marvelously efficient against unarmed civilians, especially against frightened Jews. By their terror they kept the large city of Budapest under control, which was what Veesenmayer wanted. A good many policemen and most gendarmes happily went over into the Szalasi camp.

Like the Nazis, the Arrow Cross held mystical, quasi-religious torch light celebrations, which were accompanied by solemn night marches. Thus, on the eve of their putsch, Saturday, October 14, the Nyilas noisily paraded with torches and rifles through downtown Pest. Horthy's loyal police and troops could have dispersed the unruly crowd with ease, but they received no orders. This was taken as a sign of the regent's weakness. When Horthy spoke on the radio on Sunday afternoon, October 15, and announced the armistice, his game was already up. This is why between Horthy's radio speech and that of Szalasi there was but a short interval of two hours at the most. There was a brief exchange of fire around the royal castle, but the Hungarian units were no match for the Germans. The regent took refuge at Veesenmayer's legation, of all places. Veesenmayer then had Horthy and his family removed and imprisoned in a South German castle. They remained there until the end of the war. With Horthy's disappearance the last vestiges of Hungary's conservative and aristocratic structures also vanished.

The representative of the International Committee of the Red Cross, Friedrich Born, gave an excellent description of these events. He called the Arrow Cross coup a "revolution of nonsense." A swarm of incompetent adherents of Ferenc Szalasi took over, and the events of March 19 were repeated manifold: "A wave of arrests flooded across the capital city and the entire country. All key personalities in political and economic life were imprisoned and led away to Germany. This included anyone who at one time or another had opposed the Arrow Cross or who had attracted the ire of the new power holders. Hungarian police, party organization and military gendarmerie, also the German Gestapo began to arrest and imprison 3,000 important personalities. It was clear that most of them would serve as convenient hostages to be used on a suitable occasion."

Urged on by Eichmann, Arrow Cross chieftains made inflammatory statements against Jews on the radio and in the papers. Their bands moved about the city, searching for their victims wherever they could find them. They removed labor-service men from a camp at

Obuda, drove them to St. Margaret Bridge, shot them, and threw their bodies into the Danube. Even German military units participated in the killing spree. Included in these units were many Hungarians of German ethnic origin, who were known for their antisemite spirit. During the night after the takeover, a hand grenade was thrown onto a platoon of German soldiers marching along Maria Valéria Street. None were killed or wounded, but excited rumors arose. Some said that a Jew had thrown the grenade from the window of a nearby "yellow star" house, just opposite the Hotel Dunapalota. The incident was not investigated, nor was the presumed killer found or identified, much less arrested. No one was formally accused and brought to trial. But the "yellow star" house was immediately surrounded. Only elderly people, women, and children lived in the building; not one of them was of military age, none could seriously be suspected of throwing a hand grenade. The Germans ordered the 200 inhabitants of the "yellow star" house out into the street and executed them.

*　　*　　*

Inspired by the easy "success" of this attack, the Nyilas tried to create similar incidents at some of the Swiss protective houses. But the Chalutzim were always on the alert, and Consul Lutz, as a precaution, detached loyalist policemen from the legation and the glass house to patrol Poszonyi Road. The Arrow Cross bands were normally too cowardly to contemplate attacks when they realized there would be resistance. However, the new minister of the interior, Gabor Vajna, went on the air and issued the ominous words: "No Jew should think he can hide behind any foreign government. All Jews living within Hungary are under the control of the Hungarian state. We shall not tolerate any interference in our internal national affairs."

The black Packard of Consul Lutz was seen throughout Budapest. He reassured the vast crowd that pressed against the glass house on Vadasz Street, telling them he would do his best to protect them. He calmed the nervous staff of the Emigration Department inside, who were overwhelmed by the onslaught and who were constantly on the lookout for the Nyilas. He spoke to the loyalist policemen who kept watch outside and to Lieutenant Fabry's platoon in order to reassure himself of their dependability. He went to the Danube shores when he heard that the Nyilas were once again lining up their victims for execution, calling out to those who might have his protective letters. There were always those who timidly answered and waved a Schutzbrief. Then he would ask if there were others who claimed his protection. If he could not prevent the killings from happening at all, he hoped at least to confuse the murderers, slow them down, and prevent more murderous bullets. Calmly the consul would open the car door and let the persons who claimed his protection enter, much to the dismay of the Arrow Cross. Those rescued were painfully few, but it was better than nothing. Such open interference, as Vajna would call it, was highly dangerous, because Lutz could have become a victim himself. His enemies — Veesenmayer, Eichmann, and Vajna — could have wished nothing more than the occurrence of such an "unfortunate incident." In Veesenmayer's correspondence to German foreign minister Ribbentrop, more than once the minister poured out his wrath over the uncontrollable Swiss consul. But the fact that his commanding figure descended from an expensive, chauffeur-driven automobile, that he was impeccably dressed and walked like an aristocrat, and that he talked in German impressed the uncouth killers, who in their short lives had seen nothing but the savage violence of the poor and had heard nothing but instructions in hatred. They also knew that it was best to leave important-looking people alone.

One scene was related by Geoffrey Tier, the English professor-spy, who happened to accompany the consul on several of his dangerous tours. Lutz heard shots coming from the Danube shore, near the House of Parliament. He made Szluha speed in that direction. The three men came upon one of the rivershore executions. When the Packard drove up and braked to a noisy stop, the consul found a Nyilas band, which, having completed the execution of a group of Jews, stood by the river shore watching their victims being carried away by the rapidly flowing water. Here and there they shot a bullet after them, if they detected signs of life. When Lutz and his companions rushed out of the car, a woman shouted from the water: "Consul Lutz, Consul Lutz, help me!" She had been shot in the stomach. She pressed one hand on the wound and splashed in the water with the other, trying to stay afloat. Lutz knew she would soon lose her strength and drown. The woman managed to swim to the wall where the consul stood. There was a staircase leading into the water, where in more peaceful times small boats were moored. Without a moment's hesitation Lutz went down the staircase. He stood in the water up to his waist, and when the woman came near, he grabbed her. The ice cold water, which would have frozen her to death within minutes, had an unexpected beneficial effect, in that it luckily closed off the wound. With her teeth chattering she tried to explain to the consul that he himself had given her a protective letter. He answered that this was not important now and that she should not talk. Paper or no paper, she was protected by him. With Tier's and Szluha's aid he pulled her out and placed her in the backseat of the Packard. Like a madman Szluha raced off to Freedom Square. Luckily, among the refugees in the basement of the former American legation there was a Jewish surgeon, who immediately organized a primitive operating room and performed surgery. The woman survived. Having observed actions such as these close at hand, Tier's admiration for the consul knew no bounds. Years later, in London, during a talk about Carl Lutz to Swiss students of English, the professor exclaimed glowingly: "He was the greatest man I have ever met!"

* * *

A confusion of orders and counterorders poured out from the Szalasi government. This was caused not only by the ideological disarray inherent in Arrow Cross "philosophy" and the muddleheadedness of the new leaders, but by the simple fact the "new Hungary" was not independent by any stretch of the imagination. Hungary had become a full German colony, and, besides, large parts of its territory were now occupied by the invading Red Army. The confusion centered on how to deal with the Jews.

Eichmann, who had left Hungary during the last few weeks of the Horthy regime for lack of work, returned in order to finalize his job, the deportation of the Jews of Budapest. But he and his Hungarian accomplices could no longer simply round up the victims and deport them to Auschwitz. The giant death camp was no longer in operation, and the

183

Obersturmbannführer was simply unable to command cattle wagons for shipment to an "ersatz" labor camp. Railway equipment had become scarce and was entirely reserved for military purposes. Moreover, Veesenmayer interfered with Eichmann's arrangements. The minister demanded from Szalasi a labor force of 50,000 Jews, to be sent to Germany for the construction of underground airplane factories. The Nazi minister of industry, Albert Speer, was badly in need of supplementary slave labor if he was to prevent a collapse of German war industries, now that even middle-aged and older factory workers had been drafted into the armed forces. He had recently requested no less than 450,000 Hungarian Jews, whose industrial and administrative skills he believed to be high. The SS and the Gestapo were under some embarrassment when they told him that most of these people were "no longer available." Speer, when he heard of this mass murder, was utterly dismayed, as he later wrote in a self-serving autobiography. The Nazi state had shot itself in the foot, thereby hastening its downfall. Hitler's ferocious determination to get rid of all Jews worked at cross-purposes with the labor requirements for Germany's war production. But it is hard to believe that Speer, a top Nazi, was as ignorant of the Führer's Jewish policies as he pretended.

As a miserable second choice, Eichmann made Szalasi agree to sending another 50,000 Jews to Germany, or 100,000 altogether, an agreement he did not intend to honor. What Eichmann or Veesenmayer failed to mention to Speer was that this Jewish labor force consisted mainly of women, old people, and children, who would be of limited use. The majority of young and middle-aged men whom Speer really needed had been destroyed long ago. Even though this reduced labor force was needed urgently, it was treated so badly that within weeks or months all were dead. Whether they went to a labor camp or to Auschwitz, the final effect was the same.

Under these circumstances the protection of thousands of Jews by Swiss Consul Lutz and other diplomats could hardly make the German representatives and the Arrow Cross firebrands rejoice. The neutral diplomats kept too many working hands away from Speer's vast slave labor system. Thus, the Germans demanded that the Arrow Cross apply new pressure on the neutrals. What relieved the dangerous situation somewhat was that the various members of the Nyilas government worked at cross-purposes. One group, the most extremist, which was supportive of Nazi Germany, was lead by Vajna; it wanted to break all existing promises concerning the Jews. This faction was backed by the party rank, essentially the Nyilas bands. Through public statements and press releases the firebrands kept whipping up wider "popular" support. Then there were others with cooler heads who thought that the neutral states would cut off diplomatic relations if the persecution of all Jews resumed unabated. The recognition by the neutrals of the dependent putschist government was precious, because it symbolized the last and only claim of the Arrow Cross usurpers for international legitimacy. In their mind, the "honor" of Hungary was at stake. Until the end of the war this pathological desire would be skillfully used by Consul Lutz and his neutral colleagues as the one "weapon" in their efforts to protect Jews.

But then the Swiss government made a move that seriously weakened the consul's position vis-à-vis the Arrow Cross authorities. Within days of the Arrow Cross coup it recalled Minister Jaeger because it wanted to express its "disapproval" of the putsch and to question the new government's legitimacy. The action was dictated by popular feeling in Switzerland, which ever since the Auschwitz deportations had been hostile to a Nazi-dominated Hungary. The idea was doubtless good, but the effects on the Lutz operation could have been disastrous.

Lutz felt left out in the cold. Not only did he miss the minister's advice and encouragement. Worse, he feared that his overall diplomatic cover was being pulled away. Anton Kilchmann, who had been the legation's first secretary, became Swiss chargé d'affaires, a substitute minister of lower rank. But within weeks the new man suffered a nervous breakdown and left also. Henceforth the direction of the Swiss legation was in the hands of thirty-one-year-old Harald Feller, the juridical advisor, who in the legation's hierarchy ranked third. The Hungarian foreign minister, Gabor Keményi, was much put out by this seeming lack of respect. He threatened to retaliate by closing down the Hungarian legation in Berne, which would mean that all Swiss diplomats in Budapest would be expelled. This was very uncomfortable for the consul, because all arrangements concerning the glass house and the protective houses, not to speak of the tens of thousands of

Schutzbriefe, could be cancelled. His protégés would immediately fall into the hands of the Arrow Cross.

But apart from unkind words nothing happened. In fact, Feller's nomination turned out to be a stroke of immense luck. He was a tough young lawyer who had no intention of letting himself be impressed by the Arrow Cross. Lutz, now almost fifty, at first resented being formally placed under someone almost twenty years younger, but in the end he benefited from the change. Feller had no fear of confronting the Arrow Cross government. He stood up to it with unwavering courage, and his support of the consul remained steadfast. Nonchalantly the young diplomat steered his rump legation through the final stormy phase of the war. Through his presence at the helm of the legation, Swiss diplomatic cover for the Lutz action was not diminished, but became stronger.

Angel Sanz-Briz, the Spanish chargé d'affaires, also left, and the other legations of Portugal and Turkey closed down and moved to Sopron in western Hungary, which the Arrow Cross government considered safer. Of the other top diplomats only Angelo Rotta, the papal nuncio, and the Swedish minister, Carl Ingvar Danielsson, remained at their posts. The latter was substantially supported by the Swedish Red Cross and Raoul Wallenberg, the recent arrival. Finally, there was Friedrich Born, the Swiss delegate of the International Committee of the Red Cross, who also decided to stay in the capital. To varying degrees, with Carl Lutz in the lead, their main objective was to rescue Jews. Cooperation between the neutral diplomats was excellent.

They were forced to play the self-destructive and opposing poles of the Arrow Cross off against each other skillfully. The first was represented by hardliner Gabor Vajna, the minister of the interior, as stated above, and the second by Foreign Minister Keményi. The latter was an impoverished and simple-minded nobleman, a former journalist, who had drifted into the Arrow Cross party despite his background, without ever becoming an extremist firebrand. In the government cabinet Vajna and Keményi usually cancelled each other out, so that the consul and the other diplomats always had to see both, in order to make agreements stick. This cost time and nervous energy.

The deal with Nazi Germany about the 100,000 slave laborers had barely been signed when the jumpy Arrow Cross government changed its mind, this time not without reason. Every night, as the poorly prepared ministers sank into their beds, happy over their new and unlimited power, they were inevitably forced to hear the remote thunder of Soviet guns, which brought them nearer to reality. How could Budapest be defended? they asked, panic stricken. Their very survival depended on this crucial question. Defenses must be built. But who would dig ditches, construct the dams, create gun emplacements? Hungary, like Germany, had not only sacrificed its Jews but also lost the substance of its manhood on the battlefields in the east, ever since they had foolishly attacked the Soviet Union in 1941. For the first time, ideological friends quarrelled seriously and Szalasi risked a shouting match with Eichmann, when he told the Obersturmbannführer that at least 40,000 Jews had to be kept back for erecting defense walls around Budapest.

Not even Veesenmayer succeeded in changing Szalasi's mind. The German minister's bones chilled when Ribbentrop cabled him to return to Berlin for consultation. The Führer, no less, gave Veesenmayer a terrible tongue-lashing, treating his proconsul to Hungary like a small boy. He called him an utter failure. Veesenmayer, he shouted, had not only been unable to control Horthy. Even Szalasi, who was really a stupid man, entirely dominated by Germany, was escaping him. Hitler's mood was dangerous. He looked nervous and his gestures were fidgety. The attack on his life on July 20 and the bad news from the collapsing fronts were making their imprint. He said he had a good mind to have Veesenmayer executed for sabotage. Then the Führer relented and told his envoy he would give him another chance, but he had to deliver the full 100,000 Jewish workers. If Veesenmayer had been a courageous man, which he was not, he could have replied that it was not he but the unfailing Führer himself who had ordered the great deportation of the Hungarian Jews to Auschwitz, and that, if they were still alive, Speer would not have to worry now about his industrial production. But no one ever talked back to the Führer and lived. And Veesenmayer already had plans for his own future.

Szalasi remained adamant when Veesenmayer came to see him again after his return to Budapest. His priority, the Hungarian chief of state said, was the defense of his own capital. If the city withstood the coming siege, he would gladly reconsider helping the Germans with their industrial production. Whatever they would do with the Jews after that was no concern of his. He, too, wanted all Jews to vanish from Hungarian soil, because the country must return to its original purity. But Berlin remained pitiless. Hitler wanted these slave laborers now. In the end Szalasi gave way. All right, he sighed, let the Germans take the entire lot. But Eichmann, the transportation specialist, no longer knew where to find the necessary cattle wagons in order to transport the 100,000 to Germany. Another solution had to be found.

*   *   *

Thus, at the end of October 1944 the Nyilas bands broke into the "yellow star" houses and drove 40,000 Jews to various assembly points at the edge of Budapest. They also searched out Jews wherever they might find them. This was easy, because countless "Christians" confided to the Arrow Cross where they were hiding, such as private apartments, hospitals, or sanatoria. Jenö (Eugene) Szatmari, an opposition journalist to whom Lutz had given refuge at the former American legation and who went about Budapest with false Swiss identity papers, described the depressed human columns driven by the Nyilas:

> The exodus is upsetting also to the observer. Only children and old people remain at home, without help, because all those who normally take care of them have been called up. There are many thousands who do not obey and they go into hiding. The collection points are closed off hermetically, no one may speak to those inside. Mobile commissions investigate each case. There are however officers who often display much humanitarian spirit, and who sometimes make those women return home who carry babies in their arms. There is no shelter for such masses. They have to camp in the open. From the collection centers they are brought to different camps, on foot, of course. I was told that these people were needed in order to build fortifications.

A lucky few who came with foreign passports were also allowed to go home. But those who "merely" came with protective letters, even though they were registered on collective passports, were forced to remain in these makeshift camps and enter labor service.

The telephones rang without interruption on Freedom Square and on Vadasz Street, and the Chalutzim brought alarming messages to the Swiss consul. The Nyilas were not respecting the Schutzbriefe, they said, because Vajna had told them they were worthless. The black Packard criss-crossed Budapest without interruption, searching for those who claimed the consul's protection. Lutz argued with Arrow Cross bandits and with army officers, and he literally tore the victims from their grasp. Several times a day and also during the night he went to the glass house, and he was in constant communication with the inhabitants of the protective houses on Poszonyi Road, reassuring them that they were safe.

The consul and the other diplomats decided to act together, as they had in the past. They brought their protest to Keményi, Szalasi's foreign minister, and patiently explained that according to international law a new government was obliged to keep all inter-state commitments entered into by previous governments. Moreover, ever since the League of Nations had been created in 1920, all states of the world had a legal and moral duty to respect minimal human standards for all of their citizens. When Keményi answered that the League of Nations no longer existed, Lutz replied that this was a formalist answer, and that international law existed on its own, as long as a majority of all countries supported it. Then he asked on what grounds the new government ignored the heritage of Hungary's chivalrous traditions, of which everyone had always been so proud, including Mr. Szalasi himself? Did Hungary really want to become an outlaw nation?

The question of the consul hit its mark.

Rotta and Wallenberg pressed Keményi further. They said it was impossible to establish a rational relationship with the new government if he, Keményi, agreed to one thing and Vajna said the opposite. They were forced to tell their home governments about these fickle see-saw decisions, and this made a bad impression. Lutz added that several times he had come across Arrow Cross bands which had impertinently torn

Schutzbriefe into pieces, because Interior Minister Vajna had allegedly said they were worthless. How could the neutral governments consider Hungary to be a reliable partner state?

The foreign minister apologized. He realized that not only Hungary's honor but his own position inside the cabinet was at stake. The conflict no longer took place between him and the neutrals but increasingly within the Hungarian government itself, that is, between Keményi and Vajna, with the cloudy-headed Szalasi maneuvering between the two. The upshot was that on October 30, 1944, radio stations and the press announced that holders of foreign passports and protective letters were exempt from being drafted into labor service. This was a remarkable victory for the diplomats. But the victory had a price. The numbers of those whom they could officially protect were terribly small, not more than 14,500, not the tens of thousands to whom they had given protective letters already. Inside that overall number Consul Lutz was, once again, back to his 8,000. Wallenberg was "given" 4,000. And the rest, 2,500 all told, were divided between Rotta and Born, with a few Spanish and Portuguese protégés thrown in. Nevertheless, the neutral diplomats congratulated each other, knowing full well that, as before, they would not respect such limits. They had obtained their main objective, namely the recognition of the protective letters as such. Although Vajna was unhappy that he had been outvoted, everyone knew that behind him stood Veesenmayer and Eichmann, who in turn were under pressure to fulfill "the Führer's wish."

Among the threatened Jews of Budapest the news of the agreement caused a furor, as the journalist Szatmari reported:

> The reason for the undeniably big success [of the agreement with Kemény] to become recognized by the neutrals. It is clear that the neutral governments will avoid this, but the success is undeniable and it has to be exploited. And it is exploited. After a conversation with Krausz, the head of the emigration department, Lutz directs him to issue as many protective letters as possible. The offices in Vadasz Street are stormed. People line up by the thousands, in order to obtain the miraculous paper. And indeed, the paper is miracu-

lous, because its holders are dismissed from most labor camps and labor companies. There are cases, where agents let themselves be paid for obtaining the certificates, but these are relatively few. What is important is that the certificate offers the possibility of escaping the labor camps in order to hide in Budapest. The emigration department works under high pressure. Each single paper means a human being saved — this is the motto.

Lutz even went as far as giving secret orders to his staff to aim for as many as 100,000 Schutzbriefe, because this was the number of Jews whom Veesenmayer and Eichmann wanted to send to Germany.

Consul Lutz broke all diplomatic standards in order to engage in this high-risk gamble. In summary, he made himself "guilty" of a three-fold trespassing of his authority, each of which could cause him serious trouble:

First, he exceeded by far the number of protected persons agreed upon with Keményi (8,000). In this way, as already stated, he thwarted the "Führer's wish" to murder all remaining Jews, a move that in itself was dangerous. This was not a mere legal matter; from now on, his very life was in danger.

Second, while Consul Lutz informed his superiors in Berne about the new agreement, he did not trouble to tell them that he was going far beyond the official figure of 8,000, namely to 100,000. Each Schutzbrief holder, having lost his/her Hungarian citizenship, became a virtual Swiss citizen. If they had known, the unperturbed lawyer-politicians at the Swiss foreign ministry in Berne would have been horrified, because Hitler — they reasoned within their narrow frame of reference — could have decided to dump the still undeported masses of Hungarian Jewry upon Switzerland, perhaps in revenge against the stubborn consul in Budapest who resisted his "wishes." But the Führer was incapable of such subtleties. Even while going to his final doom, he still wanted to kill all Jews.

And third, the "Swiss problem" was connected with that of the British, who thought they could hide behind the provisions of the Palestine White Book and its top limit of 75,000 immigrants. The affair of the deliberately unmet quota of 40,000 had made clear that the British government had no intention of keeping its word. The well-groomed hair of British foreign minister Anthony Eden would have stood up straight had he known that "his" representative in Budapest was issuing 100,000 protective letters, and more if possible. These letters were like so many uncovered checks that the British government would ultimately have to pay and to explain to the hostile Arabs. This would be the end of the White Book and perhaps of the British hold over Palestine and the Middle East. As long as the crisis of the Hungarian Jews lasted, the British government suffered from the nightmare of these masses descending upon Palestine, via Switzerland or directly. Fortunately, slow and deficient wartime communications and press censorship kept the consul in distant Hungary from being the cause of what might have become a devastating international scandal.

The spirit of Carl Lutz made him stand up against brutality, legalism, and political indifference, an unholy trinity. Only a person with profound human and religious convictions could withstand the tensions arising from them.

Under these enormous pressures the consul's marriage eroded further, which was the price for the daily outpouring of his energy under nerve-racking conditions. Whenever the consul thought Gertrud wasn't looking, he furtively reached out and touched Magda and she responded in kind. Although they all tried to respect conventions and feelings, the former British legation turned into a curious ménage à trois. As the situation outside the walls of the former British legation became ever more deadly for Jews, Gertrud knew that she could not send Magda and her little daughter, Agnes, away. They had no safe place to go, except perhaps to Poszonyi Road, but Gertrud had no heart to send them into those crowded buildings, especially not little Agnes. Moreover, Carl would never agree. At the same she did not want to leave her husband, as she was tempted to, because such a flight could endanger the thousands whose lives depended on the consul alone. He might carry on an affair with another woman, but he could also crack and break down if she, Gertrud, left. Perhaps, once he had had his fling, he might come back to her. She knew such derailments happened in seemingly spotless marriages, when middle-aged husbands went astray for no apparent reason, perhaps because they feared they were missing out on life, or if a lively wife got bored with a sterile husband and took a lover, or for reasons which only the couple itself knew. Carl Lutz himself, finally, did feel guilty over his illicit love. His puritanical background demanded extreme sexual discipline, and he knew he was violating these "laws." He went to the local Methodist superintendent and confessed his unfaithfulness. The pastor advised him to drop the affair and to straighten his marriage out. But the consul said that while he highly respected Gertrud and in some ways still loved her — she was a great and exceptional person, her advice was precious, etc. — she was too straightforward and too much down-to-earth and offered little romance. The new woman, on the other hand, was more dreamy, more refined, and, why not, more erotic. He was, after all, only a man with the desires of a man, may God forgive him. There seemed little the superintendent could do, although the two men kept seeing each other. The triangular relationship continued unchanged and they all waited for "the great event" that would somehow resolve all problems.

*   *   *

On November 2, 1944, the last murders of Jews took place in Auschwitz-Birkenau. The gas chambers were partially destroyed and their elements taken to other concentration camps. The Nazis intended to eliminate all traces. On November 26 the last 204 members of the (Jewish) special command were liquidated, because even these last surviving witnesses of horror could not be allowed to tell the world of the millionfold deaths they had seen. The Red Army reached Auschwitz only on January 27, 1945. The Soviet soldiers understood immediately what they saw, despite all German attempts to hide the crime. They discovered 648 unburned bodies and 7,600 survivors, mere skeletons. Since the erection of the camp two-and-a-half years earlier, two million Jews and two million Soviet prisoners, Polish political prisoners, Gypsies, and other non-Jews from all over Europe had been brought there. Even today, over half a century later, Auschwitz has remained the symbol of human-made hell.

*　　*　　*

Despite the agreement between Keményi and the neutral diplomats, which had been formally endorsed by the entire Szalasi cabinet, Vajna and the Arrow Cross bands meant to destroy the remnants of Hungarian Jewry. Thus, on November 8, Laszlo Ferenczy, the chief of the gendarmerie, who had Magyarized his former German family name, appeared on Poszonyi Road, in order to find out how many Jews had found refuge above and beyond the authorized 8,000. As expected, he told Vajna, the minister of the interior, that he had found double, perhaps triple the authorized number. He was not even counting the 3,000-4,000 who were hiding inside the glass house on Vadasz Street. During the course of his search, Ferenczy reported, he had also "discovered" that many Swiss protective letters were mere imitations of the originals, with fake signatures of the consul. This was intolerable, he exclaimed. Did Lutz realize that they could declare him persona non grata?

Lutz did not accept the rebuke when Vajna and Keményi confronted him with the "evidence." He said he was glad that at last they could talk openly instead of beating around the bush and trying to be polite. Of course there were many more people in the Schutzhäuser on Poszonyi Road than there were supposed to be. Of course he had signed more protective letters than officially agreed. Of course there were unauthorized and inauthentic protective letters in circulation. The reason for this "triple" problem, however, lay neither in his supposed lack of control over his consular administration nor in any ill will toward the authorities, as the Hungarian officials were claiming. The real reason was the desperate and inhuman condition in which so many thousands of Hungarian citizens were kept by these same authorities — not because they were political opponents, but simply because they belonged to a minority. How could he, Carl Lutz, ignore those whose fear was written all over their faces when they came to appeal for help? They kept coming to him and to other neutral diplomats because they were afraid, because they were mercilessly hounded by undisciplined Nyilas. His employees were working day and night preparing protective letters, lodging and feeding the asylum seekers. It was ridiculous to keep the numbers of Schutzbrief holders and inhabitants of protective houses down to 8,000. Even the production of so-called fake papers, which personally he didn't like, were the actions of a desperate people. The consul readily conceded that there might be some self-seeking elements at the fringe of the Chalutzim, and that some outsiders probably copied protective letters for sheer personal gain, taking the last pennies out of the pockets of the poor and the frightened. Moreover, was it not conceivable that the Arrow Cross themselves fabricated copies, in order to embarrass him and to make money on the side? This led to one last question, why was Mr. Vajna unable to keep his Nyilas under control? And why was it necessary to threaten the last remaining neutral diplomats? The Hungarian government was mistaken, he added as Vajna's face became dark red, if it thought that by such behavior they could obtain the recognition of the neutral states.

The discussion settled nothing. Keményi was embarrassed and Vajna angry. They realized that it was useless to impose more "agreements," because they knew that neither Lutz nor the other neutrals would respect any further inhuman consignments. But the Hungarians were pressured hard by Veesenmayer and by Eichmann to get the "contracted" laborers underway. Since the minister's visit to the Führer they both had little to laugh about. This would be Eichmann's last deportation, and he knew it. Once he was done with it, the war would end and he would return to the dreary insignificance whence he had come. As autumn turned into winter, the decomposition of the state, which had begun on March 19, reached a further stage.

*   *   *

In early November 1944, advance units of the Red Army reached Gyal-Puszta, only thirteen kilometers from the city limits. Cleverly Eichmann used the general confusion to further his own aims. Despite Szalasi's refusal to turn over the 40,000 to labor service, Eichmann directed the Arrow Cross to pull back the forced labor units from the incomplete defense works. The Nyilas preferred to obey him rather than their own chief of state — with Vajna's secret approval. This did not make sense to the ordinary uninformed Hungarians, and even less to the tortured Jews, who were forced to march this way and that. But this was how Eichmann got the 100,000 service laborers for Germany together. However, in the meantime these had been so badly mistreated by the Nyilas that their number was diminished, though no one knew by how many.

Under great brutality Nyilas bands drove the defense wall builders back into Budapest, together with the others whom the criminal youths had found elsewhere. They formed new columns that converged upon St. Margaret Bridge and continued in the direction of Obuda. This was a run-down suburb north of Buda, which was probably the oldest human settlement in the region and which now became the meanest. The place used to be inhabited by Suabian artisans, but these had long ago been replaced by ill-paid industrial workers, who occupied rows and rows of unsavory one-story brick lodgings. But Obuda's main feature was a large brickyard that was walled in on all sides. This was ideal for a temporary concentration camp. It was to become an interim stop for the exhausted marchers. Now, as the November nights lengthened and cold, fog, rain, and snow settled in, the tall, dead chimneys, the shacks which sheltered the burnt-out fire ovens, the cranes, and the rusty rails looked more depressing than usual. Ultimately, several tens of thousands of human beings were packed inside the compound. They stood, sat, or lay in cold mud, sometimes knee-deep. The main road from Budapest passed through Obuda. It proceeded along the Danube, all the way to Vienna.

The journalist Szatmari described the disaster as follows:

> The situation of the Jews is rapidly becoming worse. The government, the police and the army barely bother with them any more. They are completely in the hands of the Nyilas. From all houses not only Jewish men between 16 and 50 and women between 16 and 40 have been taken away, but also children and old people. In pouring rain the unfortunates are led on foot to the brickworks at Obuda, where 30,000 people are now concentrated, without roof, food or water. Hundreds line up for the toilet. The armed snot noses are not in the least concerned with identity papers, which means that hundreds of Schutzbrief owners are among the prisoners. One would have to intervene in thousands of cases.

During these days of acute tension, before the wretched columns reached these indescribable brickyards, Consul Lutz would often drive alongside them, trying to signal to the tortured that they had not been completely forgotten and that perhaps not everything was lost. This may have been a small sign of encouragement, but for him it was ten times more important to be out near them than to keep busy at his office concerned with administrative matters. Inevitably, the Nyilas guards would come running each time they saw the Packard, and point their rifles at the consul.

Under Veesenmayer's and Eichmann's pressure the erratic Szalasi now gave up his objections to the delivery of the 40,000. Thus, the entire mass of the 100,000 was once again available to the Germans, insofar as they could be found. But the Nazi authorities were also becoming confused, now that the prospect of defeat was increasingly disturbing their minds. According to the latest decisions from Berlin, the Jewish victims were no longer to work for Albert Speer's war industries. This particular understanding had never been much to Eichmann's liking. Instead, they were to raise defensive walls around Vienna, the ancient Habsburg capital. Eichmann really intended to use the Vienna Road as a marching death camp to replace Auschwitz. Obuda was his assembly point. The enclosures of the brickyard could hold a maximum of 30,000. When it was filled up, the slave laborers would be driven out onto the overland road and forced to march all the way to the German border at Hegyeshalom, 185 kilometers away. From there they would continue toward Vienna. After they had gone, Eichmann would assemble the next 30,000. And so on.

*   *   *

Again the Arrow Cross regime returned to the "problem" of the allegedly falsified protective letters. This talk of a scandal in which the Swiss consul and his staff were said to be involved also suited Eichmann, who thought this would be a good way of undermining Lutz's moral standing and to destroy his action. Once Lutz was discredited, the remaining diplomats could be handled with ease. Loudly the Obersturmbannführer proclaimed to anyone who cared to listen that Lutz and Wallenberg would now be punished for the "mess" *(Schweinereien)* they had caused. He encouraged Vajna and the Arrow Cross chiefs to annul all agreements concerning the Schutzbriefe.

Thus, Vajna used the "scandal" to tighten the screws on the Swiss consul. Cynically, he suggested that Lutz himself decide which protective letters were authentic and which were not. Lutz vigorously protested. This was placing an undue responsibility on him, because whenever he declared a Schutzbrief false, its bearer would be condemned. Coldly, Vajna answered that if he refused to cooperate, all protective letters, without exception, would be cancelled and their bearers deported.

In later years Lutz remembered the task of sorting out good from false Schutzbriefe to be the most "heart-rending" job of his life:

> Hundreds of Schutzbrief holders had already been brought to the brickyards and countless identity papers needed to be controlled. For us, this was doubtless the most painful task ever undertaken. At one time my wife [Gertrud] and I stood four hours in snow and ice inside the ill-famed Obuda brickyards, performing this sad business of sorting out Schutzbriefe. We witnessed soul-searing scenes. Five thousand unhappy human beings stood in one row, freezing, trembling, hungry, carrying small bundles with their belongings, and showed me their papers. I shall never forget their fear-ridden faces. Again and again the police had to intervene, because the people almost tore off my clothes as they pleaded with me. This was the last upsurge of a will to live, before resignation set in which usually ended in death. For us it was mental torture to have to sort out these documents. On such occasions we saw human beings hit with dog whips. They fell to the ground with bleeding faces, and we were ourselves openly threatened with weapons, if we tried to intervene.

To the horror of Carl and Gertrud Lutz, one of the Arrow Cross chieftains whom they saw at Obuda was Zoltan Bagossy, the giant, whom they remembered threatening the Jews who tried to enter the former American legation when the Germans occupied Hungary on March 19.

The former bodyguard of Ethiopian emperor Haile Selassie did his best to keep the desperate people in line by shouting and using his enormous fists. Gertrud quietly watched him for a moment. Then she tapped the giant on his muscular arm and asked whether he was participating in a boxing match. He made a glowering face as he looked down on her. Then he relaxed, looked ashamed, walked away, and hid behind a brick pile.

There were at least two kinds of imitation protective letters. On some not even the name of the Swiss legation was spelled correctly. For instance, instead of "Légation de Suisse" it would say "Légation de Susse." Others had been produced at some underground printing shop, where an unschooled printer used black instead of red ink for the field that surrounded the Swiss cross. Sometimes there were more clever imitations, noticeable only to a trained eye, such as that of the consul himself, but not necessarily to the Arrow Cross or the SS man who supervised control procedures. Whenever the consul realized that his "companion" did not notice anything, he would not hesitate to declare such papers authentic. Surprisingly, Bagossy, whose muscular body dwarfed Lutz, turned out to be the most tolerant of all "supervisors." At one moment the giant was fascinated by a beautiful young girl who had false papers. He whispered to Lutz to take her back to Poszonyi Road and to give her proper papers. It would be a shame if she got killed.

As the task in terms of numbers was enormous, the consul asked Gertrud to organize a checkline of her own. She later recalled the terrible scenes at Obuda as follows:

> We felt like judges dispensing death penalties. I accompanied my husband several times, often at four or five in the morning, when we were called out to the brickworks, in order to see whom we still could get free. And this was probably the worst thing I ever did in my entire life. However, if we had not done it, then those whom we saved, would not have been saved. Sometimes, it happened that we were not forced to tear a family apart. For instance, I told one German guardsman: "I do not pretend to fool you. By now you know quite well which protective letters are authentic and which are not. You do not need us to sort them out. But I shall not separate this

mother from her child." At another time, I recall this elderly woman. Her two sons had valid papers, but she did not. It happened that the Germans would close an eye when I insisted, but at other times they did not.

Those whose papers the Lutz couple declared authentic were freed immediately. The weakest, who were unable to stand on their own feet, were invited to climb into their Packard. They would slowly precede the foot column along the Danube and across St. Margaret Bridge to the protective houses on Poszonyi Road, as it was important to keep stray Nyilas from interfering. It was a happy reversal of the death marches. At other times a few courageous Chalutzim would transport the rescued by trucks that belonged to the Swiss legation, and which were normally used to carry food and bedding to the Schutzhäuser.

In the haze of dawn after their work was done, the worn-out consul and his wife would sometimes stop on St. Margaret Bridge and watch the column of their protégés pass. It would be frosty, as the dark-grey November night sky gave way to the silver streaks of dawn. Below them the mud-colored Danube rushed rapidly toward the sea. They were satisfied with the lives they had rescued from the jaws of death, but sad for those whom they had lost. The faces of the condemned remained engraved in their memory, the men, the women, and the children. As they looked across the restless ribbon of the Danube, the skyline of Budapest would slowly emerge from the dark. It was marked by the House of Parliament on the left and the hill of Buda to the right. To the east and to the south the dark night clouds regularly reflected flashes of red. The flashes came from Soviet guns firing at the German-Hungarian front. Within seconds each flash was followed by muffled thunder.

Once, to their surprise, Bagossy joined them on the bridge, watching the silent column pass. He, too, looked at the red flashes in the clouds and said that he had doubts whether the front could hold much longer. What was he going to do? the consul asked. Bagossy said he didn't know. So far, throughout his life, he had always been on the losing side. His father was a poor farmhand, unable to feed his many children. He himself had tried boxing, but this was a miserable job. It got him nowhere. An agent came by one day and talked him into going to Ethiopia. He became one of Haile Selassie's bodyguards. The emperor paid miserably, but at least he was able to eat and send some money home. Then the Italians pushed his boss from his throne, and after he returned Bagossy entered the Arrow Cross. What else could he do? In this wretched Hungary of the few rich and the many poor there was no chance for the underdog, try as hard as he might. Most Nyilas were poor devils like him. This was why they behaved so badly. In their heart, despite their loud talk and violence, they knew that the end was near. Now, Vajna, that idiot, had told him to sit in Keményi's office at the foreign ministry, in order to keep an eye on him. He could not be trusted, Vajna had said of the foreign minister. But he was sorry for Keményi. Despite being a baron he was really a poor bastard, he had no money. Some day those who won the war would hang him, too, for being with the Arrow Cross.

It was the first and perhaps the only time that Carl and Gertrud Lutz felt sorry for the Nyilas.

*   *   *

On November 10, 1944, the Jewish foot columns began to march from the Obuda brickyards toward Hegyeshalom. They, whom the Hungarian state was "lending" to Germany for its war effort, were entirely at the mercy of savage and uncontrolled Nyilas bands. The condemned walked in columns of 1,000 each, hungry, weak, and tired. The Red Cross delegate, Friedrich Born, was among the first to drive along the Vienna Road to find out what was going on: "Old people, men and women, young men and girls, but also children," he reported, "staggered slowly along towards the setting sun. Soon, even the lightest baggage was dropped by the wayside. In their weakness the walkers were unable to carry them. During the frosty late autumn nights, they would crouch by the roadside, without cover, without food and terrified about the aim of the voyage, only to be driven on again at dawn. Sometimes shots were heard, when overtired marchers were utterly unable to continue. The Vienna Road became a road of dread and it will probably remain engraved in human memory as the road of hatred. Forty columns of a thousand each were driven towards Germany to their death."

201

The death march did not remain unnoticed. Diplomatic couriers drove from Vienna to Budapest in the opposite direction and passed the long columns during their journey. When the couriers came to Budapest they minced no words about what they had seen, the beatings of the defenseless, the shootings, and the hundreds of bodies lying by the roadside. There were even German officers, they said, who told the Nyilas to be more merciful. But as soon as they were out of sight, the "snot noses," as Szatmari had called them, acted like wild beasts as before. The local populace and the Catholic and Protestant clergy in the villages and towns along the road acted with courage and helped the marching Jews, now that they themselves saw with their own eyes the terrible consequences of church-inspired antisemitism. Whenever the Arrow Cross were not watching, these people provided the marchers with food and fresh water, and to the stronger they confided secret escape routes. But each time a helper was caught in an act of mercy, he or she was executed immediately.

Once the marchers had left the confines of the capital it became difficult for the neutral legations to intervene. The diplomats knew that many of the victims still had protective letters. But they lacked the system of communication provided by the Chalutzim inside Budapest. After all, the province had long ago become judenrein, clear of Jews. No network was possible. Of course, the neutral diplomats, jointly and individually, lodged protest after protest with Keményi and Szalasi, and one formal agreement followed the other. But these were of little use, since Vajna ignored government orders. Even when the minister of the interior imposed restraint on his "troops," perhaps in rare moments of self-pity motivated by fear, they disobeyed. The Arrow Cross government was visibly falling apart and the Nyilas bands became a law unto themselves. On several occasions Lutz and Wallenberg followed the columns with their automobiles, but the best they could do was to wrest a few unfortunates from the claws of the Nyilas. It would have been too risky to dispatch the Chalutzim with trucks on rescue missions. As Jews they would have been exposed to as much danger as the walking victims.

Nevertheless, at one point the neutrals were able to mount an unusual coup. Reliable information on this incident comes from Alexander

Grossman, who together with other leading Chalutzim at their head-quarters in the glass house on Vadasz Street was one of the moving spir-its of the action. He described how help came from an unusual side:

> In November 1944 Hungarian police captain Dr. Nandor Batizfalvy
> came both to Consul Lutz and to Wallenberg from the Swedish le-
> gation and offered them his help in the strengthening of their hu-
> manitarian activities. On the 22nd of that month there was a confi-
> dential meeting in the building of the Swedish legation on 4 Ülloi
> Street. Batizfalvy reported on the death march of the deportees in
> the direction of the German border. He described the terrible condi-
> tions of the marchers who had set out from the Obuda brickyards
> and how the survivors were handed over to the Germans at the bor-
> der crossing of Hegyeshalom. According to Batizfalvy, 10,000 hu-
> man beings had already lost their lives before reaching the border —
> shot dead, beaten or starved to death or by suicide. On the day after
> this encounter, delegates from the Swiss, Portuguese and Swedish
> legations, from the papal nunciature and from the International
> Committee of the Red Cross, drove to the border under Batizfalvy's
> guidance, in order to get those deportees back who could show pro-
> tective letters. The Swiss legation sent Dr. Arje Breszlauer and
> Laszlo Kluger (both Chalutzim). The appearance of the haunted,
> who ranged from 12 to 80 years of age, who had been driven across
> the country on foot, was indescribable. The delegation succeeded in
> bringing several hundred men and women back to Budapest.

The delegates were, in part, aided by Hungarian army drivers, whose vehicles were parked at Hegyeshalom, waiting to be turned over to the Germans. It was an admirable act of disobedience of simple soldiers.

Minister Veesenmayer was most upset about this "raid." He cabled to Foreign Minister Ribbentrop in Berlin that an entire column of 1,000 persons, destined for labor service in Germany, had been boldly "re-moved." He blamed especially Swiss consul Lutz, who increasingly acted in defiance of German interests. Veesenmayer went as far as requesting instructions as to how he should deal with the consul. Was he prudently asking his superiors for permission to "take care of" him? Berlin never answered, unless Gerhart Feine, who controlled all coded messages, suppressed the answer. Feine had on other occasions quietly succeeded in diverting Veesenmayer's ire from the consul.

*　　*　　*

Endless columns of Soviet soldiers, mostly Ukrainians, crossed the Carpathian mountains and descended into the Hungarian plains. The Soviet Union appeared to have unlimited human resources. By late November 500,000 men, well trained and well equipped with artillery, tanks, and a tactical air force, advanced toward a terrorized and dispirited German-Hungarian force of a mere 180,000 defenders of Budapest, which was commanded by SS general Karl Pfeffer-von Wildenbruch. Marshal Malinovsky erroneously thought that he faced many more enemies, ferocious fire-eaters all of them. He hesitated to push his luck, because he, like all Soviet commanders, fought the war bearing an exaggerated respect for German military capacities. Well did he remember the nightmare of the summer of 1941, when a superbly managed German force had surprised the unsuspecting Soviet Union during a gigantic attack on a 2,000-kilometer front running from Finland to Romania. History had never seen anything like it. The catastrophe of the Red Army was enormous, and Nazi Germany almost forced the communist state to its knees. Millions of young Soviet citizens were sacrificed to repulse the attackers.

Now the situation was reversed. But Malinovsky also knew that Stalin wanted to use the Soviet Union's new military power sparingly in order to redraw the postwar map of Europe. For this, he needed as many troops as could survive the war. Thus, Malinovsky did not enter Budapest immediately after the tank battle of Debrecen; he directed the mass of his army to cross the Danube at Mohacs, where in 1529 the Hungarians had been trounced by the Turks. Then he proceeded westward and northward. It was clear that he would attempt a vast encirclement of the Hungarian capital, making Budapest another Stalingrad, in order to entrap Hitler's southern army. Malinovsky's decision had fateful consequences. In the first place, it prolonged the sufferings of the Budapest Jews for many weeks. Secondly, his decision probably helped to prolong the war by three or four months. As soon as Hitler grasped the marshal's intentions, he, too, changed his tactics. He ordered the German army to make its stand at Budapest, and not at Vienna, as he had originally planned. Pfeffer-von Wildenbruch was told not to cede a foot of ground. If Budapest had fallen during the autumn as the result of a quick Soviet move, the Germans would have been thrown off-balance, and Malinovsky could have taken Vienna shortly thereafter. By Christmas 1944 the Red Army would have stood in the heart of Germany, perhaps even on the Rhine. As a result of the combined "mistakes" of Malinovsky and the Führer this was not to be so. By Christmas 1944 the Red Army had not gone beyond Budapest.

The Nyilas did not seem impressed by the Red Army menace. Or they pretended that they were not afraid. They were convinced that the good Führer in Berlin would soon unveil a miracle weapon and push his enemies back. They certainly did not rush to the front to sustain the wavering lines. They preferred to fight not the Soviets but the hapless Jews. They were less dangerous.

*   *   *

The Arrow Cross remained an undiminished danger to the Swiss consul. Horrified, the occupants of the Schutzhäuser watched Nyilas vehicles circle on Poszonyi Road one night, pointing to this building or that. Early in the morning of November 30, the day after the news of the Mohacs crossing had come in, Chalutzim in charge of the protective buildings telephoned the consul, who was just sitting down to breakfast at his Buda residence, reporting that Nyilas bands, supported by gendarmes, were attacking the Schutzhäuser in large numbers and were dragging people away.

Carl Lutz called Szluha at once, and, again accompanied by Gertrud, along with a Swiss employee of the consulate, rushed to Poszonyi Road to confront the attackers. As he often did, the consul carried his camera. He would shove pictures under Keményi's and Vajna's noses, whenever they refused to believe his words. When they arrived at Poszonyi Road, they told the Nyilas to stop troubling the protective houses, that these were international territory and that the people inside were protected by the Swiss government. Gertrud Lutz rushed to the frightened Jews to reassure them. She spoke to the gendarmes, some of whom seemed — surprisingly — embarrassed by the brutality of the Arrow Cross bandits. Suddenly, she noticed one Nyilas who had seized a woman by her hair and was dragging her along the ground, hitting her with a dog whip. She pointed this out to her husband. Immediately Lutz got his camera ready and prepared to take a shot. While he did this, Gertrud went to the Nyilas youth and told him politely that this was no way to treat people, especially women who were unable to fight back. The Nyilas, a teenager, was so dumbfounded that he became tongue-tied. Before he could think of an answer, Gertrud told him that if he promised to behave, he should come to Verböcsy Street and fetch a chocolate bar. Confused, the youth nodded. No one had ever talked to him in this way. Early on the following day he came, without rifle or dog whip, and, like a small boy, asked for his chocolate bar. He was so astonished that this strange woman was keeping her word that he forgot to thank her. Gertrud Lutz would have given anything to find out whether the boy really mended his ways.

Despite Gertrud's intervention, the incident on Poszonyi Street almost turned into tragedy for the Lutz couple. While Gertrud was conversing with the Nyilas and the consul was about to shoot his picture, a gendarmerie officer placed himself in front of him. No photography was allowed, he shouted, and covered the lens with his hand. Quietly, Lutz explained that he was the Swiss consul and that the buildings were under his protection. He wanted to photograph the misbehaving young man. Unimpressed, the gendarmerie officer pulled his pistol, ripped the camera from the consul's hands, and ordered him to go away. Lutz answered that he was here in an official capacity and that he would lodge a protest with the authorities for being impeded in his duty. The gendarmerie officer then pulled his gun also on Gertrud, shouting that she too must leave.

The Lutz couple finally managed to get rid of the excited gendarmerie officer, while the Arrow Cross kept molesting the Jews. The consul asked Gertrud and the consular employee to retreat to safety, but to keep watching from a distance. He himself would return in a moment. Szluha drove him to the foreign ministry in all haste. There, Lutz jumped out of the car and asked for the foreign minister. He hadn't arrived yet, but Zoltan Bagossy, Keményi's "cabinet officer," the consul's recent conservation partner, chanced to be there. Lutz told Haile Selassie's former bodyguard what was happening at Poszonyi Road and asked him to help in all urgency.

They were lucky. The Arrow Cross band and the gendarmes had not yet led the Jews away. Lutz pointed out to Bagossy the gendarmerie officer who had stopped him and Gertrud from doing their work. The giant went over to the man and demanded that he explain his behavior. But the gendarmerie officer, sure of his military and social superiority over a simple Nyilas chief, had no intention of explaining anything. Another gendarmerie officer appeared, accompanied by three vicious-looking Nyilas. They all sided with the first gendarmerie officer, when they heard that this big Nyilas man and the foreigners had tried to keep them from taking the Jews away. The five immediately surrounded Bagossy. They ask him to show his identity papers and pressed machine pistols against his chest. The situation was more than critical. But Bagossy had not taken bodyguard training for nothing. By using an extremely rapid move he turned the tables, so quickly that his opponents had no idea what happened. He pulled his pistol from his holster and jumped outside the circle of the five. Now he had them all before him within his direct firing range. For a moment they glared at each other. Then, making use of his towering figure and uttering threatening language, Bagossy made the gendarmerie officers and the Nyilas drop their weapons. He had them arrested and sent to a military tribunal.

It takes little imagination to think what would have happened to the Lutz couple and to the inhabitants of the Schutzhäuser on Poszonyi Road had Carl and Gertrud Lutz not stopped to listen to the life story of an Arrow Cross man, Haile Selassie's former bodyguard.

But the Nyilas continued raging against the Jews. As Poszonyi Road seemed too risky, they decided on another target. On December 5, 1944, they attacked a camp on Columbus Street that was protected by Friedrich Born of the International Committee of the Red Cross and removed its 3,000 inhabitants. No one ever saw them again.

9. "EICHMANN HAS FLED!"

B y late November 1944 the military situation had worsened and the death march to Vienna had diminished to a trickle. The impact of the Arrow Cross regime upon the Jews of Budapest was nevertheless catastrophic. Within a few short weeks their numbers had gone down from 250,000 to 190,000. For Gabor Vajna, the bald-headed, mean-faced minister of the interior, there were still too many. Thus, he decided to fall back on Eichmann's earlier, repeatedly frustrated plan to concentrate all Budapest Jews in one single place. How they would eliminate such a large number of Jews in the middle of a heavily populated city was not clear, but they were sure that a way would be found. All the inhabitants in the scattered "yellow star" houses, those protected by the neutrals and the International Committee of the Red Cross, and those hiding elsewhere, in churches, monasteries, and nunneries and with Christian friends, would be brought to this one place. The Arrow Cross, just like the previous governments, could always count on informers to tell them where the Jews were hidden.

Backed by Eichmann's Sonderkommando, the government closed off an area in Pest, which largely coincided with the former Jewish ghetto of the Habsburg days. It was bordered by Dohanyi Street, Karoly Ring, Kiraly Street, and Nagyatadi Szabo Street, and was a poor, run-down area right next to the prosperous downtown business section. This district was inhabited by 20,000 people in all, 8,000 Jews and 12,000 Christians. The Christians were moved to former "yellow star" houses, and the Jews were transferred to the old-new ghetto. The exits were boarded up, except for four gates, which were guarded by SS soldiers and gendarmes. Eichmann's orders, transmitted through Vajna, were strict. The Jews were allowed to enter the ghetto through these gates, but none were allowed to come out alive.

There was only one difficulty with this scheme. The large ghetto, as it came to be called, could not possibly absorb more than 70,000 persons at one time. Their elimination, Vajna thought, would have to be done in batches, just as at Auschwitz, until, progressively, all of the 190,000 Budapest Jews were somehow eliminated, insofar as this was possible within the city. Soon, for the first time in its history, the Hungarian capital would become judenrein, just like the province. Historic destiny, Gabor Vajna proudly thought, had called him to launch a new era.

There remained the thorny problem of the neutral diplomats: Lutz, Wallenberg, Rotta, Born. They represented nothing but selfish war-profiteering states of ridiculous size, a backward church, and a do-good organization. They were a nuisance. None of them would have a place in the new Europe of the strong and the courageous. If a deal must be struck in order to keep them happy, it would be strictly on Hungary's terms, not on theirs. It was an affront to Arrow Cross Hungary and its German ally to let these neutral diplomats continue to dictate the law and to issue far more than 100,000 identity papers. The government must no longer brook such interference. Only Hungary had the right to decide what must be done with its Jews.

Thus, Vajna made Keményi call the neutral diplomats before him once again in order to put his foot down. In the first place, he told them of the government's decision to concentrate the Jews in one single place. These would include the bearers of foreign identity papers. Second, the foreign legations would only be allowed to "protect" 14,500 all told: Switzerland 8,000, Sweden 4,000, and the others 2,500 together, as had already been "agreed." They could keep them in their Schutzhäuser or wherever. All the rest would be transferred to the one assembly point, the large ghetto.

Was this brutal order the forerunner of the final assault on the Jews of Budapest, the cancellation of months of difficult negotiations? the diplomats asked themselves. Shivers went down their spines. They remembered the concentrations in the Hungarian provinces when they were powerless to intervene. They thought of Obuda where they had to sort out "authentic" from "false" papers. They remembered the road to Vienna. The pattern remained the same. What were 14,500 Jews when compared with 190,000?

The diplomats protested sharply. They accused Keményi of going back on his word. They said they were frustrated, because the foreign minister, although well-meaning as a person, was unreliable. He had little power within the Szalasi government and regularly caved in before a roughneck such as Vajna. Once again they repeated the earlier refrain: Was this the way for the Arrow Cross government to gain the respect of the international community? The diplomats said they refused to listen to a repetition of earlier government proposals, and that he, Keményi, should inform the government accordingly. A point of no return was reached.

When Vajna learned of what the diplomats had answered, he did not choose to reply via the foreign minister. He ordered an immediate attack upon the Swiss Schutzhäuser on Poszonyi Road, which housed the largest number of all "foreign" Jews. Several Nyilas trucks drove up. The "snot noses" jumped off and entered the buildings almost unhindered, declaring that they had come to count the inhabitants and to transfer those in excess of the "agreed-upon" figures to the large ghetto. The outnumbered Chalutzim ran for cover. The Arrow Cross dragged the unlucky inhabitants out into the streets.

Alerted, Consul Lutz, his wife, and several Swiss consular employees rushed to Poszonyi Road. They hastened to one building and then to the next, always trying to intervene whenever the Nyilas and the gendarmes dragged people out, shouting that what they were doing was illegal. It was an absurd and unequal struggle. Each time Carl or Gertrud Lutz or any of the consular staff grasped the arm of one of the crazed Nyilas who was beating a victim, they could have been murdered themselves.

The consul finally managed to get hold of police captain Batizfalvy and some of the loyalist policemen who were guarding the glass house and the former American legation. The police captain detested Vajna and refused to obey him. In fact, Vajna's control over Hungary's security apparatus was no longer absolute, because policemen and even gendarmes were beginning to protest against his senseless orders. Moreover, the Nyilas had one major weakness. They were cowards. Whenever they met real opposition, minimal as it may have been, they turned tail and ran. This happened as soon as Batizfalvy showed up. He pulled his gun and the Nyilas disappeared. Nevertheless this had been the most substantial attack to date.

The frustrated Vajna could do no other than continue plotting revenge. He felt increasingly that the very existence of the Schutzhäuser complex on Pszonyi Road was an insult to his authority.

One night, not long afterwards, the Jewish owner of one of the protective houses on Poszonyi Road called the consul to report that an Arrow Cross band had broken into his building. They were pushing 300 persons into two rooms. The prisoners lacked air and would die of suffocation unless the Arrow Cross were driven away. The consul described the incident himself:

> I drove at once to Keményi's cabinet chief, Bagossy, who, the longer the war took an unfavorable turn, became increasingly helpful. He armed himself with machine pistols and three body guards and accompanied me to the house in question. We found the 300 persons in the two rooms, squeezed tightly together, without air or food. Some of the older people had already lost consciousness. I arranged for them to be moved into a larger apartment. When, on the following morning we returned with Mr. Bagossy and several officials from our legation, the Arrow Cross had already led the entire group away.

Apparently the consul had believed that the 300 would be reasonably safe. But the "snot noses" kept an eye on the building. They returned as soon as Lutz and Bagossy had gone and led the 300 away. Next morning Lutz and the giant Nyilas searched in vain for their whereabouts. One wonders how seriously the former bodyguard of Haile Selassie applied himself to the task, he who knew the inside workings of the Arrow Cross. Did the all-observant Vajna put the squeeze on him, making him an accomplice to this mass murder? If so, did the consul trust the "conversion" of this opportunist too implicitly? On the other hand, to whom else could Lutz have turned in the middle of the night, he who was without weapons? This was the only time that such a disaster befell the consul's rescue operation, but it tarnished the image of the Swiss Schutzhäuser. Carl Lutz was deeply affected by this failure. Vajna and his ilk had proven how easy it really was to break through the thin line of diplomatic defense.

Downcast and yet furious, Lutz saw the foreign minister that morning, who was already informed. He, Keményi, had been told by Bagossy, and he added that the government was sorry. Interior Minister Vajna could, however, not be reached for his version of events, Keményi said. The consul said that this cowardly refusal to face to unpleasant truths seemed typical of all Arrow Cross behavior. He did not appreciate this. Lutz's voice rose in anger. Maybe the government was sorry, as the foreign minister said, and perhaps some of the Nyilas bands were beginning to act on their own, as he had heard, so that Vajna could not be held responsible. If this was so, why hadn't the minister of the interior come to Freedom Square himself first thing in the morning, to offer his apologies and his help to find the murderers? Why could he not be reached? An apology and an offer to find the criminals would be very much appreciated by him and the entire Swiss legation. Or was this incident, the consul continued with irritation, a means of putting pressure on him to accept the unjust "agreement" that the government tried to impose on the neutrals? There was nothing Keményi could say. He promised to ask the minister of the interior to find the 300, and Bagossy added that he, too, would continue looking. The consul eyed the giant, and wondered what role he was really playing.

Then he decided to drive a hard bargain with Keményi. He forced the foreign minister to increase the number of Schutzhäuser on Poszonyi Road from seventy-two to seventy-six and the number of their inhabitants from 15,000 to 17,000. Each building was calculated to "lodge" 200 refugees.

The problem was that the pressure of desperate people forced Lutz temporarily to allow up to 30,000 to squeeze into the protected houses, far beyond the 17,000. But this exceeded any humanely tolerable limit. Moreover, the strain on food and fuel was enormous. Every single space from basement to attic, even on the staircases and in bathtubs, was densely occupied.

Of course the demand of the Arrow Cross to concentrate all Jews within the large Pest ghetto had a vicious objective, namely to concentrate the largest possible human mass for quicker seizure. Yet the measure provided relief for the congested Poszonyi Road houses. As if the agreement with Keményi on the 17,000 did not exist, Vajna made Lutz transfer no less than 25,000 to the large ghetto from one day to the next, which the consul did under protest. In one brief moment occupancy of the Swiss protective houses on Poszonyi Road was reduced to 5,000. Vajna had almost reached his aim of eliminating the protected area altogether. But Lutz refused.

And indeed, within a short time occupancy was back again at the level of 17,000, at which it remained until the end of fighting in Pest, in mid-January 1945.

In the consul's eyes the 25,000 who had been transferred to the large ghetto were a high-risk group. If they were murdered, months of hard labor and hope would have been in vain. He insisted to the foreign minister that there was no question of delivering them to the Nyilas outright. Even within the large ghetto they would remain under his diplomatic jurisdiction. Keményi agreed and Lutz secured from him the right to unlimited access to the large ghetto by day or by night. He and his staff would supervise the general condition of the 25,000 and supply them with food and medications. Keményi promised that he would inform Vajna, and when Lutz asked whether the minister of the interior would really back him up, Keményi stretched out his hand to the consul and said that he had to believe him. It was almost like the plea of a desperate man. The consul took a deep breath. The pietist arose in him. Perhaps, if nothing else worked to protect these people, there was always the power of prayer. It had occasionally been effective of late. On the other hand God seemed also to be absent most of the time, he thought.

The other neutral representatives also had little choice but to submit. The Swedes were ordered to transfer 5,500 of "their" Jews to the large ghetto; of these 2,500 were under Wallenberg's care and 3,000 were protected by the Swedish Red Cross. The papal nuncio ceded 2,500, and Portugal 800. All of them were granted the same control rights as those given to Consul Lutz. In this way the neutrals hoped to lessen the weight of the dangerous concentration.

Later, shortly before the liberation of Pest by the Red Army in mid-

January 1945, the Arrow Cross decided to move another 32,500 "unprotected" Jews into the large ghetto. This brought its total population to its capacity of 70,000.

Keményi said to Lutz a few days later that Vajna had grudgingly agreed to the right of neutral representatives to keep an eye on "their" Jews inside the large ghetto. What the foreign minister did not reveal was that Vajna had accused him, saying that, by giving the foreigners a control right, the ghetto project had become intolerably modified. This would obviously hinder his murder plans. He accused his colleague of once again falling into the trap of the neutral diplomats.

But Vajna did not have the courage to confront the diplomats directly. This dishonest and mean man would strike at them surreptitiously. The last time he hit out against Consul Lutz was when he murdered the 300. This time he chose Friedrich Born, the Swiss delegate of the International Committee of the Red Cross. This was relatively easy, since Born did not represent a government but merely an internationally recognized organization with no political or economic power. He was not a diplomat in the strict sense, but he did possess an immunity close to that of government envoys. Born had taken a large number of Jewish educational and medical institutions under his wing and protected thousands of children throughout Budapest, declaring them off-limits to police and to other official organs. He was also known for giving straight answers, thereby deflating more than one objectionable bureaucrat. He was the kind of person who is rarely appreciated by dictators.

Vajna forced Born, via Keményi, of course, to turn over 6,000 children to the large ghetto. Many of them had been entrusted to the International Committee of the Red Cross in a way similar to those who earlier had been taken into the custody of the Jewish Agency and of Consul Lutz for emigration to Palestine. Most of these children's parents were dead, having been deported or otherwise killed. Their welfare had been administered by Otto Komoly and Hungarian Protestant pastors Albert Bereczky and Gabor Sztehlo.

Born protested energetically against this extremely brutal measure, and received vigorous support by Lutz, Rotta, and Wallenberg. Half of the children, 3,000, were transferred into the large ghetto immediately.

There they suffered from unsanitary conditions and were kept without any effective supervision. Vajna refused Born's insistent plea for social workers and nurses to accompany the children into the ghetto. He had already had made too many concessions on the large ghetto, he said. As a result, many of the very small children died from neglect, cold, and starvation. The other 3,000 came to the large ghetto in early January 1945, a few days before liberation. Shortly after the large ghetto was freed, Red Cross representatives photographed some of the small worn-out, lifeless bodies, which were piled up in long rows near the Great Synagogue on Dohanyi Street. Photographs taken at that moment make for a haunting vision of hell.

*   *   *

Edmund Veesenmayer, Hitler's plenipotentiary to Hungary, may have been "a convinced national socialist," according to his own words. But he left Budapest on December 8, 1944, as soon as he realized that the Red Army would encircle the Hungarian capital. His excuse was that the government to which he was attached was moving to Sopron, on Hungary's western frontier. Veesenmayer was above all an opportunist who sought his own advancement and was not unconditionally loyal to the Führer, who had promoted him to the top of the Nazi hierarchy — certainly not after Hitler had nearly executed him. Ever since that dangerous encounter in Berlin the minister was obsessed with escaping the coming disaster. A few years later, in 1948, when this Nazi appeared before his judges at the International Military Tribunal in Nuremberg, he loudly proclaimed his innocence, similar to the wailings of all Nazis whose misfortune it was to get caught. What choice did he have but to obey Ribbentrop's orders? he lamented. He was an innocent victim of Hungarian machinations. Horthy disliked him. The rest of the old politicians hated him, too. The deportations were really unfortunate, but he had nothing to do with them; he didn't know anything about them. Astutely, Veesenmayer added that he had been a disciplined anti-communist all along, whose single-minded aim it was to defend civilized western Europe against the red hordes swarming out of Asia. He even claimed that, by making a decided

215

stand in Hungary, he played a central role in impeding the Red Army from reaching the Channel Coast. In reality, Veesenmayer had fled from Budapest before the Battle of Budapest began. Hitler's former plenipotentiary, whose major job had been to destroy Hungarian Jewry, did not have the courage to face up to his enormous crime. The Nuremberg prosecuting attorney of state set the record straight: "After having caused the annihilation of 500,000 Hungarian and Slovakian Jews, he did not succeed in the murder of the remainder, who were liberated by the Allied armies."

American military judge Maguire became enticed by the supposed merits of Veesenmayer's claim that he had defended western civilization against communism. By 1948 the Cold War was getting into full swing and perspectives were shifting. The former allies, the United States of America and the Soviet Union, were becoming enemies. They were in the process of setting up NATO and the Warsaw Pact and of dividing Europe and the rest of the world into two hostile camps and restocking it with armaments. The perpetrators of the Hungarian Jewish Holocaust were no longer seen as incredible mass murderers, but as misguided bystanders of an embarrassing historic accident. "Fighting communism," the catchword of United States Senator Joseph McCarthy and other, more respectable figures who spearheaded the new politics, became more important than raising the awkward memory of the dead of Auschwitz. The Nazis became "denazified," and most remained unpunished, as long as they joined the anti-communist campaign.

At Nuremberg Veesenmayer succeeded in using this new spirit to reduce the enormity of his crime. With a sigh of relief he learned on April 2, 1949, that the International Military Tribunal was imposing a mere twenty years of imprisonment on him, minus four years for preventive arrest. He had escaped capital punishment. Hitler's former proconsul was sent to Landsberg prison in Bavaria. But he did not even have to sit out this modest sentence. Five years later, in 1954, John McCloy, the United States high commissioner for Germany, intervened and had him freed. Adolf Eichmann, who in Hungary had stood under Veesenmayer's political orders, received no such favors, when in 1961 an Israeli court in Jerusalem condemned him to death. Neither did Sztojay, Jaross, Szalasi,

Vajna, Keményi, and others — Veesenmayer's lackeys — whom a people's court in Budapest condemned to death in 1946. Veesenmayer, the gang leader and almost the only survivor of this unsavory crew, returned to his wholesale perfume business and became a rich and well-respected citizen of Cologne. In vain Nazi hunter Simon Wiesenthal tried to have his case reopened, but among the German judges there were many who only a few years before had themselves served the late Führer. How could they deal harshly with a culprit who had been one of their own? Veesenmayer died in 1977, untroubled by law or bad conscience.

*   *   *

During late afternoon of December 24, 1944, the Red Army closed off all exits from Budapest. A few days earlier, the Germans had launched a desperate counterattack and pushed the Soviets back a little, but they were unable to maintain an open corridor between Budapest and western Hungary. The Red Army renewed its advance and broke through the well-defended German line at Székesféhervar between Lake Balaton and the capital and occupied Suabian Hill. In the end the Soviet move occurred surprisingly fast, so that Eichmann was almost trapped in his headquarters at the Hotel Majestic. Before he departed, he hastily called the Nyilas chiefs to his side, saying with remorse how sorry he was not to have destroyed all of Hungary's Jews. In his entire career, this had been his only failure. Would they please return to the city and finish the job on his behalf? They should no longer respect the immunity of the neutral diplomats who had spoiled their game. Eichmann assured his acolytes that all was not lost, because the Führer still had a secret weapon up his sleeve and that he would win the war and that he, Eichmann, would return.

From Suabian Hill the Red Army continued northward and reached the Danube at Esztergom, where Cardinal Serédi had his official residence, and disrupted the Budapest-Vienna road. No Jew would ever again be forced along that infamous highway.

Given Vajna's mood, Consul Lutz knew that another attack from the Nyilas was coming, despite the desperate military situation. He alerted Lieutenant Fabry's detachment at Vadasz Street, which was composed of army deserters and disillusioned policemen, whom he financed. He placed part of the detachment in a defensive position around the former American legation on Freedom Square; another segment was posted near the glass house on Vadasz Street and in front of the annex building on nearby Wekerle Street. A third detachment, which was composed of thirty policemen who had deserted and who asked the Swiss legation for asylum, was stationed around Eszterhazy Palace next to Mathias Corvinus Church in Buda. Harald Feller had moved the chancellery of the Swiss legation into the basement of that great palace, because he feared that the Swiss legation building on Stefania Street would soon be captured by the Red Army. Eszterhazy Palace was located only 300 yards from the Lutz residence in the former British legation. The Eszterhazy family thought that their residence would be safer if it hosted a neutral legation.

No such precautions were taken by the Swedish legation and its dependent buildings. Minister Danielsson seemed sure that he was sufficiently protected by his extra-territorial immunity. The Arrow Cross noted the absence of armed guards. Eichmann had barely left when Nyilas trucks stopped in front of the legation. "Snot noses" jumped off and attacked the building, knocking down doors, breaking windows, destroying office furniture, and carrying away files with names and addresses of Swedish protégés. They stole Minister Danielsson's paintings, food supplies, and his expensive wine. The minister escaped through a back door and fled to the papal nunciature. As Rotta's residence was too small and provided little safety, Danielsson moved on to the Swiss chancellery at Eszterhazy Palace, where Feller, who had reinforced his police guard further, hid the Swede in the cellar. Danielsson remained there until the end of the war. Wallenberg vanished, but showed up at the Swiss legation later. Lars Berg, a legation attaché, Yngve Ekmark, a consul, and two women, Asta Nielsson and her secretary, Margareth Bauer, both from the Swedish Red Cross, were less lucky. The Arrow Cross kidnapped them and carried them away. They were freed by Friedrich Born a few days later. Not counting the repeated raids on the Swiss Schutzhäuser on Poszonyi Road, this was the first full-scale attack on the central seat of a neutral legation.

*　　*　　*

In the later recollections of both Carl and Gertrud Lutz, this last Budapest Christmas was the one bright moment in the midst of gruesome happenings. 1944 would also be the last time they celebrated Christ's birth together.

Carl Lutz, the inveterate romantic, did his best to make this Christmas the best celebration ever, as if in defiance of the fate that had brought him to this indescribable conjuncture. There would be a large candle-lit tree in the great hall of the former British legation for a Christmas Eve fête. On Christmas day itself, the 25th, he and Gertrud and several of his staff — Magda and Agnes would be kept out of sight — would walk over to Eszterhazy Palace, bearing cakes and small presents, and continue having a good time with Harald Feller and his Swedish guests. Carl Lutz remembered how his father and mother used to gather their expectant brood around the Christmas tree in their low-ceilinged living room in Walzenhausen. The candles were so expensive in those days! But they shed a marvelous, warm light. Then, Ursula, his mother, would read the Christmas story from the Bible: "In those days a decree went out from Caesar Augustus that all the world should be enrolled. . . ." If he thought about it, he could even now recite the entire text by heart and sing all of the verses of half a dozen Christmas carols. The children would receive presents, perhaps a pair of warm hand-knitted socks, made by Ursula's nimble fingers after the children were in bed. There was no money to buy toys. The one toy they did have was a wooden horse, made by his father, Johannes. He'd better not think of it, otherwise the tears would flow and he could not show himself in public. What would his mother think of him now? She would certainly approve of his protecting thousands of Jews. But what about Magda? God forgive him! She was there when he returned home at night. Her little daughter, Agnes, was a bright and cheerful little girl. It was inevitable that she brought him to her mother or her to him, knowing that Unkie, as she called him, liked her, without gathering the depth of their mutual attraction. He remained courteous to Gertrud, they even slept in the same room, they talked about the events of the day, and Gertrud accompanied him on his dangerous missions, but their sexual relations had ceased. There were nights when she searched out his side of the bed, only to find that it was empty. Iron-willed they maintained a united front toward the outside, though everybody in the household and probably beyond knew what was happening. Perhaps Ursula would have understood. There was no one he had ever met, who, like his mother, had had such an incredible capacity of looking at a person and knowing what were his or her innermost secrets. The Künzlers, from whom she descended, were said to be a religious family, but to some there was a mystery about them. They had produced inventors, travelers, introverts, poets, philosophers, and people who knew how to explain the world. Carl himself probably had inherited more of the Künzler strain than he knew.

During the afternoon of the 24th, the consul assembled his staff at his office on Freedom Square around a candle-lit Christmas tree. He had insisted on this, even though his secretary had balked at first, saying that even such a modest celebration seemed inappropriate when the city was under fire and they all were so terribly busy. The consul ignored her, and when his people trooped into his office, he told them that they were an unusual and dedicated team and that he thanked them for their cooperation throughout the year, a year full of dangers. He wished he could be more positive about what was in store for them all, but he hoped that these tribulations would soon end. He said that as a religious person he was sure that the Almighty still held his hand over them. This was followed by small talk. Gertrud had offered small cakes, which was a rarity for most. Although it was still early in the afternoon the consul allowed those who lived away from Freedom Square to return home at their pleasure. He was looking forward to seeing them after Christmas, he said, as he shook hands with the parting staff.

Among the staff there were two newcomers, two young Swiss business executives by the name of Peter Zürcher and Ernst Vonrufs. Zürcher was a corporate lawyer who had descended from a distinguished family of pastors and legislators. He had come to Hungary shortly before the war, where, young as he was, he had been directing a textile conglomerate, which belonged to Swiss investors. Warfare had ended this highly successful venture, but Zürcher did not return to safety in Switzerland, because tender bonds attached him to a beautiful young Hungarian woman. He had come to Consul Lutz, asking for a temporary assignment.

The other was Ernst Vonrufs, who was a few years older than Zürcher, his friend. He had come to Budapest during the mid-thirties, was married, and had two small children. He, too, was in the textile business. Vonrufs had built up two flourishing mills and had gathered together a modest fortune. When, during the summer of 1944, war came near, he sent his family back to Switzerland. He himself remained in Hungary, because he wanted to remain within reach of his enterprises and to save what he could of his properties. He, too, had asked Lutz for work, in order to spend his time usefully while impatiently waiting for the war to end.

This was in November 1944, when the crisis over the "illegitimate" Schutzbriefe was at its height and the consul needed every help to bring matters under control. The Chalutzim were dedicated, he said, and several had lost their lives while working for him, not forgetting that most had lost all of their families. Many were psychologically damaged, which explained perhaps why some were disorganized and unruly. He wanted to keep Vajna or any other of his enemies from making the "disorder" an excuse for declaring him persona non grata and closing down the entire operation. There were tens of thousands of protective letters in circulation, perhaps close to 100,000, and he thought the department needed stronger day-by-day guidance. One problem was that the Schutzbrief action had grown out of all proportions far too quickly. Moshe Krausz, the head of the department, was not capable of giving direction to such a vast operation. Moreover, he didn't get along with the Chalutzim and he increasingly withdrew into himself, wondering only whether he and his family would survive.

Zürcher and Vonrufs agreed to take charge of the operation, to Lutz's great relief. The consul asked his superiors in Berne to confirm Zürcher and Vonrufs as temporary staff executives at the non-diplomatic level. The hiring of these two energetic young men was one of the finest moves of his career in Budapest.

When the Christmas party was over, the consul kept Peter Zürcher and Ernst Vonrufs behind after the rest had left in late afternoon. He told them that as the Soviet guns were now shelling from nearby, the Soviets would occupy the city within two or three days, hardly more. The Germans could not resist long. It was therefore possible that the bombs and the fighting could prevent him from driving across the Danube from his home to the office for a short while. The bridges might even be blown up. If this were the case, would Zürcher and Vonrufs be prepared to act as his temporary representatives for the Pest side? This meant that they would probably have to make early contacts with the Soviet forces, once they reached the center of Pest, negotiate with them, if need be, keep an eye on the former American legation, explain to them the glass house and of course the Schutzhäuser on Poszonyi Road. Above all there was the large ghetto, where 25,000 "Swiss" Jews were interned at high risk. The two young men should of course share responsibility with the other neutral representatives for the safety of the entire ghetto of 70,000. This was the most exposed link of the protective system of the neutrals. They knew as well as he that this was a dangerous assignment, especially if things went from bad to worse. Dr. Zürcher planned to marry and Mr. Vonrufs had a family. They should think about it.

Without hesitation they said yes, as if it was the most natural thing to do. The consul was relieved. For the first time he felt that he was no longer alone. He signed a paper authorizing Dr. Zürcher to act on his behalf in Pest, in case this would become necessary, supported by Mr. Vonrufs. Then Lutz wrote a corresponding note to the foreign ministry, just in case, and asked his secretary to deposit it with Keményi on her way home, or if the foreign minister had gone to Sopron like everyone else, to leave the paper with Bagossy.

Then Lutz made the rounds of the legation building, wishing a merry Christmas to those to whom he had given protection. There were 150 of them, and most came forward wanting to shake hands. The woman he had rescued from the cold Danube waters walked on crutches. She was recuperating well and he gave her a hug, reassuring her that she could stay inside the legation as long as she wanted. Then he took the little Christmas tree and a handful of candles and walked over to the glass house, with Szluha following behind in the Packard, shaking his head, wondering why the consul insisted on going on foot, carrying tree and candles with his own hands. It was cold and snow was falling, and the noise of battle was more muffled. The glass house was terribly crowded. An incredible 4,000 refugees were crammed in there and in the two annex buildings. There was barely space for setting up the tree, small as it was, and the candles burned uncertainly for want of air. The people were glad for the break in their monotonous existence, however, and wished the consul a happy Chanukkah. He encouraged them to hold on, because in a few days surely the war would be over and they could go home. When he saw Rafi Friedl and Alexander Grossman, he took them apart and whispered an invitation into their ear to celebrate Christmas Eve at his residence that evening. He would have liked to invite all of the Chalutzim, but he obviously couldn't do that. He simply wanted to express his appreciation to them in this way. He would send Szluha to fetch them in his official car, for safety's sake.

The consul ordered his chauffeur to drive him to the Great Synagogue, where the large ghetto had its principal entry. He left him waiting, while the SS guards opened the gate. They let him through without a check. Once again, he continued on foot. For an hour he walked up and down the ancient cobblestone streets, knocking occasionally at the doors of the old run-down houses. The inhabitants peeked out suspiciously, but they relaxed when they saw it was he. They were living badly, they complained, they were cold and hungry, sometimes the Nyilas came and threatened them, but they were surviving. The children were worse off, because no one took care of them and they were already weak when they came in. The consul answered that he would send in more food and fuel, and that he and his colleagues from the other legations were keeping an eye on the large ghetto and that they were not abandoned, although inwardly he did worry and they knew it.

When he came out, an early mid-winter darkness had engulfed the city. It stopped snowing. The air was icily cold and he saw a few stars. He ordered Szluha to head up Andrassy Avenue. The snow had made the surface slippery and Szluha was driving with care. The consul went to pay a brief call on the Methodist superintendent, wishing him a merry Christmas and leaving a pound of coffee with him. Occasionally the diplomatic pouch brought such rarities to Budapest, and he knew that the superintendent and his family had not seen coffee for months, if not years. Perhaps he should have left the gift at the large ghetto, where people had nothing at all, but what good was one pound among thousands? The pastor thanked him profusely. Then he raised his eyebrows and the consul shook his head. No, he hadn't changed his relations with . . . her.

On his way home, before crossing St. Margaret Bridge, he drove along Poszonyi Road, stopping off at several Schutzhäuser, wishing a merry Christmas or a happy Chanukkah to the Hechalutz guards and to some of the people he happened to see. It was evident that they all lived a miserable life. They were wrapped up in blankets and looked underfed, though perhaps not as badly as the inmates of the large ghetto. Their one concern was whether the Nyilas would come back and make them disappear like the 300. The consul reassured them that this was unlikely. He would keep an eye on Poszonyi Road, they knew that, didn't they? Lutz asked that his greetings be passed on to those on the upper floors. They should be told that they would soon be free.

He posted himself in the middle of the long road, looking up and down the buildings that used to belong to a fine middle-class neighborhood. At the windows hundreds of faces pressed against the glass, staring at him, wishing to be free. If it were not for him, they knew they would be small heaps of ash in Auschwitz or skeletons by the side of the road to Vienna. They were human beings, each with his or her personal story. They were not numbers. It was important to remember this uniqueness when he faced his enemies, those brutes, who only talked in numbers, in mathematical units. He knew he was taking risk upon risk to save these people, which gave the Nyilas new excuses to return and do their evil deeds.

But the consul was tired. Why, O God, was the struggle so long? If only the shells stopped screaming and exploding, at least at night. What if a single bomb hit one of these crowded buildings? This was a nightmare.

It was seven o'clock by the time Szluha drove the Packard through the gate of the former British legation. As he got out, he did not know that he had just returned from his last round of Pest as the Swiss consul. He would never again even see his office in the former American legation.

The consul ordered the chauffeur to return to Pest in order to pick up Friedl and Grossman.

*   *   *

Gertrud had also thought of Christmas. She wanted to make a counterpoint to war and to the distress of her own situation. Of course she was not one to let anyone peek behind the disguise that concealed her feelings. But Christmas was a time of emotions, when even strong persons could break down, cry, stamp their feet, or create angry scenes. Above all, no one knew whether one would survive this terrible war, this hurricane that was reaching its culmination. Perhaps, after it was all over and the dust had settled, normality might return, also in her relations with Carl. She must not be too hard on him, because for months he had been going through hell, being in the forefront of a gigantic battle in order to save tens of thousands. Stronger men would have collapsed under the weight of such responsibility. Perhaps Professor Tier was right when he said that Carl was imbued with greatness. But then Tier tended to exaggerate, and what she herself saw was not an imposing strength, but an ordinary being, whom circumstances had propelled upward to battle demons. Carl, she admitted, was nevertheless fighting extremely well. If he had been an ordinary person, for instance a simple bureaucrat, like many other consuls, he would have said that saving Jews was none of his business, because officially it was not. Such people didn't even have to be antisemitic. Indifference and laziness sufficed, because involvement always meant trouble, problems with superiors, blocked careers, danger from enemies. Most people on earth belonged to this category, she thought. In that sense, yes, Carl had greatness, because he did care. But then there was Magda. How did his weakness for her pair with greatness? Even if Carl dropped her and sent her back to her husband, would their own relations ever be the same again? But then, Magda, with her beauty and her enticing warmth, made up for what she, Gertrud, seemed to lack, even though she herself surely was not bad looking, and even if she, in her way, was a warm person. Her rival was really a very intelligent and a well-mannered person. One could see that she came from a distinguished family. Under normal circumstances the two women could even become friends. But had the seed for her and Carl's estrangement not been laid ten years earlier, when she, Gertrud, wanted to cancel the wedding because she had met that young architect? Carl had not appreciated her waywardness. He had taken her aside for a serious talk, almost like a father scolding his rebellious daughter. He had been almost forty and she a young girl of twenty-three, after all. The difference in age was considerable, but surely not decisive. Or was it? They never again talked about this story, but a certain rancor must have remained in both their hearts. Then there were no children. . . .

Gertrud resolved that there was no point going round in circles and racking her mind over past and present. So she threw herself instead into the preparations for the feast. They all would share. Geoffrey Tier would humor them with stories, perhaps about his mishaps with the British Secret Services, whether they were true or not. Magda, why not, was a good cook and she knew how to play musical instruments. Agnes could make cookies, as soon as she, Gertrud, found some flour. Szluha would find a pine tree, cut it, put it up, and light the candles. Carl could read from the Bible and give a talk. He always did that well. And she, herself, would find the food supplies, without which Christmas was impossible, and she would supervise everything.

When Gertrud heard on December 21 that the Red Army had been evicted from Biske, a small town west of the capital, where the Swiss legation had rented a rural manor house to serve as a refuge in case it got bombed out of Stefania Street, she "borrowed" Szluha and the Packard and drove there to find food supplies for a good Christmas, and, if possible, additional stores for the uncertain days to come. There was a farm attached to the manor, which made contacts easier, all the more as she was going to pay the tenant with hard Swiss currency instead of the anemic Hungarian pengö. When her household was concerned she used all the advantages of her position as the wife of a consul. Gertrud thought of eggs, a sack of flour, and, why not, an entire pig. If her Jewish house guests were hungry — as they doubtless were — they would not mind dining on a well-roasted pork chop. They could always ask for God's forgiveness, if they suffered from pangs of conscience. Surely, the Lord in heaven understood and forgave, especially if he himself had ever gone as hungry as they.

Gertrud found the house of refuge and the adjacent farm unharmed, despite recent battles (both would be razed when the Red Army took Biske a second time). She wrote later about her "shopping trip":

If one wanted to build up an adequate food supply, it was necessary to forage like a hamster. Whoever owned an automobile drove to the countryside as often as possible, in order to return with large bags of potatoes, flour, fats and meat. Because of the lack of transportation, these supplies were short in Budapest. Ration cards were of no use in the city, while in rural areas the farming estates offered an abundance of such products, which often couldn't even find buyers.

The journey, though relatively short, was difficult, because the road was swarming with German and Hungarian soldiers, who fled westward, all trying to escape the Soviet encirclement. Shortly before the Packard arrived in Biske, low-flying Soviet planes machine-gunned the road, and bullets hit adjacent fields.

Despite such hair-raising incidents, Gertrud's food-gathering journey was a success. The trunk and the backseat of the car were loaded down with potatoes, onions, flour, and half a dozen geese, stripped and cleaned by the farmer's wife. Gertrud agreed with the farmer that she would return on the following day. He promised to kill no less than three pigs, and cut and prepare them for her to take back. This would be a marvelous Christmas feast for her household, for people who hadn't eaten meat for weeks or months. She paid the farmer in advance. Gertrud and Szluha left Biske after nightfall, hoping that darkness would protect them from low-flying airplanes and other mishaps. But at one point Szluha braked sharply, because in the obscurity the shape of a huge tank coming toward him loomed up. It rumbled across the road right in front of the Packard, inches away. "My God!" Gertrud exclaimed, raising her hands to her mouth. Almost at the same moment she noticed tanks moving all around them. They had driven right into an advancing armored column of the Red Army, which was crossing the road toward the north. Szluha maneuvered with dexterity and escaped the steel monsters. For a moment both Szluha and Gertrud thought they would be crushed.

Luckily, the Packard was black and could not be easily seen at night and none of the guns in the turrets turned in their direction. The Soviet tank commanders, if they saw the vehicle at all, must have wondered why an American Packard with a Hungarian diplomatic license plate was crossing their battle-poised column, as if negotiating city traffic.

Despite this close call Gertrud decided to return to Biske on the next day, in order to pick up the meat. The entire household forgot its worries and talked about nothing but the wonderful Christmas dinner that was to come. The consul thought his wife should not take such terrible risks and pleaded with her to stay at home. But once she had made up her mind, he knew that no power on earth, her husband least of all, could shake her determination. She'd be back, he didn't have to worry, she said. The Christmas fête would be one they'd remember always. The consul patted her cheek, and from his brief glance she judged that his love for her had not entirely died.

Gertrud and Szluha took off shortly after the break of day, hoping that the machine-gunning airplane pilots would ignore them. The road seemed strangely empty. The flight of soldiers and civilians had apparently stopped. There was battle noise in front. They heard the heavy booming of artillery and wondered why machine gun and rifle fire seemed to come from so close at hand, interspersed as it was by hard short strikes of tank artillery. A surprised German post stopped the Packard. The sergeant in charge could not hide his astonishment at a civilian vehicle running around a battlefield. He looked at Gertrud's papers and said there were limits even to diplomats and if life was dear to Frau Konsul she must not advance further. She had to pick up some merchandise in Biske, Gertrud insisted. Biske had fallen to the Soviets during the night, the sergeant explained. Gertrud shook her head, perplexed. So that was what those tanks were doing, she mused. What tanks? the sergeant asked. Never mind, she answered, it was too complicated to explain. "We had to return without having achieved our objective," Gertrud recalled factually, when she talked of this incident later. "Russian soldiers probably ate our splendid Christmas dinner. Nevertheless our supplies were satisfactory. I thought they would last us for four to six weeks."

*   *   *

Even the normally imperturbable Szluha was upset when he deposited Rafi Friedl and Alexander Grossman at Verböcsy Street on Christmas Eve. He called the consul into the courtyard and recounted breathlessly what had happened after he had gone to pick up the two Chalutzim at the glass house. When they were crossing the chain bridge a Nyilas post ordered him to a halt, even though he was driving a diplomatic vehicle. Without any warning the "snot noses" tried to pry open the door. They probably wanted to throw them out and steal the car. Fortunately they had managed to lock all the doors in the nick of time. The Nyilas banged against the sides with their boots, shook the Packard dangerously, and ripped off the Swiss consular pennant. Their leader seemed to be an especially vicious fellow, Szluha said. The only solution was to break through and race away. The bandits sent a few bullets after them but hit nothing. Szluha was sorry for the damage they had caused to the beautiful car.

The consul looked the Packard over. He saw nothing but a few scratches. No bullet holes, nothing serious, he said, he had more pennants in store. Rafi said that if the Nyilas had opened the doors, he would have fought the criminals like the devil. He would have thrown their leader over the railing into the Danube, like they always did with the Jews. Grossman said he noticed that the gang chief was dressed in black, not in green as the Arrow Cross usually were, and that he looked like a priest. He could have been a priest, he added on second thought, he had heard of a Nyilas group chieftain, one Father Andras Kun, who was killing Jews in the name of Jesus Christ. Lutz shuddered. What an aberration, he exclaimed, in the name of Jesus the Prince of Peace, who had been a Jew himself!

Before they entered the house, Grossman took the consul aside. He said he had heard an interesting rumor running about town, namely that Eichmann had fled Budapest during the afternoon. He said he wasn't sure if it was really true, but he hoped it was. Eichmann! Lutz exclaimed. Had they at last got rid of the monster? An inhuman human, a multiple murderer, who was married and had children, but who sent other people's children to the gas chambers, and who fainted when he saw blood? He hoped he would meet his just reward some day.

In the great hall of the former British legation on the hill of Buda it was the night before Christmas. Consul Lutz decided to start a new diary, because he thought that he was about to face events of great portent. He wanted to record them while they were fresh in his memory, a written photo album, so to speak. Despite war and horrors, his first entry was marked by a touch of romanticism, which was typical of most of his personal notes: "The tree radiated a most fabulous light. In the great hall we were all assembled together. The windows were rigorously blacked out, because the front lines had come dangerously close to Budapest. If one went outside one could see lightning and fire signals, and the sound of cannon made our windows rattle. But all of this distant fury vanished under the gentle tune of Silent Night, Holy Night which came from the harmonium in the next room."

It was a moving celebration, even for Jews who had never seen a Christmas tree or who did not know any of the tunes. Former days, Chanukkah commemorations, the Feast of Light, came to their mind, long before there were race laws, yellow stars, and cattle trains. There were tears and empty stares; there was also a new feeling of security and belonging among a group of people, most of whom had not known each other the year before. Where would they be the next Christmas? With Agnes by his side, the consul read the obligatory Christmas tale in a sonorous voice: "In those days a decree went out . . . , the story about that Jewish baby, whose young parents of uncertain status were robbed by unscrupulous tax collectors, of soldiers sent by a tyrant to kill babies, and of a flight into exile by night. It seemed as if this familiar Christmas tale was written by someone today, Geoffrey Tier exclaimed. When did human beings ever stop oppressing others? God's hand was over the child, the consul answered. But why didn't he send his angels to protect our children? Alexander Grossman asked. He got up and walked around the hall, his hands behind his back. He struggled to maintain his composure. He wished he had the answer, the consul replied softly. Instinctively, he patted Agnes's blonde head, but stopped when Grossman turned, looked at them, and wanted to say something, but did not.

Another Christmas carol followed, "O Come, All Ye Faithful." Gertrud Lutz later remembered that in the middle of this hymn a grenade suddenly struck the next building and caused a frightful explosion. Several windows of the legation were shattered and cold winter air streamed in. But no one panicked: "For the sake of the children we continued this little celebration crossing our fingers and with self-discipline," she wrote later. "We prayed fervently for protection and that there be Peace on Earth soon."

Two days later, on December 26, another shell struck the house next door. All of the windows of the former British legation flew to pieces. The consul learned to his dismay that the German commander of Budapest, SS general Pfeffer-von Wildenbruch, and his general staff had chosen the old historic wine cellars below the neighboring residence to be his headquarters. The location had been betrayed to the Soviets, and Marshal Malinovsky now directed his aircraft and his heavy artillery at the site, hoping to wipe out the German command post. This meant that the former British legation was almost in the direct line of fire. "There were several explosions on that day," the consul wrote in his diary. "I ordered all the women and children to move into the cellar. The five policemen guarding our building had to move couches, rugs and upholstered furniture into the cellar, including a large metal container full of food supplies. Next to this cellar there is another one, interconnected with the first by a long corridor. We installed toilets and wash basins."

At frequent intervals the walls of the cellar trembled. Henceforth, Lutz and his household sat in near darkness, brightened by a mere candle, left over from Christmas. There was no more electricity. The few candles had to be used sparingly, because no one knew how long the Red Army would keep pounding the German headquarters. It was a nerveracking experience, all the more so as Lutz could not avoid remembering that four feet below the surface of the inner court of the former British legation, directly above the cellars, there was the container filled with 3,000 liters of gasoline, which the British minister had installed in case of need. The gasoline container had now become a potential bomb.

The consul's diary stopped here, after the second or third entry. It was barely possible to write in darkness, in the midst of the tremors. From now on he and his household lived one single uninterrupted night. They were cut off from all outside communication. Lutz had brought a battery-run radio into the cellar, but the sound was weak, as the battery was nearly exhausted. Each evening at seven they captured the thin voice of the BBC. This is how they heard the news confirmed that Budapest lay under siege from all sides and that the Germans were in vain trying to lift it. After a few days the battery gave up the ghost and they were cut off. Lutz wondered whether they had escaped Veesenmayer and the Arrow Cross only to be crushed by Soviet bombs.

The consul could not know that on this Christmas Eve his troublesome next-door neighbor, SS general Pfeffer-von Wildenbruch, had wired the Führer for permission to capitulate. His forces were exhausted and outnumbered, he explained, and ammunition was running short. Two days later, on the 26th, the crazed man in Berlin angrily replied that such dishonor was out of the question. Officers who capitulated would be executed. "To the last man . . . !" he ordered.

10. THE LAST ASSAULT

The siege and the shelling did not mean that the Arrow Cross were giving up their evil designs inside the beleaguered city. A few days after Christmas, the Nyilas trained their sights on Harald Feller, the young Swiss legation chief. They were sure he was hiding Danielsson and other Swedish diplomatic staff members, but could not prove it. Moreover, the Nyilas were convinced that Feller was hiding Jews in his own private apartment on the western slope of Buda hill. Some suspicious neighbors had sent them a hint. Both rumors were of course true. Feller was sheltering Danielsson and most of the Swedish legation staff, except for Wallenberg, who wanted to maintain his independence and sought safety in frequent address changes. And Feller did hide thirty Jews in a rescue action of his own. There were children among them, and one young woman was about to give birth to a baby.

One night shortly after Christmas Zolton Bagossy came to Feller's apartment to find out. The giant had resumed his old ways as an ordinary Nyilas gang chief. If his suspicions were confirmed, he was determined to remove these Jews by force, regardless of whether Feller's apartment was extra-territorial or not. Bagossy pulled up outside Feller's house with a truck. He made his companions wait outside; they must not come in until he called them.

Feller could not refuse the dangerous visitor, but before Bagossy began a room by room search, the diplomat made him sit down. He placed a whiskey glass in front of him, and kept filling it for hours on end, fetching an-

233

other bottle as each one emptied. Simultaneously, he kept the Nyilas chieftain engaged in vigorous conversation. Feller's lively spirit, his training as a theater actor, and his rich knowledge of literature enabled him to find new conversation topics endlessly. At two in the morning, the Swiss top diplomat to Hungary, who himself did not scorn Scotland's finest, dragged his unwelcome guest out into the street and dropped him into the arms of his astonished Nyilas fighters. Feller said their boss was sleepy, and he asked that the gentlemen be so good as to bring him to a soft bed. As the Nyilas drove off, the young man took a deep breath.

For the moment the thirty Jews were safe. But early next morning Feller moved them in all haste from his apartment to the Swiss chancellery at Eszterhazy Palace, where he placed them in the deepest recesses of the noble structure. It took eight or nine trips before they all had disappeared inside the great palace. Finally, he moved his own belongings. He assumed that once Bagossy became sober he would lose no time and return in a vengeful mood. The gangster would, however, find his apartment empty. But it all meant that the Arrow Cross would be gunning for him personally.

Thus, the next incident followed quickly, on December 29. Feller could not handle the situation with the same ease. On this occasion he became personally acquainted with the mysterious Arrow Cross priest, Father Andras Kun. The Swiss diplomat never knew whether he was attacked because of the Bagossy incident or for another reason, but he was sure that Bagossy had something to do with it. On the evening of that day, after nightfall, Feller decided that despite the constant shelling he wanted to give encouragement to the few staff he had left behind at the regular Swiss legation on Stefania Street. They were bravely risking their lives, he felt, by waiting for the critical moment when the Germans withdrew and the Soviets arrived. This was likely to be his last visit on Stefania Street. The front was now only minutes away. Feller took along Baroness Valeria Perényi, his secretary, who of late had become his fiancée, an undaunted and fearless person like himself. At night at least the Soviet airplanes did not swoop low along the avenues and machine- gun moving vehicles. The only danger came from the artillery, whose grenades exploded throughout the city, also at night. But there were also the roaming Arrow Cross gangs. When Consul

Lutz heard of the venture of Feller and his fiancée he called it an act not of courage but of folly by a young couple.

Harald and Valeria raced down the Buda hill slope to the Danube, crossed the chain bridge, and soon they were driving along Rakoczy Avenue eastward. The city was dark — only the lightning flashes of war and an occasional burning building showed the way and helped them avoid gaping shell holes. The occasional military posts waved them through with an indifference that announced the approaching end.

Suddenly they were stopped by an Arrow Cross roadblock. Feller showed his papers and said he was a diplomat. This did not impress the Nyilas, and they ordered the couple to follow one of their trucks. One young man entered the backseat and held his rifle to Feller's head. A few "snot noses" sat on top of the truck in front and pointed their rifles at them as they rode through the dark streets. Within minutes they reached the Arrow Cross headquarters. This was a large, gloomy building at number 60 Andrassy Avenue. Feller and the baroness shuddered when they followed their captors through a gigantic entrance gate and entered the inner court, where they were told to leave their car, but to leave the key in the ignition. They had heard countless rumors about torture chambers in this building, and in the darkness they thought they saw two or three lifeless bodies lying alongside one of the walls.

They were led to a small cellar room with a desk and a few chairs. A large German swastika and an Arrow Cross flag hung on the wall. Feller protested again when he and the baroness were ordered to sit down. He repeated that he was a diplomat and could not be arrested or questioned and that the baroness was a diplomatic staff person with similar rights. He said he knew several Nyilas group chiefs, Bagossy and others, and that he maintained good relations with them; he wanted to see them. But the Nyilas only laughed when they heard these names and gesticulated obscenely.

The door opened suddenly and a black-dressed young man with a clergyman's collar and a black hat entered. The Nyilas stepped back respectfully, seized his hand, and kissed it. This was evidently the ill-famed Father Andras Kun, the gang chieftain. With cynical sharp black eyes the priest looked at his guests. He studied their papers. Then he looked up and exclaimed that they had apparently caught some rare birds. Herr Doktor Feller, the Swiss chargé d'affaires! And an authentic baroness. What an honor. They needed to have a serious conversation together, didn't they? The priest turned Feller's briefcase upside down. Several papers and 100 old Napoleon gold coins fell out. Did the Jews pay him all this money for hiding them? he asked. Or did he finance spies with this gold? They belonged to a Swiss citizen, Feller answered, who wanted him to place them in the safe of the Swiss legation until the war was over. Why should the legation on Stefania Street, a few minutes from the front, be a much safer place than Eszterhazy Palace in Buda? the priest asked, as he pocketed the gold coins. He changed the subject without waiting for an answer. Where, he asked, was Minister Danielsson? Feller answered that he did not know. He was lying, Kun said with an undertone of menace. As a priest he knew when people lied and when they did not, he said. How about those Jews he was hiding in his apartment? There were none, Feller answered. If the father would like to find out, he should go and check himself. If they were not there, where were they? Feller said he had no idea about any Jews. Why did he make Bagossy drunk? The whiskey was good and they were both drunk, was his answer.

He would soon find out, the priest said, and he waved to one of his men, whispering into his ear. The Nyilas nodded. How about a persuasive argument such as pulling out fingernails? Kun asked. The Nyilas returned with a set of long, pointed pliers. These, the priest explained, would be introduced just under Feller's nails. Then the pliers would be pressed together and slowly they would pull the nails out. This method made everybody talk, he added. As if to protect his fingers, Feller rolled them together until they made a fist and brought his hands down by his sides. Kun noticed the movement, smiled, and said, Feller seemed to understand. Once they had taken care of him, they would turn to his lady friend, and he, Feller, would be watching from close by what they did to her. This method, too, made boyfriends and husbands wince and talk. Did he need to be more specific? With a long wooden staff Kun hit both of them over their heads, which was very painful. Harald and Valeria made a grimace of pain but did not cry out. Kun apparently wanted to see how they might react to torture. In the end they would be shot, Kun added, like those people they had seen in the courtyard. How about the truth now, without more ado, quickly?

When Harald Feller talked about this terrible scene in later years, pain showed in his face. He said that when everything seemed lost, a miracle happened, which he could not explain. A Nyilas suddenly opened the door and peeked into the room. He shouted that a truck full of boots had just arrived. They really belonged to the German SS, but one of their comrades had sidetracked the truck and brought it here. If they hurried, they could get what they wanted. Without another look at their prisoners Kun and several of the Arrow Cross rushed out to steal these goods from their comrades-in-arms.

Feller recovered his wits. They might have a fighting chance to get out, he realized, but he and the baroness would have only a few seconds, at the most a minute, before their torturers came back. Using his best acting, he tried a bluff on the few Nyilas whom Kun had left behind. He recalled having overheard a chance remark made by one of them, that he had a cousin in Berne by the name of Szilagyi, who represented the Arrow Cross government in Switzerland. Feller said to him that if he and the baroness were tortured and put to death, the Swiss government would execute that diplomat Szilagyi immediately. Did he want that? There was a hasty debate among the Nyilas, at the end of which Szilagyi's cousin opened the door carefully, looked up and down the corridor, and told Feller and the baroness to vanish. The two, hardly believing their good luck, hastened out of the room, ran up the stairs, came to the inner court, jumped into the car, and raced through the gate before the guard there knew what was happening.

*   *   *

Revenge for the escape came quickly and mercilessly. On New Year's Eve, two days after the near-murder at the Arrow Cross headquarters, the Nyilas came to attack a major Swiss installation, the glass house, which housed the Department of Emigration of the Swiss legation, from where the Chalutzim communicated with the Jewish community throughout Budapest, and where 4,000 people were hiding. This was really the focal point of the resistance organized by Consul Lutz, who had inspired all the other neutral legations. The glass house must be eliminated. The moment was favorable. Consul Lutz was neutralized in his cellar, and his friend, Foreign Minister Keményi, that wolf in sheep's clothing, who was more worried about Hungary's image abroad than anything else, had gone to Sopron.

No less than forty to fifty Nyilas raced into narrow Vadasz Street. The assault happened so fast that Lieutenant Fabry and his military detachment around the corner did not realize what was going on, until they were told later.

The few policemen standing guard hastily withdrew inside the glass house and locked the door. The "snot noses" threw a hand grenade. The door cracked into a thousand splinters. One Nyilas jumped off a truck and pushed his machine pistol through the opening and started firing inside. There were frightful shouts. Three Jews were killed, among them the wife of a rabbi. Then the other Nyilas jumped off their trucks, entered the building cursing, and drove 800 persons out into the cold. They pretended they were concerned for their security and wanted to move them to the large ghetto.

Rafi Friedl and Alexander Grossman felt they had nothing to lose. They took courage, stepped forward, and told the invaders loudly that they were top executives of the Swiss legation. They spoke in German, not Hungarian, which made the uneducated Nyilas think they were foreigners, perhaps Germans. They became unsure. With imposing gestures Friedl and Grossman pulled paper pads out of their pockets, pretending that they had to write a report to the consul, and the consul would contact the highest Hungarian authorities, asking that these authorities confirm the transfer officially, inasmuch as the Nyilas group seemed to have no written order. There would of course be an official investigation into the broken glass door and the deaths. The police would establish a protocol. As they talked like this they advanced toward the surprised young assailants, writing at the same time. The Nyilas became less boisterous and turned into what they really were, insecure teenagers who did not know how to behave. They finally admitted they were hungry and had come to get some food. They were told the Jews in the glass house were much better fed than ordinary Hungarians. Rafi Friedl asked why they hadn't said so right away. They would have given them something to eat without a problem, had they only asked decently. Look at the broken glass and the dead people!

At this point Arthur Weisz, the owner of the glass house, who had rented the premises to the Swiss legation, joined the conversation. He said he would see to it that they got food, but he had to make a list of the kind and quantities of food they needed and then see how much they could spare. He, too, started to write importantly as he talked. Weisz's intervention gave Friedl and Grossman a chance to withdraw without being noticed. Grossman ran to Freedom Square and alarmed Zürcher and Vonrufs, and Friedl alerted Lieutenant Fabry. In less than fifteen minutes the surprised "snot noses" were cornered by policemen and soldiers. In an authoritative voice Dr. Zürcher asked them to leave, as they had entered an extra-territorial building. The Nyilas beat a hasty retreat, uttering curses and threats. Fabry thought it was better to let them escape instead of shooting at them. If only one Arrow Cross was left dead, the entire mob of 3,000 to 4,000 Nyilas from all over Budapest would converge upon the glass house within the hour. There would be a slaughter.

But this was not all. On the same day, almost at the same time, Nyilas bands attacked a Swedish Schutzhaus on Poszonyi Road. Whether the two attacks were coordinated cannot be established. It is possible, however, that the Arrow Cross really meant to raid a Swiss-protected Schutzhaus in revenge for their failures, but did not know the difference between Switzerland and Sweden — that is, if they cared. This second attack had far worse effects than the first. The "snot noses" seized all of the 290 inhabitants of that building, brought them to the Danube shore, executed them, and threw their bodies into the river. They claimed that this was the just punishment for someone firing at a passing Arrow Cross band.

After these multiple murders the time had come for Peter Zürcher to go into high gear as the Pest representative of Carl Lutz. Since Christmas the situation had undergone profound changes. If Consul Lutz had still managed to deal with a structured, though increasingly confused, government, Zürcher barely knew to whom he must address his complaints and, if he did, how much authority the addressees possessed. He decided at this point that he must lodge his protests with one Ernö Vajna. This was, Zürcher was told, the brother of Gabor, the obnoxious minister of the interior, who had fled to Sopron with the rest of the Arrow Cross government. He had been appointed the official representative of that government in Budapest and had established his headquarters in city hall, an impressive late-nineteenth-century building in Pest. Ernö Vajna was at least as violent and hateful as Gabor.

Zürcher came to the important man accompanied by Ernst Vonrufs. The two Swiss businessmen were inseparable, as they crisscrossed shell-torn Pest on their extensive and highly dangerous journeys by foot. Vonrufs functioned as a witness to Zürcher, his bodyguard and trusted advisor. And vice versa. Upon seeing Vajna, Zürcher first protested vigorously about the outrageous crime committed at the Swedish Schutzhaus. Vajna counterattacked violently, eyes protruding from his forehead, fists pounding on his desk. His inborn violence came to the fore. He said that this was no concern of Zürcher's. By what right did a Swiss representative act on behalf of a third country? Zürcher answered as politely as he could that there were times when national distinctions lost all meaning, that is, when such horrible crimes were taking place. What difference was it if those unfortunate Jews were protected by the Swiss or the Swedes? At any rate, the Swedes had asked him to protest on their behalf. Both Minister Danielsson and Mr. Wallenberg would have come themselves, had the Arrow Cross not threatened to murder them. Zürcher reminded Vajna, if proof was needed, how the Swedish legation had been deliberately destroyed on Christmas Eve. To date the Hungarian had not even offered the slightest excuse. And why did they hound Wallenberg? Would Mr. Vajna now be good enough to deal with him, Zürcher?

The government representative grumbled that "the Jews" had fired from the Schutzhaus and had to be punished. Courteously, Zürcher answered that there had surely been no young or middle-aged men in the building who could even hold a rifle, and that, even if the shooting had taken place, all civilized countries would first proceed with a proper police enquiry. Only if guilt was established would they make a formal accusation, which in turn would serve as the basis for a court trial. Ernö Vajna listened open-mouthed. He had no inkling of juridical procedures. But like all stupid men he could not allow anyone to question his authority. He said he did not wish to continue discussing the matter further and dismissed Zürcher and his companion. The "conversation" was ended.

*　　*　　*

Not knowing that Hitler had ordered Pfeffer-von Wildenbruch to hold out "to the last man," Lutz at first had believed that fighting inside the city would not last more than two or three days and that his absence from the scene of action would be short. After that, he thought he would quietly return to his office on Freedom Square and await the return of the diplomats whose interests he had been representing in wartime Hungary. Naturally he would also do his best to help "his" Jews to return to normal life, devastated as it was.

However, Lutz and Zürcher were separated from each other from Christmas 1944 until mid-February 1945, though Zürcher's own responsibilities ended on January 18, when the Red Army occupied Pest. Buda, however, fell only on February 12. Lutz would doubtless have taken different dispositions had he known that the siege of Budapest would be so agonizingly long. Now he and his entourage were caught in the basement of the former British legation. Soviet artillery pounded all the buildings along the edge of the hill of Buda. One of the policemen guarding the legation was killed, and the consul had him buried in the garden. Another one, who had been sent out to fetch fresh water, was also killed. He fell on Verböcsy Street, and the water from the overturned pail that he was carrying mingled with his blood.

At any rate, the consul could not have chosen two men better equipped than Peter Zürcher and Ernst Vonrufs to represent him in Pest. Like the consul, Zürcher originated from the Appenzell hill country, from a village near Walzenhausen, where people combine toughmindedness with human concern. Unlike the slim-figured Lutz, Zürcher was a solidly built man. He wore dark-rimmed glasses and bore himself with an air of authority. The reports that he laid daily on the consul's abandoned desk were couched in the cool, no-nonsense language of a lawyer-businessman. They listed the essence of events, persons, subject matters, and the time. Only after this evil period was over did Zürcher reveal a personal reference to the acute physical dangers due to war and Arrow Cross threats through which he and his companion had passed.

But Zürcher's and Vonrufs's stepping in at this juncture was not only necessary for the legation. It turned out to be indispensable for the survival of the remaining Jews of Budapest. It was they who in the end kept the project of all of the neutral diplomats from ending in disaster.

Starting on Christmas Eve 1944, the Danube bridges toppled into the river one by one. The telephone cables were cut between the two parts of the city. After Pest was occupied by the Red Army, the front line followed the Danube shore directly. Heavy Soviet artillery lined up on the Pest side and in unprecedented concentration threw fire and brimstone upon the historic buildings of old Buda. When Pfeffer-von Wildenbruch capitulated on February 12, Buda was razed. By that time Consul Lutz and his entourage had been seven weeks in hiding, not knowing from one moment to the next whether one of the innumerable missiles fired at the German headquarters would find its way into the cellar of the former British legation. In his recollections this was the darkest and most harrowing period of his life. Had it not been for Gertrud's desperate "shopping trip" to Biske, the entire group might have died of starvation.

Peter Zürcher and Ernst Vonrufs had to face the combined terror of war and of the dangers of Arrow Cross hostility alone. It was an appalling time.

The immediate problem was how to face — once again — Arrow Cross revenge for their frustrated attack on the glass house. On New Year's Day 1945, Arthur Weisz, the owner of the glass house, was murdered. He was made to pay for having tricked the attacking Nyilas by engaging them in conversation and giving Friedl and Grossman time to alert Zürcher and Fabry. He fell into a Nyilas trap. He was enticed to leave the building and a few hours later was found murdered.

On the same day, Otto Komoly, who had frequently been in touch with the consul and who became one of Friedrich Born's major organizers to save Jewish children, was entrapped and murdered. He had been one of the finest Hungarian Jewish leaders, a highly decorated officer of World War I with four years of frontline service.

Then there were twenty-five American citizens, who had been interned together on Festetich Street and who came under the consul's special care. The Nyilas removed them to the large ghetto. They were not killed, but their lives remained in great risk.

The large ghetto of Pest, however, remained Zürcher's and Vonrufs's largest worry. They knew that this large concentration of Jews was an open invitation to their enemies for murder. He and his staff visited the ghetto daily. So did the representatives of the Holy See, Spain, and the International Committee of the Red Cross. From their meager resources they provided food and fuel, but above all encouragement, so that the 70,000 would not give up hope. But they also feared that the various murderous acts to date were nothing but the forerunners of the final assault. In Zürcher's mind there was no longer any question of *whether* but only of *when* the Arrow Cross would pounce on the ghetto.

*   *   *

The first days of January 1945 passed, one by one, terrible, cold, and threatening.

One day, Zürcher and Vonrufs learned that within the shifting power game of the Arrow Cross a new name was cropping up, Sédey. This cruel man in his mid-thirties, who had emerged from Nyilas riffraff, had named himself mayor of Budapest and was rivaling Ernö Vajna.

The two young Swiss were told that among the Arrow Cross chiefs, who were fighting among each other, they must see Sédey, who as the new mayor was gaining momentary importance. On January 2 they set out to see the unknown decision maker, darting from house door to house door, listening to the whistling of artillery missiles and ducking their heads, until they came to city hall. The great man was occupied inside his office and they began talking to his councillor, a Nyilas called Pal Szalay, who sat in the front room as receptionist. To their surprise this councillor turned out to be a reasonable young man, one of the few who admitted that the atrocities committed by his colleagues-in-arms gave the Arrow Cross a "bad reputation." How true. Never before had Zürcher and his colleague met any Nyilas who was critical of his own. Even greater was their astonishment when they heard Szalay admit that Arrow Cross structures were falling apart and that the different groups could no longer be controlled.

Suddenly the door opened and a bulky figure in Arrow Cross uniform stepped out. This was Sédey. Suspiciously he eyed the two visitors. Zürcher came directly to the point. What did his excellency, the mayor, think of extra-territoriality? he asked after having introduced himself as the representative of Consul Lutz. This, in a nutshell, was the debate the consul and his other neutral colleagues had waged with the various Hungarian governments ever since March 19, 1944. Sédey's answer was grim. He said that the legation buildings were of course protected, but not the Jews inside. To which Zürcher answered that he made no distinction between Christian and Jewish employees. Sédey just shrugged his shoulders. The conversation was short. Zürcher did not even have the chance to sound out Sédey on the large ghetto, but the exhange did not reassure him.

To whom else could Zürcher turn?

In his predicament he and Vonrufs decided to head straight into the lion's den, the Hotel Astoria, where the SS had its headquarters. When he and Vonrufs neared it they saw that the building had been hit by a Soviet shell and that its top floors were burning. There was confusion and shouting. SS soldiers rushed hither and thither, loading bedding and office furniture and files onto trucks. Zürcher wondered where in this beleaguered city they could flee. He was grimly satisfied seeing this elite unit, which had terrorized Europe for so many years, in headlong flight. Someone gave Zürcher the name of the commanding officer, a General Remlinger, who, he learned, was also the military commander of Pest. At the same moment they saw him walking through the hotel lobby. He was on his way out. Hastily, Zürcher planted himself in front of the important man and told him that Mayor Sédey had threatened to disregard the extra-territoriality of the buildings protected by Switzerland. A massacre could occur if Sédey had his way. Could the general help?

To Zürcher's and Vonrufs's surprise the SS general said yes, he would help. He admitted, however, that he could do little to protect all Budapest Jews against the designs of the Arrow Cross, who were uncontrollable. But at least he would see to it that the former American legation was safe. He would order an artillery battery to be stationed on Freedom Square. They should get in touch with its commanding officer, and he would tell the Nyilas to stay clear of the place. Zürcher then looked up at the burning top floors and asked the SS general how long the Germans hoped to resist. Remlinger raised his hands. What did it look like? he asked, turned around, and walked away.

The two Swiss hastened back to Freedom Square, and to their surprise they found that the SS general was keeping his word, except that he was not dispatching an artillery detachment, but a simple infantry patrol, commanded by a middle-aged sergeant. This was better than nothing, however. The sergeant was a gregarious Bavarian, who said he had gone through nearly six years of war. He had seen so much bloodshed and death that the time had come to protect life. He had no problem with looking after the building on Freedom Square. All that the Swiss had to do was to shout across the square: "Swiss legation in danger!" or fire three times, and they would come running. Two days later, however, a stray bullet hit the sergeant and the patrol withdrew. SS general Remlinger was captured not long afterward. He was brought before a Soviet military court and executed. His last good deed in Budapest did not balance out years of depravity.

Nevertheless, the former American legation and the glass house were no longer troubled. Word had got around to the green shirts that the two buildings were under the special protection of the SS and the German army, even though that protection was evaporating as quickly as it had been extended.

*   *   *

Not surprisingly, the "snot noses" turned again on the Swiss and the Swedish Schutzhäuser on Poszonyi Road, about whose security Zürcher had not had time to talk to Remlinger in their hurried conversation. In the early morning of January 6, some Swedish protective houses came under attack by a Nyilas band commanded by a chieftain called Hidassy. This criminal had been briefly washed up from obscurity to leadership by the "revolution of nonsense." The attack was serious. The "snot noses" were driving 400 to 500 Jews onto the street in their usual brutal way of pushing and beating people, in order, as they said, to bring them to the large ghetto where they would be safer. A Hechalutz found Wallenberg in his hideout. The young Swede immediately raced to Hidassy's headquarters on Varoshaz Street. Mastering his anger with polite words and promises, Wallenberg succeeded in persuading the young gangster to withdraw his band for twenty-four hours. Hidassy said that he first needed to talk to Ernö Vajna about how best to effect this transfer so that they would really be safe. This was no small matter, he added importantly. In reality Wallenberg hoped that within twenty-four hours the Soviets might have occupied all of Pest.

Zürcher and Vonrufs were also alerted, and without knowing of Wallenberg's intervention, they, too, rushed to Hidassy's headquarters. They got there shortly after the Swede had left. Hidassy was also gone, apparently to order his band to stop the attack. Immediately, Zürcher and Vonrufs proceeded to the city hall, where they wanted Vajna to issue strict orders to all Nyilas not to attack any of the Schutzhäuser. Vajna was not at city hall, but Zürcher and Vonrufs pushed into Mayor Sédey's office. He was in a bad mood. The Jews from the Swedish protective houses had once again fired upon the Arrow Cross, he said, just as the Hidassy band was peacefully marching past. Not only was the agreement with Wallenberg null and void, but the Swedish protective houses would all be closed down and their inhabitants moved to the large ghetto. Moreover, all of the inhabitants of the Schutzhaus from which the shot was fired had to die.

This story seemed repetitive. The same accusation had been raised a few days earlier: "Swedish" Jews firing against peaceful Arrow Cross. It seemed as if these terrified people, who were locked up in their crammed apartments, had nothing better to do than to provoke the gun-happy outlaws. He asked Sédey whether he really believed the story. Was it perhaps not the other way round? Was it not Hidassy who had ordered the shot fired so that he would have a "reason" to kill more innocent people?

Zürcher realized that he was raising his voice. Might it be the case, he asked more calmly, that some of these group chieftains were engaging in actions of this kind in order to embarrass the Hungarian government? He pronounced "Hungarian government" very respectfully, which was not lost on Sédey. Rather than allowing Hidassy to proceed with his unauthorized evacuation, Zürcher said, might it not be better to have him suspend what he was doing and submit the matter to Dr. Ernö Vajna? If the neutral governments saw that Hungary was adhering to proper legal procedures, recognition for the Arrow Cross government might be forthcoming more easily.

Yes, Dr. Zürcher had a point, Sédey admitted. It was better to take one's time on such life and death matters. He realized, he said, that the Arrow Cross often proceeded without much reflection. Now that they ran the government they must learn to act more responsibly. The mayor talked as if he saw months and years ahead of him in quiet government service, while at the same time his world was collapsing all around him. But the mayor was also afraid of Vajna and suspected that perhaps the brainy Zürcher was influential with his superior.

Hidassy was called to order, and the inhabitants of the protected houses were allowed to return. For several days, it was as if Zürcher was playing poker with the last leaders of the declining Arrow Cross regime. Sédey and Vajna tried to cope with the disorganization in the lower ranks, even though they were rivals. Zürcher had an advantage in that he was often fed confidential information by Szalay, whom he began to trust. Szalay was looking for a way out by jumping off the running train before it crashed. But as soon as Sédey met Ernö Vajna again, the two Arrow Cross chiefs invented new obstacles. They questioned diplomatic immunity at all levels. Forgetting that he himself had approved Sédey's order that Hidassy's band withdraw from Poszonyi Road, Vajna suddenly insisted that the Swiss were not allowed to protect more than 8,000, and that the "excess" must be moved to the large ghetto. This figure he evidently had heard from his brother, Gabor, who long ago had got it from Veesenmayer. Ernö Vajna had no inkling that Consul Lutz had made the Arrow Cross government accept an increase from 8,000 to 17,000 several weeks previously. Vajna moreover did not realize that the large ghetto could not absorb more than 70,000. He did not understand that it would be difficult, if not impossible, to make tens of thousands of additional undernourished and sick prisoners shuffle along the streets of Pest under bombs, shells, and strafing airplanes, and under the eyes of the general public. Then again, Vajna asked what protective letters really were. Finally, he wanted to see a list of all Schutzbrief holders with their addresses. His decisions became more jumpy and contradictory each day. His memory grew defective. Vajna came late for appointments, and when he did arrive he had forgotten what the discussion was to be about. His mind was obviously focusing on escape.

The day arrived when Zürcher and Vonrufs came to the city hall and waited in vain for Ernö Vajna. None of the Nyilas who sat at the desks playing cards, sharpening pencils, or reading cheap novels had any inkling where he was.

The Arrow Cross bands started to dissolve. The Nyilas threw their green uniforms away. Some of them had already retreated with Eichmann's Sonderkommando before Christmas. The end of the war would find them in Germany. Zoltan Bagossy vanished, and no one ever saw him again. Others merged with the population and reappeared later as active members of communist youth organizations. Certain bands stuck together until the very end, such as the one commanded by the perverted priest, Father Andras Kun. On January 11 he and his group committed what may have been the last deed of horror of the Nyilas. The killers, some young women among them, entered a Red Cross–protected Jewish sanatorium at Maros Street in Buda, ten minutes on foot from where Consul Lutz and his household were hiding. They murdered ninety-two persons, sick, old, children, including doctors and nurses. The Nyilas tried to cover up their misdeed by burying the bodies in the grounds of the hospital. After Buda fell to the Red Army in mid-February, most of this Nyilas band was captured and brought back to the scene of the crime, where it was forced to unearth the victims. Andras Kun managed to hide, aided by his mother, and prepared to escape. Following a hunch of Alexander Grossman, the Chalutzim detected his whereabouts. The priest was caught. He, too, was tried before a war crimes court and executed, together with the rest of his band.

On the day of the attack on Maros Street, January 11, the Swiss legation on Stefania Street was occupied by Red Army soldiers. They broke into the building, emptied Minister Jaeger's splendid wine cellar, stole money, watches, and jewelry, and arrested Max Meier, the visa officer, believing he was the minister. Then they closed the legation down.

Peter Zürcher wrote about these three most dangerous weeks of his life:

> Until the arrival of the Red Army it was our job to assure the security of the former American legation. The offices of the Department of Foreign Interests of the Swiss Legation were located in this building, which also contained substantial material valuables from the former diplomatic representation of the United States. At the same time we had to guarantee the lives of thousands of nationals protected by us, including the employees of our department. Finally we had to defend the so-called protective houses from being attacked by militant Hungarian national socialists, where lived those Jews who had been given Swiss Schutzbriefe. After Jews were hanged on trees or were shot in front of the legation and their bodies thrown into the Danube, we had no other choice but to help. To us the interrelationship between our rescue action and emigration to Palestine as part of our representation of British interests was a mere pretext. The specific subject matter of our negotiations became less important each day. Our main objective was to gain time until the Red Army arrived. At all costs we wanted to prevent the most feared final atrocities against the legation, its staff and the persons it protected. All of the Jews, who on the basis of these negotiations remained inside our protected houses, survived until the Red Army came.

*   *   *

By and by the Red Army occupied the suburbs of Budapest, and its huge columns advanced in a convergent manner upon the center. The heaviest Soviet guns fired day and night from the industrial Danube island of Csepel toward the royal castle in Buda and downtown Pest. No one, it seemed, could survive such an inferno of steel and fire. The Hungarian-

Jewish military historian and eyewitness Peter Gosztonyi described the unendurable conditions in the besieged city as follows:

> A front in the ordinary sense no longer existed. It crossed streets, houses, often apartments and cellar holes, where small independent groups fought on their own. In the face of enemy fire, sporadic messengers maintained communication between the various command posts. Smoke rose from the city, and rubble piles rose steadily higher in the streets, which looked as if they were dead. The population withdrew into the depths of its cellars, where it vegetated without electricity, gas and in most places also without water. Its losses increased by the day. No one came to extinguish the fires or to bury the corpses. The wounded bled to death where they had been hit. There was no one to help them. Under the impact of artillery fire, which hammered at the city without ceasing, ammunition dumps blew up, killing hundreds of civilians in gigantic explosions. Soviet loudspeakers were pushed forward into the city and announced the next artillery barrage or the target of air bombardments. The speakers asked enemy soldiers who were hungry to surrender with their cooking utensils and to get food.

All over Budapest the women were shuddering when they thought of what was in store for them. Horrible tales had reached the city ahead of the Red Army of thieving and raping in Hungary's smaller cities and towns, though there were those who insisted that many enemy soldiers behaved decently. Was such pillage and rape their revenge for the indescribable Nazi war of annihilation against the East, in which Hungary had participated on its own volition? Surely, every single Soviet soldier must have a personal reason for wanting to get even for the severe wound inflicted upon his own people.

On January 15, 1945, the Soviet front in Pest lay no more than a normal ten minute walk from the eastern end of the large ghetto, somewhere between the devastated city park and Rottenbiller Boulevard. On this freezing winter morning the fate of the 70,000 Jews of the large ghetto of Pest hung by a thin thread.

This was to be the day of the last assault.

Chalutzim awakened Zürcher and Vonrufs at the former American legation with rumors that something seemed afoot and that they had better come and find out. The Chalutzim were probably also in touch with Wallenberg, whose hideout was known to only a few, but who at this moment was getting ready to cross the Soviet front. As he no longer dared to appear in the open, it is likely that he, too, communicated with Zürcher via Chalutzim runners about the rumors he himself had received. This may have been his last communication with anyone in Budapest.

Without shaving or taking breakfast, Zürcher and his faithful assistant Vonrufs raced through the dangerous streets of downtown Pest towards city hall. Although the distance was short, getting there seemed to take an eternity. Firing was constant and ear-shattering. The two young men ran, jumped, stopped, crouched on their knees and held their ears whenever an artillery grenade whistled by, holding their breath as it exploded. Finally, they stormed into the safety of Szalay's basement office. The young green shirt was the only one left with whom they could talk inside the enemy camp. He might be a traitor, but what alternative did they have?

He knew why they had come, Szalay exclaimed. They, too, must have heard rumors of what a police officer had just told him, namely that at the Hotel Royal some 500 German soldiers, SS among them, and 200 gendarmes and countless Nyilas were assembling. Machine guns and hand grenades were being distributed. Out of curiosity the policeman had asked what it was all about. Were they going to the front? Some of the Nyilas had laughed. It was then that the police officer realized that this armed mob was about to attack the large ghetto. If the assembled Jews could no longer be deported, they would be killed right where they were. The police officer — Szalay didn't even know his name — hastened to city hall and told him. Would he please let Vajna know? he asked.

Vajna was still here? Zürcher and Vonrufs looked at each other. He had apparently tried to escape the beleaguered city, perhaps with a small plane, but hadn't succeeded. Now he was caught like everyone else.

What now followed was Pal Szalay's "finest hour," or rather the finest five minutes in the life of this simple Arrow Cross youth from a modest background, who had been taught nothing but hatred. What made Szalay go through such an evident "conversion"? His encounters with Zürcher, Vonrufs, or Wallenberg? Or did he perhaps remember a beautiful Jewish girl walking past him toward deportation and he couldn't get her out of his mind? He rose and said to Zürcher and Vonrufs that he had been thinking about everything. He had made a serious mistake in becoming involved with the Arrow Cross, who had promised a new Hungary, but had brought nothing but death. Perhaps he could do something, even if it cost him his life. Whatever happened, the 70,000 in the large ghetto must not die. Could he help him? Zürcher asked with concern. No, Szalay answered solemnly. He and Mr. Vonrufs had already helped him by just coming to city hall and asking the right kinds of questions. Without them he wouldn't even have begun to think straight. He rose, straightened out his green shirt, walked to Ernö Vajna's office door, knocked, and entered without waiting for an answer. His face was white.

Through the closed door, Zürcher and Vonrufs heard a brief exchange, subdued at first, ending with shouting and fist-pounding. Within two minutes Szalay came out again and slammed the door. His face was no longer white, but red and furious. He said that the obnoxious Vajna told him he knew about the killing plans and did not object, even though he did not himself plan to participate. He knows about it! Szalay shouted. Vajna was a man without principles. He said this so loudly that Zürcher and Vonrufs thought Vajna would surely hear, come out, and shoot his rebellious subordinate. He did not.

They were still talking when the commander of the SS Division Feldherrnhalle, General Schmidthuber, arrived and told Szalay that he wanted to see his superior, Ernö Vajna. Another incredible scene followed. Szalay, the little Nyilas, planted himself in front of the powerful SS general, who was astonished that an unimportant underling was blocking his path. Szalay said, looking the general in the eye, that he had heard that at this very moment officers of the general's division, which he knew to be one of Germany's best fighting units, were plotting at the Hotel Royal, together with many Nyilas. They planned to kill the 70,000 innocent and defenseless men, women, children, and old people of the large ghetto. They were arming themselves with hand grenades and machine guns. Did he, the general, know about this? And, if so, did he wish the SS Division Feldherrnhalle to soil its reputation with such an evil deed just before the end? Szalay did not wait for a reply. With a loud, trembling voice he said that if the general did not prevent this crime, he, Szalay, would see to it that he be brought before a military court and tried for war crime.

If the SS general had been in a bad mood he could have had the impertinent Nyilas arrested to be court-martialed for insulting an officer and executed. Or he simply could have pulled out his revolver and shot him dead, as the SS had always done. He was clearly irritated over the young man's impertinence. But Schmidthuber was no fool. He realized that Zürcher's and Vonruf's eyes rested on him. He decided to keep a cool head, which he did not want to surrender to the hangman's sling. Schmidthuber grunted, turned on his heels, and drove straight to the Hotel Royal. There, at gun point, he ordered the bloodthirsty assembly to disperse and to go and fight the enemy. Then he replaced the excitable Arrow Cross guards around the large ghetto with reliable German SS soldiers under his direct orders. No one, least of all the Arrow Cross, he commanded, was to enter the ghetto. He sent a messenger to his superior, SS general Pfeffer-von Wildenbruch, and reported what he had done. The supreme commander of Budapest confirmed the decision.

The last assault did not take place.

During the night of January 15 to 16, a few hours after the near mass execution, the Red Army broke through the German defenses and reached the edges of the large ghetto. The unthinkable happened: grateful Jews showed the parting SS a passage to safety.

The Red Army men broke down the wooden fences that blocked off the large ghetto. They walked down the narrow streets and knocked at each door, telling the inhabitants to come out, they were safe. Endless rows of pathetic and emaciated figures climbed out of the cellars, pushed the ruins aside, and emerged from the overcrowded old houses. The old men and the women held undernourished, hollow-eyed children by the hand. These were the remnants of the once flourishing Hungarian Jews, 750,000 of them, a people that could not believe that they were heading toward catastrophe. Some of the Red Army men, who after a long and frightful war believed themselves to be steeled against atrocious sights, were so overcome that they wept. They tore the yellow stars from the clothes of the Jews and shouted: "Now you are free!" But what was the meaning of freedom for a people whose hurts were so much more than physical?

Just inside the main gate, near the partially damaged Great Synagogue on Dohanyi Street, an even worse sight awaited the soldiers. There, in the small garden of the synagogue, 2,000 unburied bodies lay in a disordered heap. During the last few weeks, war conditions had impeded their transfer to the cemeteries, and in the end there were no Jewish grave diggers left, because the Arrow Cross had systematically murdered them. Among these dead lay innumerable children, who had earlier been removed from the care of the International Committee of the Red Cross and abandoned.

When the Soviet soldiers arrived it was snowing. Like a shroud a thin layer of snow mercifully covered the garden of horror by the Great Synagogue.

Hundreds of additional bodies were found in the former Jewish steam bath on Kaczinka Street, in a number of interior courts, and in storage houses of former commercial enterprises.

The Red Army buried the many bodies as best it could. The garden behind the Great Synagogue became a mass grave, above which a memorial was later erected.

*   *   *

The "international ghetto" on Poszonyi Road was liberated by the Red Army on January 16, hours after the large ghetto was freed. As if by a miracle not one of the overcrowded Schutzhäuser was hit by artillery shells or bombs, although these had exploded all over the city, destroying one-third of all buildings and killing thousands. On the day of liberation the protective houses of all of the foreign legations held 25,000 persons, of whom 17,500 were shielded by Consul Lutz.

On January 17, 1945, the first Red Army soldiers cautiously passed the glass house on Vadasz Street and curiously looked at the hundreds of faces staring at them from the inside. Then they came to Freedom Square. Peter Zürcher and Ernst Vonrufs came to the entry and explained that this was the American legation, which the Swiss had held in trust and planned to return to the United States government as soon as its diplomats arrived.

On that same evening the Germans withdrew from Pest into Buda and blew up the last remaining Danube bridges behind them. On the 18th the residual pockets of German resistance in Buda surrendered or were wiped out. The front line now followed the Danube shore, and for nearly four more weeks the concentrated fire of the Red Army fell upon hapless Buda, all the way from the royal castle to Vienna Gate. The former British legation caught fire and burned for three days and three nights. By sheer luck the 3,000-liter gasoline tank in the inner court did not explode, which would have meant certain death for the consul and his household. When Peter Zürcher and the horrified legation staff watched the fire from the roof of the former American legation, they were certain that the consul and his entourage were dead.

On February 11, at eight in the evening, SS general Karl Pfeffer-von Wildenbruch decided to break through the tightening Soviet ring around Buda. He was left with 5,000 men out of the 180,000 whom he had commanded when the siege began. He requested Hitler's permission for the action, but wrecked his radio equipment immediately thereafter, so that he would not have to receive the Führer's reply. The break-out attempt turned into disaster, because, once again, Marshal Malinovsky knew all the enemy's plans in advance, due to inside information. When the Germans tried to break out along the narrow exits leading from Buda westward, a dense barrage of artillery and rifle fire erupted. Only 785 men survived. They were captured, including their wounded commander.

An eerie silence had fallen upon the aching city the following morning, when Consul Lutz, as the first person of his household, ventured forth and let himself be blinded by the light of day. The first thing he saw was that the walls of his beautiful residence had come down. The ruins were blackened by fire. His Packard in the courtyard was a wreck of twisted metal. It still stood exactly where Szluha had parked it on Christmas Eve. Every single house of historic Verböcsy Street was in ruins. Dead German soldiers lay everywhere. Lifeless horses were still harnessed to their vehicles, all testifying to the savage fire power that had stopped the break-out attempt the night before.

Three hundred meters further south, splendid Eszterhazy Palace also lay in ruins, but Harald Feller and his Swedish guests emerged unscathed. Only Raoul Wallenberg had disappeared, though Feller and Danielsson had known for some time that he was planning to cross the Soviet front lines. He apparently wanted to urge the Red Army commanders to advance more quickly, so that the endangered Jews could be rescued. Later it became known that he had indeed succeeded in crossing the front lines on January 17, but that he was arrested right away. But by then his intervention — if that was what he intended — had become illusory. The Red Army was already in full control of Pest on that day. Hungarian-Jewish historian Jenö Levai, who was usually well informed, believed that the young Swede was murdered shortly after his crossing the front lines, although he was not sure who the murderers were and what their motives could have been. Others thought that Wallenberg was taken to Moscow and kept imprisoned in the Soviet Union for several years before he died. At any rate, after 1945 the name of Raoul Wallenberg sank into oblivion for ten years. It was as if no one, either in Sweden or elsewhere, cared to remember him. His name suddenly reemerged at the height of the Cold War, when John Foster Dulles, the former American legal counselor of the wealthy Wallenberg family, directed United States foreign policy. The case of Raoul Wallenberg was given great publicity, evidently in an effort to embarrass the Soviet Union, America's Cold War enemy. The surprised Soviet Union was either unable or unwilling to explain the fate of the young Swede. Recent serious research, since 1989, has moreover turned up no viable new facts in Russian archives about Wallenberg's ultimate fate. During the course of the years he became a cult figure in some western countries, next to whom all the other actors on the scene in Budapest dropped away to insignificance, regardless of what their real merits may have been.

Harald Feller was more lucky. He, too, was seized by the Soviets. But after one year of imprisonment in Moscow, the Swiss government obtained his release and he returned to Switzerland.

The Soviet occupation forces did not allow Consul Lutz to go back to his office at the American legation. Neither was he permitted to wind up the affairs of his vast Department of Foreign Representations. He could not even explain his Jewish rescue action to the Soviet commander. In a primitive third-class compartment he, Gertrud Lutz, Angelo Rotta, and others were sent by train to Istanbul. Friedrich Born got off in Bucharest and took up a new assignment. Arriving on the Bosphorus, the travelers discovered a run-down Swedish liner, the *Drottningholm,* which carried them to Lisbon. From there they continued to Switzerland, again by rail. Peter Zürcher and Ernst Vonrufs remained in Budapest longer, in order to wind down the affairs of the Department of Foreign Interests. As soon as hostilities in Europe had ceased, they were allowed to return home by the direct route. Magda and Agnes remained in Hungary, but not for long.

MELDEGG

"Meldegg was the place where my thoughts flew to from America, from distant Palestine and from Budapest. Even when the bombs made our air raid shelter tremble, Meldegg appeared in my phantasies, along with a strong desire to be there."

In early September, Meldegg is bathed in clear golden sunshine as at no other time during the year. A slight haze hovers below over the multiple valleys and the large lake to the left. This precursor of autumn fog, it is said, helps mature the apples and pears and grapes on the slopes below, giving them their full aroma. The haze tells the people that harvest can no longer be postponed, that it will thicken into fog and that winter is coming soon like a thief in the night. But it is above the haze where the view is most glorious, where the sun paints the distant Alpine peaks with a soft but clear yellow glow, September gold. The dark blue firmament arches like a giant dome over the vast landscape and suggests the Mediterranean Sea beyond, over there, behind the snow-capped mountains.

On a day like this, in 1945, the consul came to Meldegg for the first time since his return from Hungary, four months earlier. He came up from the valley by cable car, which stops in front of the Grand Hotel in Walzenhausen, walked through the village, sauntered past his old family home, which now belonged to other people, and peeked into his father's dark and overgrown stone quarry. Then he walked up the grassy slopes, past tall pear trees and small wooden farm houses, and into the woods at the top. He stopped at the hilltop inn for a coffee, talked with the owner,

258

and signed the guest book. To the local people he was one who years before had left home as a poor boy for far lands and who now returned as a personality of renown. The press had begun to report that Carl Lutz, one of their own, had saved thousands of Jews in Budapest in the middle of the war. How he had done this, no one quite knew; they had become shy of him and did not dare to accost him outright when they saw him. The Lutzes were anyway not people who readily talked about themselves.

After leaving the inn he glanced at the nearby ruins of the castle and thought of that baron in Budapest whose medieval ancestors had been the local knights and whose Hungarian descendents still bore the name Meldegg. He wondered what had become of the gentleman. Then he sat on the bench for hours.

The landscape and the sound of the peaceful bells were like balm to fill his emptiness. He was astonished that the world could concentrate so much magic in this one spot, where everything was so familiar and yet so strange after his long absence.

He reflected on what had happened to him. Only a few days earlier he had left the clinic in Zurich, where he had spent several weeks. He had come home undernourished, the doctors reported, and his nerves were shattered by months of tension due to fear and shelling. His marriage was in ruins, and the woman he loved was far away. The cure had taken a long time. He was much better now; the clinic had done marvels. But he wasn't really cured.

He remembered when he and Gertrud had returned to Switzerland, after a long detour via Istanbul, the Mediterranean, and Lisbon. They had not expected music and flowers and speeches when they reached the Swiss border at Geneva on May 5. But the reception, if one could call it that, was sobering. Carl and Gertrud heard a bored customs official ask: "Do you have anything to declare?" Of course not, he answered, as he showed his diplomatic passport. They looked up and down the long station quay for someone from the foreign ministry to welcome them, at least one person saying, "Welcome home! Thank you for everything you have done!" It would have been enough. But there was no one.

Again, when they came to Berne, there was no one.

At the Federal Palace Lutz wanted to brief his superiors. He had so much to tell. He had prepared a substantial report during the boat journey across the Mediterranean. Above all, he wanted to talk. Surely, someone would be interested. Marcel Pilet-Golaz was no longer there. His successor was still new, learning his way about. The officials of the foreign ministry scurried past him like rabbits. One of them took his report on how he had rescued Hungarian Jews. Very interesting, no doubt. He would give it to the new foreign minister, Max Petitpierre, who might call him some day. But at the moment everybody was busy. They were receiving and dispatching countless cables and diplomatic notes concerning the armistice. Very important, certainly. Then there were the western Allies, especially the Americans, who raised questions about Swiss economic involvement with Nazi Germany. The government was nervous. A new international order was being set up and the Swiss must not be left out. This would be disastrous for the economy. The officials were kind in their way, but they were indifferent.

The foreign minister could have told the Americans about Carl Lutz, but he didn't, simply because he hadn't troubled to inform himself. The consul had saved many Jews, but was that important? Lutz's report lay at the bottom of some drawer. Official Switzerland preferred to fight for its postwar rehabilitation on purely economic grounds, which was the only field in which it excelled.

Then the blow came. Carl Lutz was hardly home, still waiting to be invited for a debriefing session, when he was ordered to appear before a judge. He was told that the government had decided to hold an administrative juridical investigation on the Swiss legation in Budapest. Strange happenings were reported of how the legation had conducted its business. For example, why had Consul Lutz ignored orders from Berne to slow down his efforts to rescue Jews, and why had he issued Swiss identity papers without authorization — did he not know that thousands of such people could claim Swiss citzenship? — and why had he, as the representative of foreign interests, become involved in saving Hungarian nationals, which was none of his business? But questions were also raised concerning Feller's behavior. Above all, what had made Dr. Harald Feller, the chargé d'affaires and top Swiss diplomat in Hungary, engage in drinking bouts with Arrow Cross chieftains? He must have been thick with the Nazis, some said. Lutz couldn't tell the doctors at the clinic that such a reception by his superiors troubled him more than he cared to admit. The investigation went on for months and wasn't finished by the time the consul climbed up to Meldegg. It continued even after Feller returned from his Moscow prison.

It was a heart-wrenching affair. But the judge in charge of the investigation was a wise man. He understood. He knew that Carl Lutz had risked his health and his life in saving thousands of human lives, and that he was a great man because he had stood up against the limited vision of his superiors. He also understood that Feller had offered strong drink to killers because, if he had not done so, the lives entrusted to him, and his own, would not have been worth much. The personnel of the Swiss legation had conducted the affairs of the nation honorably under extremely difficult and dangerous circumstances, the investigating judge said firmly. He scolded the government for launching the investigation in the first place, which he considered an insult to the persons concerned.

But the government did not apologize, though it refrained from punishing Carl Lutz. He was even promoted, if slowly. He represented German postwar interests in eastern Switzerland during the early postwar years and later became Swiss consul and general consul in Bregenz, Austria. He refused several honorable appointments because they were too far away from home. But once mutual mistrust had become rooted it remained. Lutz no longer enjoyed good relations with the foreign ministry. When Harald Feller returned from his imprisonment in Moscow and was faced with the investigation, he took a more radical step. Feller simply quit the diplomatic service in disgust and became an attorney of state in his hometown, Berne, which he performed brilliantly. The austere Swiss republic is hard on its great men. The mediocre always seem to win out.

After their return Gertrud asked Carl what he had in mind about Magda. Was his fling over, and did he want to come back to her? He didn't. He wanted to marry Magda and take in Agnes as well. Thus, during the course of that summer, Gertrud moved out and started her own life. She joined the United Nations Children's Fund (UNICEF) and became a field worker in Yugoslavia, Finland, Poland, Turkey and Brazil. It was a brilliant career. Gertrud never remarried.

Magda married Carl in 1949, and she and Agnes settled in Switzerland. Agnes became his daughter.

Sitting on the bench in Meldegg, Carl Lutz felt completely emptied.

Children's laughter awakened the consul from his reveries. A dozen boys and girls ages five to twelve came near, led by a young woman. She could not have been more than eighteen, but she had a sparkling spirit and evidently held the children's attention. Lutz looked up and noticed that the children were speaking different European languages, French, Dutch, German, and even Hungarian. He nodded and smiled and they stopped. A small girl sat next to him. She said hello, and he asked in German where she came from. She answered in Dutch: "From Holland!" "And I am French!" an older boy said in his language. "Me, I am Hungarian!" a girl answered in German but with a strong Hungarian accent. "Oh," Lutz said, "I have been to Hungary, too!" They all surrounded him and eyed him with interest. The young Swiss supervisor explained, in dialect, so that the children would not understand, that these were Jewish children who had found refuge in Switzerland. Their parents had been deported. A pastor by the name of Paul Vogt had established a home here in Walzenhausen, where they were given shelter until it was decided what was to be done.

Lutz looked at her. He knew of Pastor Vogt, he said. He had done a marvelous job in alerting both the Swiss public and the government on the fate of Jewish refugees. He, too, had helped Jews to stay alive, or at least he had tried to, though not in Switzerland, but in Hungary. The young girl looked at Lutz in astonishment. Then he must have met the famous Consul Lutz everyone was talking about? He had heard of him, Lutz answered. But what did she mean by famous? As far as he knew, the consul had simply done his duty. Well, yes, perhaps, the girl mused. But down at their home, everybody thought that Consul Lutz was the greatest, because he had no fear of the high and mighty.

If she only knew, the consul thought as he rose to leave.

He shook the girl's hand and said that if she helped these children to find their place in life again, she was doing the greatest job there was. She agreed cheerfully that she must do exactly that.

The people who lived around Meldegg were unlike the officials in Berne.

*   *   *

The total Jewish population in Hungary before the Holocaust is difficult to calculate. For one thing, the Hungarian frontiers between 1938 and 1941 changed several times. Some former provinces were reunited with "Trianon Hungary" (1920), only to be lost again in 1945. Second, 60,000-80,000 Jews had converted to Christianity since World War I. In the religious sense, they were of course no longer Jews. But on the basis of the absurd "race laws" of the 1930s, these people were counted among the Jews and had to suffer accordingly. There were, in addition, continuous debates about how to classify "half-Jews," "quarter-Jews," or "eighth-Jews," etc. Hungarian statistics, corroborated by internal Jewish counts, suggest that on March 19, 1944, the day of the German occupation, a total of 762,000 Jews lived in Hungary. Of these 440,000 were deported to Auschwitz, directly from Hungary or via camps in Germany. This left a total of 322,000 Jews in Hungary and the surrounding area, of whom 250,000 were in Budapest. Over 100,000 died during the Arrow Cross period. At the end of the war a total of 219,000 Hungarian Jews survived, both in Hungary and in the rest of Europe. The total loss due to the Holocaust amounted therefore to 501,000, of whom 100,000 were children.

Shortly after liberation in 1945 Professor Imre Heller and Professor Jozsef Waldapfel, who had been protected by Consul Lutz inside the former American legation, calculated that 124,000 had survived in Budapest. One hundred thousand were kept alive by foreign diplomats and the International Committee of the Red Cross. Of these, a major share, or 62,000, were rescued by Consul Lutz. If one adds the 10,000 children whom the consul helped to go to Palestine between 1942 and 1944, the total number was 72,000.

But what do these figures express about people with a face, with feelings, hopes, and desires, about a lively culture wiped out, about an entire generation vanished, and a Hungary, a Europe impoverished because it had been deliberately put to death? Hitler could not have accomplished his aim, if he had not been abetted by helpers and by indifferent masses, not only in Germany, but everywhere else.

One of those who opposed him was Carl Lutz.

GLOSSARY OF NON-ENGLISH WORDS

Endsieg	final victory
Greuelmärchen	tales of horror
Götterdämmerung	"twilight of the gods," the notion that at the end of time the gods would destroy themselves
Helachutz (pl. *Chalutzim*)	"pioneers," young Jews who worked for the development of Israel as a Jewish homeland
Hitlerjugend	Hitler Youth
Judenräte	Jewish Councils
judenrein	purified, cleansed of Jews
Kadima	the Jewish boy scouts
Königlicher Hofrat	a member of the Hungarian royal privy council
Kriegsgreuel	war horror stories
Nyilas	a member of the Arrow Cross party
Nyilaskeresztes Part	Arrow Cross party
Obersturmbannführer	lieutenant colonel SS
Ostjuden	eastern, Yiddish-speaking Jews